Theatre and Performance in Digital Culture

Theatre and Performance in Digital Culture examines the recent history of advanced technologies, including new media, virtual environments, weapons systems and medical innovation, and considers how theatre, performance and culture at large have evolved within those systems. The two Iraq Wars, 9/11 and the "War on Terrorism" are read through the lens of performance studies, and Matthew Causey argues that the era of *virtuality* and the age of *simulation* (such as the televisual presentations of Gulf War I) have given way to a more troubling model of *embeddedness*, a problem of materiality and embodiment (such as American embedded reporting from Iraq). Led by new strategies of the performance of war and terror, mediatized and technologized cultural systems resist simulating signs of the real to mask the real, and instead practise a technique of embeddedness, infecting the real from within information patterns and biological entities, seeking to coerce through a type of *shock and awe*.

Drawing on the writings of Giorgio Agamben, Alain Badiou and Martin Heidegger, alongside the dramas of Beckett, Genet and Shakespeare, and the theatre of Kantor, Foreman, Sociètas Raffaello Sanzio and the Wooster Group, the book positions theatre and performance in technoculture and articulates the processes of aesthetics, metaphysics and politics. The wide-ranging study reflects on how the theatre and performance have been challenged and extended within these new cultural phenomena, and asks the question that if contemporary technoculture operates under the regime of embeddedness that seeks to infect information from within while colonizing the body through science and technology, and if the new site of the struggle for sovereignty within bio-political systems is the *bare life* of the individual, how can theatre produce an effective response?

Matthew Causey is Senior Lecturer in Drama at Trinity College, Dublin, Ireland.

Routledge Advances in Theatre and Performance Studies

Theatre and Performance in Digital Culture

From simulation to embeddedness

Matthew Causey

Routledge
Taylor & Francis Group

LONDON AND NEW YORK

First published 2006
by Routledge
2 Park Square, Milton Park,
Abingdon, Oxon OX14 4RN

Simultaneously published in the USA and Canada
by Routledge
270 Madison Ave, New York, NY 10016

Routledge is an imprint of the Taylor & Francis Group, an informa business

© 2006 Matthew Causey

Typeset in Garamond by Keyword Group Ltd
Printed and bound in Great Britain by TJI Digital, Padstow, Cornwall

British Library Cataloguing in Publication Data
A catalogue record for this book is available from the British Library.

Library of Congress Cataloging in Publication Data
A catalog record for this book has been requested.

ISBN10: 0-415-36840-5 (hbk)
ISBN10: 0-203-02822-8 (ebk)

ISBN13: 978-0-415-36840-7 (hbk)
ISBN13: 978-0-203-02822-3 (ebk)

For DG

Contents

PART II
Embeddedness (after)
*The performance of 'bare life' and the bio-politics
of digital culture*

Figures

Preface

This book represents ten years of theoretical questioning, practical application, and teaching in the field of performance and technology. However, the story begins a bit further back than that, and just so the reader doesn't get the wrong idea, I promise to withhold any other biographical material from the rest of the book. My use of the preface is to explain where the book came from, and since this is my first book, it comes from a ways back. I began my avocation in the theatre some thirty years ago in the founding days of Cal-Arts, where I spent two years training as an actor with Bea Manley, formerly of San Francisco's Actor's Workshop of Herb Blau and Jules Irving. She was an exceptional teacher and a great inspiration. Cal-Arts of the early 1970s was quite an impressive space for a young person brought up in suburban northern Louisiana, where the only real claim to fame remains *The Residents*. Cal-Arts was the type of place where John Baldassari pursued conceptualism, the early feminists of the Woman's House performed, the Gamelan group performed, the African Dance Ensemble danced, the abstractions of Paul Brach were exhibited, the happenings of Alan Kaprow happened, early video art was screened, and students like Bill Viola, Mike Kelley, David Salle, Paul (aka Peewee Herman) Rubens, and even the indefatigable David Hasselhoff (long before the talking car or the beach runs) were in attendance. I carry with me that spirit of interdisciplinarity, artistic outrage and comic juxtapositions. It was only 1972, but postmodernism had set in with a vengeance. Through Cal-Arts and later NYU, I was raised on the radical theatre theory of the day: Artaud's *Theatre and Its Double*, Blau's *The Impossible Theatre*, and Grotowski's *Towards a Poor Theatre*. I was ready for no more masterpieces, happy to rethink theatre from the inside out, join the 'day that is holy', and if necessary take part in any revolution deemed necessary. I was of the times, and like so many of the time, ran through my own theatre collectives and experimental companies.

In the same decade I attended NYU to study with Michael Kirby and Richard Schechner and I remember Richard bringing a guest lecturer, Victor Turner, to a seminar on theatre and the social sciences, in what turned out to be the early days of Performance Studies. It was a time when Kirby brought out the special issue of TDR on *Theatrical Theory*. I remember being at a party with Michael, and telling him how I liked the issue and his suggestion that you could tell the intellectuals from the rest of the crowd by their reaction to that publication. I was arrogantly flattered, although he probably meant it the other way around from how I took it. NYC, at that point, was ridiculously active with theatre works that now seem like singular moments of theatre history. In one-two year period, I remember seeing Richard Foreman in his loft on West Broadway directing *Rhoda in Potatoland* (the ticket price was five dollars); the opening night of Robert Wilson and Philip Glass's *Einstein on the Beach*, where the only place you did not want to be was in front of the exit door as the crowds streamed out in mid-performance; *Pig, Child, Fire!* by Squat; the opening works of *The Wooster Group*; not to mention the early days of Punk at CBGB's. My own theatre work was staged at the Open Space in Soho, the Envelope at the Performance Garage, and at Soho Books during the time.

When I returned to academia after a ten-year absence working in film, video, and theatre, mainly in New York and Los Angeles, I carried the memory of these performances and the creased copies of the texts with me. At Stanford I combined my interest in alternative performance with the skills I had picked up in video and filmmaking, which led me to research the areas of digital culture and technoculture and the theory and practice of performance and art that responded to the field. Of particular influence was a seminar at Stanford led by Alice Rayner on technology and narratives of identity that drew in the work of Heidegger, Avital Ronell and Donna Haraway. The reading list of that seminar echoes through the bibliography of this book. At the end of the day, as I have learned to say in Ireland, it was probably my laddish love of technology that drove my research, as I am often most comfortable in a kind of *Man Who Fell to Earth* environment of multiple monitors, several sound systems, video, text, and sound all working from different sources.

At Georgia Tech, I founded the Performance Technology Research Lab, a loosely formed supplement to the Master's Program in Information and Technology within the School of Literature, Communication, and Culture. It was there that I began to work in earnest, attempting to create a performance vocabulary that combined live performance and new media technologies. In an article for *Theatre Forum* (Causey 2001), I documented some of that work for those who may be interested. I continued that practical research at Trinity College, Dublin School of Drama, with a more focused approach to digital media as an end in itself.

However, through all of these permutations, my constant concern has been to ask questions about how theatre means and how its technologies might create a space of illumination, a room for thought, be it outraged or anguished, enlightened or disillusioned, bitter or joyful, but always alive. I hope this book continues that course of action.

MDC
Dublin, Ireland
2006

Acknowledgements

A grant from the Trinity College, Dublin Faculty of Arts (Letters) Arts and Benefaction Fund facilitated the completion of this book, and I am thankful for the College's support. Additional support from the Provost's Fund for the Arts at Trinity facilitated areas of practical research in digital media that continue to inform much of my theory. I want to thank all of the members of the School of Drama at Trinity for their collegiality, support, and intellectual stimulation. In particular, I am grateful to Professor Dennis Kennedy whose leadership of the School, direction of the postgraduate seminar in research, and personal mentoring have maintained a very high standard in the department.

Much of the writing of this book has been rehearsed at conferences of the American Society of Theatre Research, the International Federation of Theatre Research, and, to a lesser extent, Performance Studies International and the Association of Theatre in Higher Education. I thank those organizations and their members for the opportunity to present my research and for the valuable feedback I received.

My colleagues at Georgia Tech (1994–2000) were instrumental in my early thinking on the subject. My collaborators and students in Tech's Performance Technology Research Lab (PTRL) helped to realize genuinely useful and viable performance experiments, including the productions of *The Bacchae*, *Faust* and *Electricity*, and to all those involved I give my thanks. Specifically, I wish to acknowledge Phil Auslander, whose friendship and intellectual challenges are a continual source of inspiration.

I would like to thank the US National Endowment for the Humanities for a grant to attend the summer seminar *Modern Theatre/Postmodern Performance*, convened by Herb Blau, whose writings and thoughts reverberate through this book. I want to thank sincerely Stanford Professor Charles R. Lyons, whose direction of my dissertation all those years ago was of such value. I learned to rethink the theatre through his seminars, and I am indebted. I want to thank Nicholas Johnson and Elizabeth Mannion for their invaluable assistance in proofreading the text.

All of the rest goes to my family, DG, Tennessee and Walker, for making the times worth living, and to my Mom for giving me a hideaway to wrap it up.

I would thank the photographers Paula Court, Bob Van Danzig, Luca Del Pia and Eduardo Kac for their kind permission to reprint their work. For assistance in gaining access to the photos I thank Gilda Biasini of *Societas Raffaello Sanzio*; Ruth Kafensztok, who is studio manager for Kac; Clay Hapaz at *The Wooster Group*; and Morgan Pecelli at the *Ontological-Hysteric Theatre*. At Routledge I would like to thank Terry Clague for his patience during the process of completing the book.

An earlier version of Chapter 1 appeared in *Theatre Journal* 51, 4 (December 1999). An earlier version of Chapter 2 appeared in *Essays in Theatre/Etudes Theatrales*, 13, 1 (November 1994), which is included by kind permission of the editors. An earlier version of Chapter 3 appeared in *Cyberspatial Textuality*, (December 1998), which is included by permission of Indiana University Press. The chapter includes a series of citations from my entry 'cyber-theatre' in the *Oxford Encyclopedia of Theatre and Performance*, which is included by permission of Oxford University Press. An earlier version of Chapter 6 appeared in *Gramma: Journal of Theory and Criticism, Special Issue on The Theatre(s) in the Age of New Technologies*, 10 (Aristotle University of Thessaloniki, 2002), which is included by kind permission of the editors. An earlier version of a portion of Chapter 7 appeared in *Theatre Research International*, 26, 2 (Spring 2001) and *Crossings: An Electronic Journal of Art and Technology*, Vol. 1, Issue 3, http://crossings.tcd.ie/issues/2.1/Causey, which is included by kind permission of the editors. The chapter contains reworked material from 'Mapping the Dematerialized: Writing Postmodern Performance Theory', a review/essay of *Postmodern Performance* by Nick Kaye for *Postmodern Culture: An Electronic Journal of Interdisciplinary Criticism*, 5, 2 (1995).

Introduction

A willing suspension of disbelief for the moment

Socrates: If we continue like this, one of two things will happen. Either we shall find what we are going out after; or we shall be less inclined to think we know things which we don't know at all.

(Plato, *Theaetetus* 187c)

The Father. And how can we ever come to an understanding if I put in the words I utter the sense and value of things as I see them; while you who listen must inevitably translate them according to the conception of things each one of you has within himself. We think we understand each other, but we never really do.

(Pirandello, 224)

I have several suggestions on how to read this book. It is advice I hope will be roundly rejected. First, you might regard my arguments as a type of *fictive theory*, which requires *a willing suspension of disbelief*, at times, to allow the discussion to play out or sustain trust. Pierre Bordieu, has already challenged theoretical reasoning for what he calls the *theorization effect*, a 'forced synchronization of the successive, fictitious totalization, neutralization of functions, substitution of the system of products for the system of principles of production' (86). He is arguing for a logic of practice, and I take that admonition seriously, and attempt to ground my theory and philosophical questioning with the concrete mattering of theatre, while maintaining a clearing for thought that pushes against the cracks in the facts and undermines the surety of the material base. Because it seems that after an initial enthusiasm for theoretical discourse in the late 1980s theatre studies has settled back to more traditional models of non-analytical historical positivism or moralizing identity and culture studies of which many strands of performance studies find themselves.

The second strategy is a bit self-protective and little cynical, drawn from Richard Foreman's advice to actors in his performances.

Always believe that when you have a line, you are saying the most intelligent thing in the world but that only a few people in the audience are going to the get it. You should play the show only for those few. That does not mean to perform in a coy, Oscar Wildean style. You should not let the rest of the audience know secrets are being passed to the chosen few. It is as if each of your lines held overwhelming information in coded form. And the audience, save for a few, are vulgar hooligans to whom you have no desire to present your wonderful ideas.

(Foreman 1992: 42–3)

I will pretend that I have profound and overwhelming information to unfold; you can *willingly disbelieve* and agree if you like, but if you do not understand, or as the Watchman from *Agamemnon* warns 'I speak to those who understand, but if they fail, I have forgotten everything' (a favourite quote of Herb Blau), then it is your fault and not my own, and the secrets of the text will be transmitted to others more adept in their understandings or be lost in time. Insert emoticon: ;-).

The third reading strategy is a bit more radical and draws its inspiration from the quote above by Pirandello. It would be to argue that everything I write about in this book never happened. It is all an illusion and the book remains, at best, an allegory of what didn't happen. Could that be true? As Blau often cautions, how seriously are we going to take the plays upon which our European and North American education in theatre studies rest? Pirandello, Genet, Ionesco, and Beckett (to remain modern and male for the moment) spelled it out rather clearly. But so did Hegel, Nietzsche, Heidegger, Baudrillard and Lyotard. There is no there there, was Stein's succinct pronouncement, which was more than just a slight at Oakland. Even though I have listened to all I have read and worked through I have refused to take it completely seriously. I can hear other voices from other rooms outside the perspective of the great European white males, modern drama, and philosophical discourse, such as what has also been learned from Amiri Baraka, or Suzan-Lori Parks, or Split Britches, or Cherrie Morraga. I offer instead a performative contradiction of the modernist tradition as I attempt in this academic exercise to make sense of it all. Yes, as Calderón implied, 'Even in a dream, it's important to do the right thing'. And so it begins (i.e. 'me to play'): the argument.

This book is a contribution to the research fields of performance and theatre studies and digital culture and technoculture studies. The work considers the history of the technological advances in the screened technologies of new media and computer environments and the manners in which theatre and performance, culture and subjectivity, and material and metaphysical conditions have evolved within those systems. I argue that the era of virtuality (a problem of illusion and representation) has given way to a more troubling model of embeddedness (a problem of materiality and embodiment). The book reflects on how the theatre and performance have been challenged and extended within these cultural phenomena.

The two sections of the book, *Part I: Simulation (before), a theoretical accounting of the history of the (dis)appearance of theatre in virtual spaces*, and *Part II: Embeddedness (after), the performance of 'bare life' and the bio-politics of digital culture*, challenge the assumptions of each other. It may help to think of the two parts as a dialectic, or even a drama in which the conflict attempts a resolution. Much of the writing of Part I is drawn from theses I developed in essays as far back as ten years ago, and they carry the historical periods and biases in the arguments they exercise. Chapters 2 and 3 and the discussions of simulation strategy in the 1991 Gulf War, the video practice of *The Wooster Group*, and theory of Brenda Laurel may seem the least current elements of the book, but they are included as essential to completing the history I am trying to tell. In a very real way, Parts I and II are separated and informed by the distance between the American and Iraqi conflicts of 1991 and 2003. The technologies of war, simulated in the case of the former and embedded in the case of the latter, motivate the question of how the theatre has responded. Part I is postmodern and carries much of the concern of an impossible transgression of late capital. Part II works within the twilight of post-structuralism and postmodernism and suggests various viable political and aesthetic positions. Part I is more Baudrillard and Virilio, Part II more Žižek and Badiou. Part I more *Wooster Group*, Part II more *Sòcietas Raffaello Sanzio*.

The argument of *Part I: Simulation (before), a theoretical accounting of the history of the (dis)appearance of theatre in virtual spaces* revisits the late twentieth century's advances in media and computer technologies, in order to map the exchanges and conversions of the televisual and live performance and the processes of how theatre happens (or does not) in virtual environments. Further questioning asks how the ideology of the will to virtuality manifests in performance and culture at large, and how subjectivity is challenged in the space of technology. Extending and critiquing Philip Auslander's litigious models of liveness, the identity politics of Sue-Ellen Case and ontological arguments of Peggy Phelan, the discussions are constructed through Heideggerian notions of technology and *world picture*, Lacanian psychoanalytic models of subjectivity, historical analysis of perspectivalism, and studies of performance, theatre and dramatic texts. The later chapters of Part I articulate the distressed metaphysics of illusion confronted by the strategies of the virtual, the problem of representing and constructing identity in mediatized culture and the possibilities of an alternative philosophical theatre.

The line of reasoning of Part II maintains that the age of simulation in which media replaced the real with the signs of the real (e.g. the televisual presentations of Gulf War I) has given way to the advance of embeddedness. The effect of simulation was that the real remained, hidden and coded, but available. Embeddedness, making its appearance in the recent American invasion of Iraq (Gulf War II), altered simulation's masking of the real with a dataflow that could inhabit the real itself and alter its essence.

Part II considers the end of the reign of virtual data by the usurpation of embedded technology and how the material bodies of the earth (through GM crops) and the human (through similar genetic modifications) are the new sites of conflict. Mediatized culture has moved from the simulated screens of the virtual to the modified bodies of embeddedness. I suggest that the notion of a virtual theatre, theatre on a screen, was dead even as it first appeared. The more interesting work of contemporary performance is concerned with the problems of digital culture, and are in fact not disturbed by the illusions and aesthetics of the virtual, but rather are dealing with the material and bio-politics of embeddedness. Here I look to Eduardo Kac's transgenic art not as a condition of virtuality, but as bodily explorations of embeddedness.

In Part II, I consider the challenge to the sovereignty of the autonomous, *free* subject in the bio-politics of digital cultures in which embedded technologies challenge the body forth toward a troubling dis-empowerment and de-materialization. Drawing from Giorgio Agamben's philosophy and political theory of post-Holocaust western subjectivity (*homo sacer*), I deliberate on the problems of the body's place of performativity in world culture and in contemporary theatre. I examine how aesthetics continues its troubling collaboration with fascism, capitalism and terrorism (i.e. all forms of ideological persuasion). I analyse the performative spectacle of September 11, 2001, the new performance territory of *transgenic art*, which, through genetic engineering, draws on the *bare life* of living creatures for aesthetic ends and on the performance of the dis-human body and dis-real stage of the contemporary Italian theatre collective *Societas Raffaello Sanzio*.

In Part I, the case is made that the virtual represented a model in late twentieth century performance practice as Lyotard defined negative dialectics, in which what is encountered is a 'non-negatable negative and abides in the impossibility of redoubling it into a "result"' (Lyotard 1989: 363). I maintain in Part I that the negative confronted by the model of the virtual is the reality/illusion pairing and the impossible redoubled result is the representational act of theatre. In Part II, the model of embeddedness cancels the dominance of the virtual, and what stands as impossible is not a problem of representation, but rather the sovereignty of the subject. What is at stake in the problem of embeddedness is the freedom of the human subject in digital culture. The question I pursue is how theatre and performance might re-establish a link with the philosophical questions of freedom and truth through a re-consideration of the nature of performance as sacrifice. I challenge the usefulness of thinking sacrificially, suggesting instead, via the writings of Alain Badiou, a subtractive logic of a theatre minus theatre that can mark a *new* place of an indiscernible event (a truth).

Methodological strategies of the book include performance analysis of the theatre and theory of Tadeusz Kantor, *Societas Raffaello Sanzio*, Richard Foreman's *Ontological-Hysteric Theatre* and *The Wooster Group*. I read the dramas of Shakespeare, Beckett and Genet against recent developments in new media art. I analyse the events of 9/11 and the Iraq wars as mediated performances, and evaluate how advanced visualization technologies of defense and medicine are shaping new patterns of coercion and subject construction. The theoretical foundations of the book are wide-ranging and are drawn from the philosophical discourses of Hegel, Nietzsche, Bataille, Heidegger, Deleuze, Agamben, Žižek and Badiou, the psychoanalytic theory of Freud and Lacan, the postmodern notions of Baudrillard, Jameson and Lyotard, the digital culture studies of Kate Hayles, and the performance theory of Philip Auslander, Herbert Blau, Sue-Ellen Case and Peggy Phelan.

There has been much written regarding, but often merely *around*, the field of performance, theatre and technology. There is more research available regarding art practice and new media, identity in digital culture, and the philosophy of science and technology. I draw from these texts and hopefully extend their useful premises. The specific texts in the field of theatre and performance studies I acknowledge in my research include *Liveness* (Auslander 1998), *Performance and Media* (Birringer 1998) *The Domain-matrix* (Case 1996), *Virtual Theatres: An Introduction* (Giannchi 2004), *Computers as Theatre* (Laurel 1991) and *Virtualities: Television, Media Art, and Cyberculture* (Morse 1998). However, outside of Auslander and Case, my own theory is less likely to draw on the earlier conclusion of theatre and performance theorists and more likely to be schooled in Heidegger, Agamben, Žižek or Badiou.

A cursory survey of the texts in the area of performance and technology show a collection somewhat erratic in approaches. Giannchi's *Virtual Theatres: An Introduction* is, as the title suggests, an introduction and serves that function well. The survey of the book helps situate what is meant by virtual theatre. Birringer's *Media and Performance* is an idiosyncratic work focused somewhat tenuously on his own dance work, but it poses important questions and did so early on and deserves credit for that. Sue-Ellen Case's *The Domain-matrix* is concerned primarily with feminist and queer theory and the ways in which virtual technologies are reconfiguring identity. It is an important work regarding gender and digital culture that informs my own text in critical ways. Brenda Laurel's *Computers as Theatre* is a theoretically challenged work that employs Aristotle's *Poetics* as a basis for constructing interactive narratives and virtual environments. Jon McKenzie (1997) has usefully critiqued the premise of the work. Laurel's book's importance is accountable by its early appearance in the field and not its current academic usefulness.

Peggy Phelan's *Unmarked* is not a book about digital culture, but it does set up an important discussion regarding the ontology of performance. As I will rehearse in the first chapter, Phelan argues that performance is defined through its non-reproducibility. The nature of performance deteriorates as it is enfolded in technological reproducibility. Philip Auslander, in *Liveness*, counters that the live is an artifact of mediatization. Liveness exists not as a prior condition, but as a result of mediatization. Both arguments are problematic. Phelan disregards any effect of technology on performance and draws a non-negotiable, essentialist border between the two media. Disputing the argument of Phelan and amending Auslander's, I suggest that the ontology of the performance (liveness), which exists before and after mediatization, has been altered within the space of technology. Auslander's text is the most important of those I have mentioned and is a touchstone in thinking through the nature of performance in mediatized culture. In the course of this book, I will fall on both sides of the argument to advance a dialectic. At times I will promote the importance of the physical presence of the other, while at other times insisting on acknowledging the always already virtual nature of the *now*. 'Absent always' is how Beckett had Hamm phrase it.

The first part of my book, *Part I: Simulation (before)*, is subtitled *a theoretical accounting of the history of the (dis)appearance of theatre in virtual spaces* and attempts to do just that. In the first chapter of the section, *The Screen Test of the Double: the uncanny performer in the space of technology*, I isolate a decisive moment in new media performance works specifically and in digital culture in general, when the presence of the *Double*, the experience of the uncanny in the space of technology, the making material of split subjectivity, the illusion of the act of seeing oneself see oneself through the mediated screens of technology, manifests. I contend that the inclusion of the televisual screen in live performance and the practice of performance in the screened world of virtual environments constitutes the staging of the privileged object of the split subject, that which assists in the subject's division, capturing the gaze, enacting the subject's annihilation, its nothingness, while presenting the unpresentable approach of the real through the televisual screens. Part psychoanalytic reading (Freud and Lacan), part textual analysis (Beckett and Genet), part film studies (Lynch and Weir), I focus on the material object wherein and upon which these performance phenomena take place, both in the nowhere of the psyche and in the lived space of the body: the screens.

Chapter 2, *Televisual Performance: openness to the mystery*, seeks to historicize the ubiquitous presence of the televisual in performance practice of the last several decades. If the ontology of performance lies in its disappearance and resists the technology of reproduction, what takes place upon the collision of the televisual, which keeps appearing and picturing, and the performative, which employs an aesthetics of dematerialization? How does the maniacally regenerating *now* of performance interact with the reproducible flow of the televisual and its economy and circulation of representations? I argue, through an analysis of a Wooster Group performance, that the *here and now* of theatre has become one of the *accidents* (the mere appearance) of the transubstantiation of performance into the technological. I suggest that the works of mediatized performance established a separate aesthetic object to theatre, a para-performative, tele-theatrical artifact wherein the immediacy of performance and the digital alterability of time and space through technology converge.

Two primary questions drive Chapter 3, *Posthuman and Postorganic Performance: the (dis)appearance of theatre in virtual spaces*. Firstly, how do the appearances of theatre *happen* (or not) in virtual spaces? Where does the *sex and death of the flesh* that seems always to have phenomeno-logically marked performance reside in the virtual? Can the fundamental and visceral property of the theatre, what Taduesz Kantor calls 'the revelatory message from the realm of death, the metaphysical shock' (114), the pres-ence of the other, *materialize* in virtual environments? Using Herb Blau's 'Universals of Performance' from *The Eye of Prey* (1987), I deliberate on the *how* of theatre in computer systems. The second question of this chapter concerns the ideology of the will to virtuality as the desire for disappearance in cyber-territories. Does the drive to be duplicated by digital agents or supplemented by simulated avatars indicate an aspiration to have done with the material and to elevate interiority, to suppress the political and to hold to the metaphysical? Drawing from the theatre practices and theory of Kantor, the dramaturgy of Genet and the philosophy of Heidegger, I argue that the ideology of the virtual is tied to a *falling into inauthenticity*, a *forgetfulness of being*, and an attempt to catapult over the shock of the body in performance toward a self-replicating immaterial material identity. My claim is that the territory of the virtual is the hearth of the homelessness of the alienated contemporary human of digital cultures. What can a theatre in a virtual environment reveal?

Chapter 4, *Perspectiva Artificialis: the duplicitous geographies of stage illusion, or, the not so splendid isolation of the actor on the early modern perspective stage and in the historical avant-garde*, argues that the history, philosophy and ideology of perspective in art, architecture and theatre design have been well rehearsed, but the phenomena of the body in performance within that artificial space have been under-theorized and under-historicized. I begin this chapter by outlining the rules and question-ing the problems of stage perspective of the early modern period and follow up with how a similar reconfiguration, or reframing of the body, took place in the historical avant-garde, including the work of the Italian Futurists and of Oskar Schlemmer at the Bauhaus. There is an implied link between these historical works and contemporary new media performance that experiment with the collage of live and mediated signs. I allege that the problem of perspective (vision in the first person) – what Heidegger refers to as the *age of the world picture*, the objectifying and abstracting of the world and the controlling impulse to the body – can be traced from the proscenium arch of the sixteenth century to the head-mounted display of virtual reality, the scientific visualization technologies that re-imagine and colonize the human body, culminating in the creation of the vision machines of the *smart weapons* of the twentieth and twenty-first centuries.

Chapter 5, *The Ruins of Illusion: theatre in the rise of the virtual and the fall of illusion*, takes a hard philosophical turn to question how the mechanics of illusion in theatre have been fundamentally altered in the rise of virtual representations. In Chapter 1, I articulated the dramatic interest in the technologically split subject, which appears as the uncanny double of the performing subject. In Chapter 2, I identify the operations of a televisual stage suggesting that the merging of the performative and the televisual produced a third way of presentation. I draw on these two theses to offer a third concerning what might be perceived in contemporary performance as a ruinous metaphysics. By this I mean that in response to the strategies and ideologies of the virtual and the phenomena of simulation theatre withdraws toward a materialism that relinquishes or merely remembers (a lifeless remembering like Agave for Pentheus) the technologies of illusion. I deliberate on a strain of resistance in Western culture and aesthetics to the slow dissolve from illusion to the virtual. The argument, expressed through Foucault's reading of Deleuze in *Theatrum Philosophicum*, Hegel's *Phenomenology of Spirit* and Agamben's reading of Hegel, suggests that contemporary theatre is a site where metaphysics, fleeing from the horror of the simulacrum, reconstructs the ruins of illusion upon the flesh of the performer and upon the remains of the stage. Theatricality becomes a mask worn by the virtual to hide its appearance. In order to make the case that the modernist (dramatic) struggle between reality and illusion is sliding toward the problem of the challenging of illusion (falseness) by simulation (virtuality) resulting in an aesthetics of the ruins of illusion, I conclude with readings of *The Wooster Group*'s Jim Clayburgh's scenographic practice as transparent industrial remains of a wasted theatricality, Richard Foreman's settings for his *Ontological-Hysteric Theatre* as re-inscriptions of the material stage upon which appear the phenomena of things in and of themselves, and Romeo Castellucci's (*Socìetas Raffaello Sanzio*) ruinous and desiccated bodies and spaces of a new tragic consciousness.

Chapter 6, *The Aesthetics of Disappearance and the Politics of Visibility* argues that the critique and encouragement of the constructions of identity and the representation of the negotiations of subjectivity in various systems of power are tasks that the theatre neatly serves. Yet I seek to articulate a problem in the reliance of some contemporary theatre and performance artists on a *strategic essentialism*, which concretizes the illusions of identity while embracing a solipsistic realism. I suggest that this is an understandable but problematic choice, given the bio-politics of digital cultures in which virtual, televisual and mediated technologies challenge the subject forth toward a troubling dis-empowerment (of expendable data). Drawing upon a disparate series of dramatic, theoretical and performative examples, I hope to demonstrate the problem of misusing strategic essentialism in the performance of identity, and point to various useful alternatives of current philosophical and technological/new media stagings. As an alternative, I ruminate on the possibility of a philosophical (impossible?) theatre that develops from a type of thinking that is not practical or economical, but which, as Heidegger suggests in 'Letter on Humanism', has no result, and whose uselessness creates a clearing for an illumination to take place. Shakespeare's *Coriolanus*, *Film* by Beckett and the performance practices of Richard Foreman and *Societas Raffaello Sanzio* reflect this model that resists the metaphysics of subjectivity and approaches the danger zone of the *unnamable*.

Part II of this study is titled *Embeddedness (After): the performance of 'bare life' and the bio-politics of digital culture*. As stated above, the argument of Part II maintains that the age of simulation, in which media replaced the real with the signs of the real has given way to the advance of embeddedness. The effect of simulation was that the real remained, hidden and coded, but available. Embeddedness alters simulation's masking of the real with a dataflow that could inhabit the real itself and alter its essence. Part II begins with Chapter 7, *Stealing From God: the crisis of creation in Societas Raffaello Sanzio's* Genesi *and Eduardo Kac's* Genesis. The performance work, *Genesi: From the Museum of Sleep* explores the *crisis of creation* brought on by the scientific revolutions of genetics and nuclear physics and the genocidal endgames of the Holocaust. *Genesi* is analysed against Eduardo Kac's art installation, *Genesis*, which combines advanced media for tele-present interactivity and genetic engineering. *Genesi* and *Genesis* relate not only in the cultural concerns of science and technology studies, but also in their interdisciplinary strategies, which include combining aspects of theatre, visual art, sculpture and technology. Castellucci and Kac engage the risks inherent in the destruction possible through creation (both aesthetic and scientific) and isolate manners in which contemporary constructions of the human are challenged. The works signal an awareness of the constantly shifting boundaries and borders of aesthetic genres and the developing convergence of the disciplines of science and art.

Having introduced Kac's work, I develop a more detailed analysis of his transgenic art that is 'a new art form based on the use of genetic engineering techniques to transfer synthetic genes to an organism or to transfer natural genetic material from one species into another, to create unique living beings' (Kac 2006). Kac has genetically altered a rabbit, fish, mice, bacteria and plant-life, so that they generate green fluorescent protein, which causes the entity to glow green when placed under UV light. These animals, bacteria and plants are placed in installations where they sometimes interact with machines known as 'bio-bots' and where local and tele-present spectators can interact or alter them in some manner. First, the goal of this essay is to ask some very basic questions about how Kac's transgenic and interactive work operates in the tradition of modern art. Second, it is to begin an inquiry into the philosophical and ethical issues that Eduardo Kac's art raises, namely, the elimination of the borders between art and life and virtual and embodied spectatorship, aesthetic genetic engineering, the ethics of robotics and the responsibilities of the artist to the art of monsters and machines.

Chapter 8, *From Simulation to Embeddedness: aestheticizing politics and the performance of 'bare life' in the bio-politics of digital culture*, notes the obvious, that the world is accelerating. Virilio has been preaching this sermon for many years, and now another shift in mediatized culture looms. I have been working in the field of live performance and technology, questioning the ideologies and power circulations of digital culture for the last ten years as a practitioner, theoretician and lecturer and I have come to believe that the critical questions posed by the collision of live performance and technology, and which have occupied so much of postmodern culture have lost their urgency. That is not to say that the questions of how identity is shaped by technology and how one might resist incursions of media into individual sovereignty, or even wondering how the aesthetics of theatre are being reconfigured, are not vital issues. However, the issues of humanness have been further traumatized through embeddedness as a new and troubling strategy of bodily (biological) and informational control. Besides the expansion of biological and genetic manipulations of the earth and human body (from cyborgs to clones), the information flow has moved from ubiquitous surveillance and simulation to embedded infiltration, creating a more devious infection of data flow and domination. My question is: how can theatre remain a useful epistemological modality, or questioning aesthetic, during this process?

I ponder the challenge to the sovereign, autonomous, free subject toward the unsacrificeable and expendable (sacred) status of the subject in the bio-politics of digital cultures in which embedded technologies challenge the body forth toward a troubling dis-empowerment and de-materialization. Drawing from Giorgio Agamben's research into the sacred human (*homo sacer*) I deliberate on the problems of the body's challenged sovereign status and its place of performativity in world culture and contemporary theatre. In this chapter I consider Stockhausen's infamous dictum that the events of 9/11 were one of the world's greatest works of art, suggesting that the image was central. The *act* was designed by the terrorists to be televisually seared into the collective imagination of the world spectator. The argument further questions how one might understand 9/11 through the damaged and weakened systems of art and aesthetics. I begin by historicizing the ongoing crisis of aesthetics through the eighteenth and nineteenth centuries' cult of the picturesque, which worked to aestheticize the natural environment through landscape painting, architecture, stage design and tourism. I extend the argument of Chapter 4 to suggest that the picturesque and the age of the world picture represent a drive to control the world through image. Digital culture is an obvious extension of the cult of the picturesque, but the simulations that drive digital culture hit a brick wall on 11 September.

The last chapter of the book is *The Theatre and its Negative: event, truth and the void*. If contemporary technoculture operates under the regime of embeddedness that seeks to infect information from within while colonizing the body through science and technology, and if the new site of the struggle for sovereignty within bio-political systems is the *bare life* of the individual, how can the theatre produce an effective response? I offer a prolegomenon to a line of inquiry questioning the artistic configurations of the theatre as a *singular* event of thought, a *truth-procedure*, and possible site of an *event*, which through a process of subjectification contributes to the appearance of the radically new, a truth, an exceptional break with the state of things as they are. I use Alain Badiou and Martin Heidegger's divergent philosophical models to understand what is meant by an *event*, a *situation* or *structured presentation*, as in the case of Badiou, and *Ereignis* (event) in terms of Heidegger, both of whom see it as a moment of radical potentiality. From this event theory, I model a theatre regarded as a sacrifice and consider what a sacrificing of theatre itself might mean (a subtractive logic of theatre minus theatre) in order to ask a final question of how the theatre event might re-establish a link with the philosophical questions regarding *truth* and *freedom*, and thereby might adequately respond to our history. My theory is that the sacrificing of theatre and the thinking of the theatre thought *can* take place and clear a space, a sacred space (the void), in which a freedom (as a comportment to allowing things to be in and of themselves) and a truth (as a radical potentiality for transformation and innovation) can happen. In this way, the book concludes in a marking of the twilight of poststructuralism and postmodernism's modulations of theatre practice, the discourses of exhaustion and continual endings, in favor of a leaning toward new potentialities and events of a radical nature.

Part I

Simulation (before)

A theoretical accounting of the history of the (dis)appearance of theatre in virtual spaces

1 The screen test of the double

The uncanny performer in the space of technology

Your reality is already half video hallucination. Soon it will become total hallucination. You're going to have to learn to live in a very strange, new world.

(Cronenberg, *Videodrome* 1983)

And if I am anything in the picture, it is always in the form of the screen, which I earlier called the stain, the spot.

(Lacan 1981: 97)

Question regarding the virtual and the real

There is nothing in cyberspace or in the screen technologies of the virtual that has not already been performed on the stage. The theatre has always been virtual, a space of illusory immediacy. Yet much of the contemporary discourse surrounding live performance and technological reproduction establishes an essentialized difference between the phenomena, from Walter Benjamin (1968) to Peggy Phelan (1993). The difference is further concretized in the critical writings of theatre and performance studies that ignore such performative mediated forms as film, television, radio and multimedia. Slavoj Žižek, in the introduction to *Mapping Ideology*, writes that it is a commonplace assumption that 'virtual or cyber-sex presents a radical break with the past since in it actual sexual contact with a real other is losing ground against masturbatory enjoyment, whose sole support is the virtual other' (Žižek 1994: 5). He dismisses that assumption by suggesting that,

> Lacan's thesis that there is no sexual relationship means precisely that the structure of the real sexual act (of the act with a flesh and blood partner) is already inherently phantasmic – the real body of the other serves only as a support for our phantasmic projections.

(1994: 5)

Lacan's argument thus challenges the assumptions inherent in the constructed binary of the real and the virtual, and thereby disputes the claims of immediacy and presence in live performance. If you accept Lacan's argument, then the anxieties surrounding the shifting perspectives on the nature of presence, aura and liveness, in regard to the ontology of the theatre, brought about by the advent of new media performance, are wholly without merit. Everything has always-already been virtual.

The debate regarding the ontology of performance and the nature of liveness and identity in mediatized and technologized culture has been well rehearsed. For the purpose of my argument, I want to point to Philip Auslander's *Liveness* (1999), a book to which this current study is deeply indebted, and to Peggy Phelan's important *Unmarked* (1993). Phelan argues that performance is defined through its non-reproducibility. The nature of performance deteriorates as it is enfolded in technological reproducibility. Philip Auslander counters that the live is an artifact of mediatization. Liveness exists not as a prior condition, but as a result of mediatization. Both arguments are problematic. Phelan disregards any effect of technology on performance and draws a non-negotiable, essentialist border between the two media. Auslander draws out a sophisticated legal argument whose dynamic materialism overlooks the most material manner of marking the live, namely death. Disputing the argument of Phelan and amending Auslander's, I suggest that the ontology of the performance (liveness), which exists before and after mediatization, has been altered within the space of technology. But how?

Question regarding performance in technoculture

Three basic assertions comprise the contemporary theory of subject construction in mediatized culture and help shape the aesthetic gestures of contemporary performance:

1. The material body and its subjectivity are extended, challenged and reconfigured through technology.
2. The televisual is the primary modality of contemporary technological representation dominating manners of thought and communication, culture and subject construction.
3. There exists an unavoidable convergence of the human and machine wherein the *slave* machine dominates the *master* human subject.

This book will grapple with all three of these claims and the manners in which they provoke performance production in culture and in art. Notable performance works created in the wake of technoculture include the theatre of the now-classical postmodernist *Wooster Group* (US); *Desperate Optimists*, an expatriate Irish company (Ireland/UK) working in performance and digital media; the altered medical body of *Orlan* (France); the obsolete body of *Stelarc* (Australia/UK); and the post-colonial cyber-performance artists *Guillermo Gómez-Peña* and *Roberto Sifuentes* (Chicano-American); *dumb type* (Japan) and *Robert Lepage* (Canada). They are all, more or less, in the process of embodying mediated subjectivity and articulating/representing that experience in performance. The developing art forms of web-based performance, interactive installations and virtual environments, including the work of *Jeffery Shaw*, *Bill Viola* and *Perry Hoberman*, are extending the boundaries of the theatre and notions of what constitutes a performance while exploring the experience of living within a technological culture. The fundamental objective of the first part of this book is to understand the processes of theatre and performance, which converge with mediated and digital technologies of representation. In the second part, I articulate some of the larger cultural performance practices of technoculture and how various artists have responded.

I pursue the question regarding the real and the virtual and the position of performance in technoculture by isolating a critical moment in new media performance works specifically and technoculture in general, when the presence of the *double* takes place through mediated duplication: the simple moment when a live actor confronts her mediated other through the technologies of reproduction. I propose that the experience of the self as other in the space of technology can be read as an uncanny experience, a making material of split subjectivity. My position is that the inclusion of the televisual screen in performance and the practice of performance in the screened world of virtual environments constitutes the staging of the privileged object of the split subject, that which assists in the subject's division, capturing the gaze, enacting the subject's annihilation, its nothingness, while presenting the unpresentable approach of the real through the televisual screens. Part psychoanalytic reading (Freud and Lacan), part textual analysis (Beckett and Genet), part film analysis (Lynch and Weir), this chapter focuses on the material object wherein and upon which these performance phenomena take place, both in the nowhere of the psyche and in the lived space of the body: the screens.[1] The goal of the tripartite strategy is to demonstrate how questions of virtuality and the real are being played out in both live and mediated performative work and across a variety of historical contexts.

'At the tone, please leave a message'

Avital Ronell, in *The Telephone Book*, writes of Freud's notion of *unheimlich*, or the uncanny, and how the phenomenon reoccurs through the subject's experience of displacement within technology. She remarks that 'the more dreadfully disquieting thing is not the other or an alien; it is, rather, yourself in oldest familiarity with the other, for example, it could be the *Double* in which you recognize yourself outside of yourself' (1989: 69). The confrontation with the *double*, the recognition of yourself outside of yourself through the echoing voice on the telephone, the anamorphic projection on the television in freeze-frame, slow-motion, fast forward and reverse, through a kind of being in technology with morphing identities that exist within the fragility of digital space, present the technologically triggered uncanniness of technoculture subjectivity. The experience of the uncanny within the space of technology seems easily constructed. When a computer screen displays a message, a question, 'how are you?' or more likely, 'what are you wearing?' or 'asl?' (code for 'age, sex, and location?') from an anonymous chatroom participant the experience is palpable. Who is it behind the text, on the other side of the screen? It is whomever or whatever I desire. The pulsating cursor, like a heart beat, anticipates the streaming text that follows, unencumbered by the appearance of the body, offering a flat screen ideally suited to project our own desires, our desiring phantasms. Increased bandwidth allows the use of video-conferencing and as a result the computer is less textual and more televisual and perhaps less illusory, now more depthlessly real. The mathematics and abstractions of text creates an unknown depth and obscurity that the video can only interrupt in its obscene clarity. The audio sampling of our voices ('at the tone, please leave a message') and the black and white surveillance video capture of our images ('is that how I look queuing up at the bank?') are now commonplace, but somehow unsettling. Why? In attempting to outline an aesthetic of the uncanny, Freud noted several literary examples that would elicit an experience of the uncanny, such as dolls, mirrors, automatons, dead bodies (televisions turned to dead channels?). When one enters a darkened room and senses a reflection in a distant mirror, or sees a figure (perhaps a child-size doll) seated immobilized in a chair with frozen eyes, the almost sublime experience of the uncanny is felt. What is sensed? Freud writes, 'this uncanny is in reality nothing new or alien, but something which is familiar and old-established in the mind and which has become alienated from it only through the process of repression' (1955: 241). The ego does not believe in the possibility of its death. The unconscious thinks it is immortal. The uncanny experience of the double is death made material, unavoidable, present and screened.

David Lynch's *Twin Peaks: Fire Walk with Me*, the feature prequel to the US television series, *Twin Peaks*, works through these issues of technological uncanniness. It is February 16 at 10:10 a.m. when Special Agent Dale Cooper enters the office of FBI Regional Director Gordon Cole. The establishing shot of the FBI Building begins with an upside-down shadow of the Liberty Bell panning up to the actual Bell, which is then echoed in a print of the Bell in Director Gordon's office. 'I was worried about today because of the dream I told you about,' Cooper confides, kneeling at Gordon's desk. Gordon nods. Cut to: an empty office hallway with a single surveillance camera hung from the ceiling pointing away from the viewer. Special Agent Cooper enters the frame, stands in front of the surveillance camera and waits. Cut to: Close-up of the surveillance monitor with Cooper looking up at the camera. Cut to: Medium shot of the hallway as Cooper walks out. Cut to: Medium shot of surveillance control room where a security guard watches three video monitors. The middle monitor displays Cooper just exiting the hallway as he enters the frame of the film and into the control room. He studies the monitor. Nothing. He repeats the sequence. Still, nothing is seen on the monitor. The editing works to unsettle the eye between monitored video space and the narrative filmic space. An elevator door opens. Pause. Philip Jeffries (David Bowie), a long lost federal agent walks up the hallway toward Cooper, who is again looking into the surveillance camera. Cooper walks back in the control room and is astonished to see himself on the live monitor and that Jeffries is walking past his image. He calls out anxiously, 'Gordon! Gordon!' Seeing himself see himself creates a startling chain of events. Jeffries, now in Gordon's office, speaks in a halting voice about an unknown Judy. The video noise of a dead TV channel, which later proves to be the sighting of the father as killer, fades in and out, superimposed upon the scenes. It is through the technological that we enter the dream space of *Twin Peaks* with its patented reverse speak. When Jeffries vanishes, it is as if he does so along the electrical wires and through videated space, as quick inserts of cabling and telephone poles are flashed. The front desk of FBI headquarters says that Jeffries was never there. Cole and Cooper confirm Jeffries's presence and Cooper's visual doubling by reviewing the video. It is not unlike the chant that went out during many protest marches concerning the Rodney King verdict, 'the video doesn't lie, the video doesn't lie!' The uncanny and videated doubling of Cooper is the warning, the crisis point, wherein the dream space of fragmentation via technology invades the real space. This crash of ontological positions and representational regimes is the situation I am pursuing.

The issues of televisual, simulated and digital culture are now commonplace Hollywood script fodder, depicting either the anxiety or desire that my life is, or should be, TV. *The Truman Show* (Weir 1998) and *EdTV* (Howard 1999) are examples from the 1990s, but newer films continue with similar technophobias such as simulation anxiety, *The Matrix* (Wachowski 1999), and biotech panic scenarios, *I, Robot* (Proyas 2004) and *The Island* (Bay 2005). Both of the earlier films and *The Matrix* offer a *Baudrillard for Dummies*, a Pirandello for those who missed modernism, through a dramatization of the theory of simulations. *Pleasantville* (Ross 1998) is a film whose twisted ideology narrates an attempted reconstruction of the televisual as flesh through a slow process of colorization. If we are trapped in the television, if our world has become televisual, then why not forget the real and make the television our reality? The designing of simulated wars for political gain is played out in *Wag the Dog* (Levinson 1997) eerily reflecting what many thought was the cynicism that lay behind Clinton's militarism in 1998–9 to counter the scandals of his presidency. However, these games of simulation in which the real is hidden by fabrication are not the critical issues facing technoculture today, but rather the problems of embeddedness in which information is infected from within so the real itself is reordered. It is that question which I will pursue in Part II of this book.

Why this ubiquity of challenge and confrontation of the real and the tele-visual, the organic and technological in popular culture? The struggle between reality and illusion is a problem that has persisted throughout Western culture from Plato's cave to Hamlet's seeming versus being, from Pirandello's *Six Characters* in search of their author to Baudrillard's *The Perfect Crime* (1996). The plethora of technological and simulation anxiety movies indicates both a long-standing fascination of philosophy as well as science fiction literature and cinema, and a more current response to the flood of mediatized experiences in current technoculture. In the following chapter I discuss this further by looking to the overpowering influence of the televisual.

The use of the technology of the screen in the films mentioned above is telling. There is often a person behind the curtain, a controlling force behind the screen or two-way mirror, that can be isolated as the cause of the mediated invasion. The Director in *The Truman Show*, the TV repairman in *Pleasantville* and the media specialist in *Wag the Dog* are the *men* behind the curtain. This reccurring narrative device of a motivating cause that can be revealed from behind the screen is a distinctly modern notion. Žižek, in an analysis of mediated technologies, writes that:

> modernist technology is 'transparent' in the sense of retaining the illusion of an insight into 'how the machine works'; that is to say, the screen of the interface was supposed to allow the user direct access to the machine behind the screen.
>
> (1997: 131)

He goes on to suggest that *postmodern* technologies deliver quite the opposite, with an 'interface screen [that] is supposed to conceal the workings of the machine.' The problem is that as 'the user becomes "accustomed to opaque technology" and the digital machinery "behind the screen" retreats into total impenetrability, even invisibility' (131). The growing opacity of the mediated screens require of the user a certain trust. The ideology of capitalism operates in this manner, looking to obscure understanding as to *how things work* while encouraging acquiescence to *things as they are*. These films dramatize the conflicts of the virtual and the real, while offering a normalizing or familiarizing operation for the subject position in technoculture.

Nothing to do with representation?

If theatre, performance, film and new media seem to share similar concerns and aesthetic gestures regarding the collapse of the real into the virtual and the construction of identity in the space of technology, are there common discourses to understand these problems? Lacan's writings on the scopic drive and modern drama's working through of the reality-versus-illusion question are two models I will put forth.

The materialist critique of the Lacanian (and thereby Freudian) psycho-analytic paradigm in film studies asserts that many of the models of its discourse (e.g. the Symbolic Order, the Real, etc.) are totalizing, idealistic and ahistorical, relying on sexual difference to articulate its theory at the expense of race and class differentiations.[2] Nonetheless, performance theorists continue to mine Lacan's *oeuvre* to help explicate the field,[3] and several notions concerning the screen and the scopic drive from Lacan's Seminar XI will help focus my argument.[4] I try to employ these works not as authoritarian or universal truth, but rather as metaphors, or even subjunctively, *as if* they are dramatic texts; not to extend the psychoanalytic discourse, but rather to tease out structures of subject construction in mediatized culture that reflect upon contemporary theatre practice. I reiterate my thesis: 'the inclusion of the televisual screen in performance and the practice of performance in the screened world of virtual environments constitutes the staging of the privileged object of the split subject, that which assists in the subject's division, capturing the gaze, enacting its annihilation, its nothingness, while presenting the unpresentable approach of the real through the televisual screens'.

The imaginary play (*The Scopic Drive*) which I construct from Lacan's texts regarding the drama of the self and subjectivity plots a division between the gaze and the subject of representation, the gaze and the eye, the subject and the other. The mediators between the two sets are the image and the screen.[5] The action of the plot follows two paths. The first concerns how the subject doubles itself as a result of the nature of being, being split, and the fascination that grows for the determining factor in that division.[6] Lacan writes, 'the interest the subject takes in his own split is bound up with that which determines it – namely, a privileged object, which has emerged from some primal separation, from some self-mutilation induced by the very approach of the real' (Lacan 1981: 83). The determining factor of split subjectivity in mediatized culture is rightly sensed as technology. The televisual screen is that privileged object that emerges from the separation of the self, but it is also the technology of the self-mutilation revealing the appearance of the double as the approach of the real. The question of the drama is not one of representation, of the thing and its reflection, but rather of the splitting of subjectivity.

The second story of the plot concerns the nature of the screen and its manipulations at the hands of the subject.

> Only the subject – the human subject, the subject of the desire that is the essence of man – is not, unlike the animal, entirely caught up in this imaginary capture. He maps himself in it. How? In so far as he isolates the function of the screen and plays with it. Man, in effect, knows how to play with the mask, as that beyond which there is the gaze. The screen is here the locus of mediation.
>
> (Lacan 1981: 107)

The screens are isolated, played among, and materialized as picture in order to map visions of the world. The screens are the technologies used to reconfigure ourselves and to see ourselves as what we are: pictures, screens. Orlan's work in digital photography and facial reconstruction resonates here.[7] The manipulations of the screens are manipulations of our subjectivity, whether we are in control or not. The mediated screens in live performance are both the opaque border of the representable object, trapping the gaze of the perceiving subject before it apprehends the object, and the site wherein and upon which the subject places its phantasmic projections, while seeing itself see itself. The televisual screen determines the split of the subject and becomes the trap for the gaze of the subject apprehending its doubling.

How do the contemporary theatre and performance artists listed above stage this drama? The performer appears live and videated simultaneously, one image in the process of living, being-undo-death, one image held in abeyance, virtually present. The doubling occurs when Ron Vawter creates a lip sync to his own visage on the video monitors and takes on the voices for all the guests on a recreation of a nude talk show in a type of technological-ventriloquist act in *The Wooster Group's Frank Dell's The Temptation of St. Antony*. In the next chapter, I will discuss this performance in detail. Another example is the videated interviewees from the Desperate Optimist's deconstruction of Synge's *Playboy of the Western World*, in which individuals fire guns on video which have real stage effects of exploding blood bags on the actors, creating a unified field of the televisual and the stage. It happens when Orlan's performative surgeries are streamed to galleries across the globe, or Stelarc's body is offered up for manipulations from keyboards throughout cyberspace, with the body of the performer extended, challenged and reconfigured through technology. It occurs when Guillermo Gómez-Peña prepares his website for racist and misogynist confessions. He foregrounds the Internet's inherent colonial structures and ethos of anonymity that promotes a disturbing honesty.

Where does the site of these sightings of the Double take place? It happens on the technological screens of television, computer and film. It happens within the biological screens of body and flesh. It happens within the phantasmic screens of perception. Lacan's well-known diagram of the scopic field maps the subject of representation and the gaze, as picturing one another through image and screen. The diagram reads the scopic field phenomenologically. The gaze is outside, so therefore, 'I am looked at … I am a picture' (Lacan 1981: 106). Or as Beckett put it, I am under the 'anguish of perceivedness' (1986: 323). The screens, wherein we see ourselves seeing ourselves, are not transparent, but opaque. The subject does not apprehend the object, whether that object is the other of her own subjectivity or the other of worldly objects, but her own phantasmic projections on the representational screen.

Videated subjects maintain a unique privilege in technoculture. Rock concerts are routinely supplemented by video projections that become the evidence of a live act. In stadium concerts the jumbotron video screens are the manner in which audience members access the performance. The competition between live performer and mediated representation of that performer for the perception of the spectator ends up as a draw at best. Why? The answer is as stated above, that the mediated subject is that 'which has emerged from some primal separation, from some self-mutilation induced by the very approach of the real' (Lacan 1981: 83). Does that mean that it is the split video image sourcing from a live feed that re-establishes the status of the real? Yes, the video image is more real than the live actor. The aesthetics of the combination of video and live images is a visual metaphor of split subjectivity. Lacan discusses a similar phenomenon in his lecture on anamorphosis. Anamorphosis, like perspective, is a mathematically derived distortion of an image that can be reconstructed with cylindrical reflection. Hans Holbein's much discussed painting *The Ambassadors* is the best known example of an anamorphic image, and Lacan makes much of the form. He argues that the image in Holbein's painting is unseen until one begins to walk away, to cease to look at it. Then the painting 'makes visible for us here something that is simply the subject as annihilated' (Lacan 1981: 88). The televisual image is anamorphic. It traps the gaze. It shows our nothingness. Yet this is not the site of pure negativity as the technological uncanny triggers the visitation of the other (in the guise of death), but is the ground upon which we dance the double in a renewal of being beyond the ego-centered and solidified subject.

> It is through this separated form of himself that the being comes into play in his effects of life and death, and it might be said that it is with the help of this doubling of the other or of oneself, that is realized, the conjunction from which proceeds the renewal of being in reproduction.
>
> (Lacan 1981: 107)

The doubling technologies of mediation act as a sparagmos, fragmenting the subject, displaying its fabrication and remembering what is other.

... Between the screen and the thing screened off

At this point in the text I drop the social science discourse I have borrowed and move to the more problematic, agitated texts of the theatre. I turn to two essential, if marginal, works from the canon of modern drama, Samuel Beckett's *Film* and Jean Genet's *The Screens*, to build my argument regarding postmodern digital culture and the doubling technology of the screen. Is there an irony in using modernism to articulate postmodernism, or a testament to the fact that the theoretical borders between modern and postmodern are riddled with gaps? My assertions on performance in technoculture through a discussion of film, theatrical modernism and psychoanalysis are, in the end, an attempt to widen those gaps and see the categories approach one another while remaining discrete.

Beckett, former Trinity College, Dublin lecturer and student cites Bishop Berkeley, former Fellow of the same institution, in his opening to the script of *Film*: '*Esse est percipi*' (1986: 323), to be is to be perceived. Thus, by way of Berkeley, Beckett marks the terrain of the text, and through a splitting of the vision of the protagonist between the eye and the object, the self and the other, the eye and the gaze, he creates a narrative of the struggle for and against self-perception. The dramatis personae of *Film* consist of one protagonist figured in the situation as two entities. Firstly, sundered into objecthood, he is *O* in flight, and secondly he is *E*, in pursuit. *E* is never seen until the end of the film, yet the film is filmed via the perception of *E* through the use of POV camera shots, as he pursues the object *O*. *E* and *O* are performed by Buster Keaton in the 1965 film directed by Alan Schneider and supervised by Beckett. There are restrictions to the perception of *E*, as he, or it, must always remain in a 45-degree 'angle of immunity' behind *O*. At 46 degrees *O* enters the 'anguish of perceivedness'.

> All extraneous perception suppressed, animal, human, divine, self-perception maintains in being. Search for non-being in flight from extraneous perception breaking down in inescapability of self-perception. No truth-value attaches to above, regarded as of merely structural and dramatic convenience.
>
> (Beckett 1986: 323)

Beckett is making clear what his film is about and what the concerns are, namely the shutting down of perception in an impossible search for non-being. But, then, in a rather ironic tone, Beckett states that 'no truth-value attaches' to what has been modelled in the work, as it is, after all, a film.

Traditional dramatic structure remains intact in Beckett's theatre no matter how impossibly reduced and condensed the work becomes: protagonist, antagonist, conflict and resolution. *Film* is no exception. *Film* is structured in three parts: street, stairs and room. The room section is itself divided in three: (1) preparation of the room wherein 'all extraneous perception is suppressed'; (2) destruction of the photographs; and (3) the 'final investment of *O* by *E* and the dénouement' (323). In the first section on the street, *O* is relentlessly tracked by *E* through a 'dead straight' street peopled with couples only, all travelling in the same direction, 'all contentedly in percipere and percipi' (324). *O* collides with an elderly couple, but moves on. *E* pauses to view the couple. The woman carries a monkey under her arm.

> She feels the gaze of *E* upon them and turns, raising her lorgnon, to look at him. She nudges her companion who turns back towards her, resuming his pince-nez, looks at *E*. As they both stare at *E* the expression

gradually comes over their faces, which will be that of the flower-woman in the stairs scene and that of *O* at the end of FILM, an expression only to be described as corresponding to an agony of perceivedness.

(Beckett 1986: 325)

The couple, each raising their second set of eyes, their glasses, is facing the perceptual force of the bodiless eye (an organ without a body, a detached gaze). They are exposed and subjected to an unblinking surveillance. They become, in that moment, the vanishing point of the image, constructed by the eye, *E*, and they figuratively vanish. What the eye sees is mis-seen and negated as that which it is not, remaining ill-seen and ill-said on the edge of the void. The agony of perceivedness is the experience of being the object of the gaze. The gaze has detached from the protagonist's eye and the couple sees, or hears, only the gaze. What do they see? How are they seen in the gaze?

In section two of the film, on the stairs and in the vestibule, *E* is momentarily out the angle of immunity, and *O* cringes at his own perceivedness, his self-consciousness, his being-ness, if we are to believe that to be is to be perceived. A frail old woman descends the stairs and meets the gaze of *E*, and like the couple in section one expresses the anguish, the pain of perceivedness to the point of collapse, and falls to the floor amongst the flowers she carries for sale.

In the third segment of the film, *O*, in an almost barren room, deliberately closes down all extraneous perception. He cannot tolerate his position as picture. He sees from one point but is *scene* from all points. The eyes of a dog, cat, fish, bird, window, painting, photographs, furniture, are all closed and hidden. Systematically, like Clov's tortuous climbing of the ladder, *O* draws the curtains to close off the window, shrouds the mirror, removes the dog and cat, and covers the fish bowl and birdcage. Sitting in a rocking chair as if at 'the end of a long day', he sees a picture of 'the face of God the Father, the eyes staring at him severely' (327). He tears up the picture in the script, and in the film version there is a grey rectangle, a trace of the picture of God, which remains on the wall. It is an outline or edge left on the wall like the pallet or section of wall from Beckett's TV play, *Ghost Trio*. The remains of what is left over in lessening and worsening the situation is made visible.

Like Krapp, *O* reviews his life not in sound but in image in the form of photographs. He looks at each picture, which forms a short history of a life, and he rips each one in quarters and discards. Unseen, or so he might wish to believe, *O* drifts off to sleep in the rocking chair, thereby allowing the investment and dénouement to take place. At this point *E* is released from the 45-degree confinement. *E*, embodied in the camera's POV, attempts to round *O*, but is forced back as *O* stirs and half awakens. *O*, now fully asleep, allows *E* to approach, to turn, or corkscrew, along the edges of the room, the walls, past the *voided* technologies of perception. The eye confronts the object. In the case of the actual film, it is Buster Keaton observing Buster Keaton. The self as perception confronts the self as other, as *E* is the double of *O*. *O* in perceivedness holds his hands to his face covering his eyes. The film presents a drama in which to see one's self is to demolish one's self, to know one's nothingness. When *E* meets *O* we see both faces for the first time, save what was revealed in the photographs. *O* is shocked at the uncanniness of seeing himself, and seeing himself see himself.

Film reminds us that the technologies of vision and their will to representation have at their essence 'no truth value attached', to be 'regarded as of merely structural and dramatic convenience'. The protagonist *O*, sundered into objecthood, races through the streets under the surveillance of the eye, *E*, in a 'Search for non-being in flight from extraneous perception breaking down in inescapability of self-perception' (Beckett 1986: 325). *Film* articulates a revulsion to seeing oneself see oneself, what Deleuze called a quest to know 'how can we rid ourselves of ourselves and demolish ourselves' (Deleuze 1989: 123). The screen in *Film* is not only the material site upon which the actual work (the film) is projected, but also the optical and virtual space which hides the object from the eye and which challenges a metaphysics of discovery. Whatever is behind the screen or embedded within the screen is unknowable. It is the *void*, not non-being, but an absent presence, whose presence hovers but is unattainable.

Genet's play *The Screens*, which narrates elements of the Algerian struggle for independence from France, pictures the eternal recurrence of the screens as a material site of subjugated peoples upon which are projected the virtual spaces presented for the use of the colonial power. The play follows Saïd, a poor thief; his Mother, who is a long time sufferer and survivor; and his wife, Leila, 'the ugliest woman in the next town'. They are the outcasts of the rejected, abjection personified; yet they know how to function in a colonial system. In this excerpt Saïd and Leila serve the French colonialists by manufacturing the images and sounds upon the material screens of the stage.

THE VAMP: It's awfully hot.

THE SON (*to Saïd*): Did you hear? Make some shade for Madame, and be quick about it.

SAÏD *kicks* LEILA, *who approaches the screen and, very slowly and carefully, draws with green chalk a magnificent palm tree.*

THE VAMP (*admiringly*): Oh! Palms!

THE SON (*to Leila*): Make a little breeze for Madame.

With her mouth, LEILA *simulates the sound of wind in the branches and with her skirt, the rush of air.*

THE VAMP (*blandly*): Thank you. I told you so: there are some lovely ones among the lot. Not everything's rotten. Those, for example, (*Pointing to Saïd and Leila*) they're no doubt supporters of ours.

(Genet 1962: 110)

The French colonialists in the characters of The Vamp and The Son demand that a world be painted for them on the eternal screens. Saïd and Leila readily submit their skills for the comforts of the ruling class. Why haven't they used those skills to better their own lot? Because they work the screens, but they don't own the screens. The stage is composed of screens upon which are drawn the material objects that are struggled over and negotiated between colonialist and subjugated other. The screens, functioning like the actual screen necessary for the projection of the film of *Film*, are the primary element of Genet's *mise-en-scène*. The screens are used to stage the stage. They are the material site of the stage but also the metaphors for colonial occupation, border zones of perception and apertures through which subjects pass through from life to death, from representation to the unknown, from one state of being to another. Genet remarks in the script that next to each screen on the stage there must be at least one real object. The contrast of screen and real object is a typical dramatic device of Genet. The linkage is to suggest that one operates at the behest of the other, not separately, or in cancellation of the other, but in a symbiotic relation; no illusion, no reality, and visa versa.

In the narrative the Algerians, through the demands of the French, operate but do not control the screens. The screens are a place, a location, wherein one can exit or enter, hide or be revealed. They are, in essence, each a tiny theatre with curtains and prosceniums, where a world is created through the pictures drawn on them. The screens are each a sign system of constructed subjectivities and identities. They are sometimes opaque or translucent or breakable. Genet's play stages the world that is created through representations, meaning the only world that exists.

The colonial soldiers understand the power of the screens to double, to mirror, and to create the illusions of volume. In order to dominate, it is necessary to replicate. One soldier should represent one million.

> Let every man be a mirror to every other man. A pair of legs must look at themselves and see themselves in the pair of legs opposite, a torso in the torso opposite, the mouth in another mouth, the eyes in the eyes.
>
> (Genet 1962: 119)

The colonial power is looking to control difference, to kill the other, through the replication of the screens as mirrors reflecting their sameness. The colonialist will not see who stands behind the screen, who moves them, or who paints them. To acknowledge their contribution is to share power and grant subjecthood.

The screens in Genet's play also demarcate the space between the living and the dead. Breaking through the paper screens into the world of the dead Kadidja, as does every other character upon entering the new space, exclaims, 'And they make such a fuss about it!' (Genet 1962: 143). The movement to the other side is a crashing through the material, a falling through the abjection, toward being on the reverse surface of the screens. The other side is the place outside the discourse of representations. The screen is the boundary at the closure of representation, and in that space laughter consumes the agony of subjugation, now finished. The Mother, having recently arrived on the other side of the screens, sees the world with new eyes.

> Those are the truths ... ha! ... ha! ... ha! ha! ... that can't be demonstrated ... ha! ha! (Her laughter seems uncontrollable.) Those are the truths that are false! ... ha! ha! ha! ho! ho! ho!'
>
> (Genet 1962: 155)

The screens, turned inside out through the subject's vanishing create a space wherein the fabrications of the other side are shown to be ridiculous, hideous and tragic.

Genet's play situates the discussion of the screens in a political and material site, by asking: who manages the screens, controls what is projected upon them and imagines what they hide? The issues of hyper-mediacy and the ubiquity of the screens is not simply an aesthetic, a dense theory, a psychoanalytical model, but rather a material, political problem. The screens cover a large portion of the earth, feeding our phantasms to the world. The screens are creating postcolonial subjects from the comfort of a Burbank sound stage, projecting the images of war distanced from the reality of the conflict, creating history's largest trap for the gaze of the world spectator.

A rebirth of tragedy

The marking of the uncanny and the performance of split subjectivity in technologically enhanced performance suggests much more than just a new aesthetic. It suggests a symptom or a way of thinking through the transitional phase Western subjectivity is undergoing as a result of mediatization. The transition can be constructed, problematically no doubt, as a re-birth of tragedy. Like Nietzsche's model of the birth of tragedy rooted in the movement from the divine body to the body inscribed and subjugated under the rule of societal law, which finds representation in the sacrificial rituals of dismemberment (sparagmos), the ontological shift from organic to technological, televisual and digital being is tragic. The tragic, in this case, finds representation and is projected in the fantasies of the fragmented and digital, medical and postcolonial body as articulated in the performance work of Stelarc, Orlan and Guillermo Gómez-Peña.

> [The] fragmented body [...] usually manifests itself in dreams when the movement of the analysis encounters a certain level of aggressive disintegration in the individual. It then appears in the form of disjointed limbs, or of those organs represented in exoscopy, growing wings and

taking up arms for intestinal persecutions, the very same that the visionary Hieronymus Bosch has fixed for all time, in painting, in their ascent from the fifteenth century to the imaginary zenith of modern man.

(Lacan 1977: 5)

The fragmented body appears at the vanishing point of subjectivity, when its nothingness is apprehended, when the double is dancing, when Pentheus's head is raised by his mother and proclaimed to be a lion, when in fact it has become the mask, the screen. When *O* meets *E* in the room shut out from all perception save one, when the screens of postcolonialism are pierced, when the other side of the screen is suggested and approaches, then tragic fragmentation is possible. Blau writes,

> Or is that we've had along with talk of the death of tragedy a twisted version of an active forgetting: the invention of aesthetic strategies that would, indeed, either anesthetize us against emotions we found intolerable, or, as eventually in body art, confront us in such a way that they could be absorbed or experienced again?
>
> (Blau 1992: 126)

Perhaps a rethinking of tragedy is possible now, but a tragedy that is removed from the tragic in a subtractive logic of lessening. In Part II of this volume I will consider this notion via the *Tragedia Endogonidia* of Socìetas Raffaello Sanzio.

Answers

I began with two questions: First, how has the ontology of the performance (liveness), which exists before and after mediatization, been altered within the space of technology? Second, how do we understand the processes of performance which converges with mediated technologies of representation? In answer to the first query, it is important to realize that performance, like the body and its subjectivity which enacts the performative, has been extended, challenged and reconfigured due to its position in the space of technology. Performance has taken on the ontology of the technological. One way to start to answer both questions is by conceiving of theatre as a medium that overlaps and subsumes or is subsumed by other media including television, film, radio, print and computer-aided hyper-media. Such a process will change, considerably, our definition of the boundaries of the theatre and the ontology of performance.

2 Televisual performance

Openness to the mystery

> Because the essence of technology is nothing technological, essential reflection upon technology and decisive confrontation with it must happen in a realm that is, on the one hand, akin to the essence of technology and on the other, fundamentally different from it. Such a realm is art.
>
> (Heidegger 1977: 317)

> Television is not only more than its technology but also more than its cultural form – it has become what we will call the televisual, and as such is definable as an ontological domain.
>
> (Fry 1993: 11)

Two interrelated phenomena of technoculture, the evolving status of the televisual and the introduction of a new performative territory in the virtual site of cyberspace, challenge the most fundamental beliefs concerning performance, including its claims to liveness, immediacy and presence. In the previous chapter, I spoke to the various positions surrounding the phenomena of the collision of live performance and technological reproduction articulated through the work of Auslander (1999) and Phelan (1993). My assertion throughout Part I of this book is that the ubiquitous presence of the televisual in contemporary theatre and the reconfiguration of performance in the virtual space of the computer establish a unique model of performance, wherein the immediacy of performance and the digital alterability of time and space through technology are subsumed and confused within each other.

In this chapter I will focus on the practice of live performance that incorporates video technologies, postponing the variety of issues surrounding computer-aided performance until the next chapter. I will attempt to position the theoretical concerns of televisual performance in relation to a technologized culture and illustrate some of the resulting aesthetic strategies.

My questioning concerning the televisual in live performance is simple, but, I believe, critical: if the ontology or essence of performance is its orbiting disappearance which resists the technology of reproduction, what takes place upon the collision of the televisual, which keeps appearing/picturing, and the performative which employs an aesthetics of dematerialization? How does the maniacally regenerating *now* of performance interact with the reproducible flow of the televisual and its economy/circulation of representation? I suggest that the *now*, the immediate, has become one of the *accidents* (the mere appearance) of the transubstantiation of performance into the technological. I will provide evidentiary material in the form of a performance analysis of *The Wooster Group's Frank Dell's The Temptation of St. Antony* via a gloss of Heidegger's questioning of technology, in order to attempt to prove this admittedly rather extreme theoretical claim. However, it is an assertion that is echoed by many researchers across various fields, who argue that identity and subjectivity are being substantially altered by our interactions with technology. Over the last ten to fifteen years there has been an immense amount of theoretical musing over the nature of subjectivity in technoculture. The aforementioned books by Auslander (1999), Case (1996) and Phelan (1993) are the most important within the area of performance studies, but within the fields of philosophy, critical theory, cultural studies, sociology, and science and technology studies there have been many more writings. These include the writings of Baudrillard, Virilio, Žižek, and Arthur and Sue Kroker. Books such as Elizabeth Grosz's *Architecture from the Outside: Essays on Virtual and Real Space* (2001), Rutsky's *High Techne: art and technology from the machine aesthetic to the posthuman* (1999), *Bodies in Technology* (2001) by Don Ihde, and Dyens's *Metal and Flesh: the evolution of man: technology takes over* (2001) are exemplary of the field. For nearly every field of study there are works in which the effects of technology are being considered. Most of the work in these areas of technoculture and subjectivity and aesthetics carry on, if recognized or not, the later work of Michel Foucault on bio-politics and its concern for the position of individual life under increasing controls of the state and culture. The foremost thinker currently in the area of bio-politics is Giorgio Agamben whose *Homo Sacer* (1998) is a major contribution to the field. In Part II of this study I will discuss the importance of the questions of bio-politics in contemporary culture and the manners in which theatre performance is affected.

Critical, cultural and aesthetic studies concerned with the effects of technology on culture and art, identity and subjectivity, have to a large extent relied on Martin Heidegger's *The Question Concerning Technology* (1977) as a primary philosophical starting point. Avital Ronell's *The Telephone Book* (1989), *Technoculture and Critical Theory* (2002) by Simon Cooper, and the anthologies *Rethinking Technologies* (1993) and *RUA/TV?: Heidegger and the Televisual* (1993) follow this model. My own theoretical strategy is no exception. However, it is crucial to note that many theorists, in attempting an understanding of the politics, ethics and aesthetics of *answering the call of technology*, have appropriated Heideggerian thought given his response to his own *call* from technology in the form of early support for Germany's National Socialism (as represented in his infamous rectorial address of 1933). Each of the above books confronts the problem in a similar fashion by questioning whether or not fascist tendencies are inherent in Heideggerian metaphysics. Philippe Lacoue-Labarthe's (1990) *Heidegger, Art and Politics* and Derrida's *Of Spirit: Heidegger and the Question* (1991) have both dealt deftly with the problem of Heidegger's politics. Continental philosophy's thinking in terms of being, essence and truth has been severely critiqued by proponents of the analytic tradition, including the marvellously succinct statement from Wittgenstein's *Tractatus*, 'whereof one cannot speak, thereof one must be silent' (1981: 151). But here I have pointed to two problems: first, the problem of thinking metaphysically about the materiality of technology, and second, the issue of fascist tendencies in Heidegger's questioning. Ronell counsels that it is important to remember where Heidegger's thinking took him, and how that process is still not quite understood: 'the asserted origin of Heidegger's relation to National Socialism began with the call of technology that has yet to get through to us' (1989: 8). To attempt to question the essence of technology is not necessary to misplace the knowledge of the intimate ties of technological advancements, nor is it necessary to forget the militaristic and fascistic cultures and governments which operate as *technocracies* that repress individuality and substantiate an order of bio-politics, placing the struggle of power on the *bare life* of the subject. For the purposes of this chapter, I take from Heidegger an understanding of 'the possibility for a free relation to technology' (Ronell 1989: 8) while remaining cognizant of the disturbing critique of that freedom offered by his actions.

The central thesis of Martin Heidegger's *The Question Concerning Technology* is that nature and humankind have become *standing reserve*, the necessary fuel for the *bringing forth*, and the revealing of modern technology in its own *interlocking path*, its *regulated course*. The scenario follows Hegel's master/slave model suggesting that the slave machine is now master to the human. Humankind, in the Heideggerian paradigm, is lost to itself as it stands ready to serve technology. Heidegger writes, 'the revealing that rules in modern technology is a challenging [Herausfordern], which puts to nature the unreasonable demand that it supply energy which can be extracted and stored as such' (1977: 296). Herbert Marcuse (2001) made similar claims regarding the loss of individuality and freedom for subjects of technocracies. In a less dystopian rhetoric, Bruce Mazlish claims that 'humans and the machines they create are continuous' (Mazlish 1993: 4) and are no longer autonomous. Richard Dienst, in *Still Life in Real Time: theory after television* (1994), and Fry, in the aforementioned *RUA/TV*, suggest the problem of agency has accelerated in technological and digital culture. Cultural memory and knowledge have been transferred to the televisual, while the subject's disembodied voices (within fibre-optics) and dematerialized bodies (transported through the datasphere and represented on the net) offer testament to a new existence in the technological. The advent of the digital worlds of virtual environments, artificial intelligence and the televisual, as well as the medical advancements of the mechanic and electronic alteration of the body in devices such as pacemakers, electronic ears, and silicon chips implanted in the peripheral nervous system to interface with robotic limbs, have reconfigured our sense of time, space and subjectivity. Humankind is not what it once was; we have entered a *post-human* phase, as William Gibson has named it, and as Donna Haraway (1990) and Kate Hayles (1999) have theorized it. A post-human culture will create a post-organic art, which is the topic of the next chapter.

Understanding subjectivity and identity in technoculture and the manners in which artists and practitioners reconsider performance, Heidegger's questioning remains a central concern. Can there be a revealing outside the interlocking path and regulated course of technology, or must performance forgo the human in order to play out the demands of technology? Or, has the human being and the being in technology collapsed in on one another, requiring the unconcealment of each to uncover the other? The binary argument of the former question is too nostalgic and reductivist to be of much use. The latter question contains my thesis.

According to Heidegger, the goal of philosophy lies in the inquiry as to the essence of a thing; *what* the thing is, the thingness of the thing. He suggests that through thinking, an attempt is made to open human existence to the essence of an object. Heidegger describes two types of thinking: the representational and the meditative (or non-representational). Representational thinking pictures the world as an object in service to human goals. The objects of the representationally thinking subject are reduced to the raw material of the subject's desire. The object is constructed as a standing reserve whose function is to serve the revealing, or simple pleasure, of the observer. The essence of the object is left concealed. In that sense, the representationally thinking subject has not yet begun to think. 'Meditative thinking is a situation of being open to what is beyond the [...] horizon of knowing' (Scheibler 1993: 128). Heidegger's theory states that the thingness of the thing can be unconcealed through an *openness to the mystery* of non-representational thinking.

In the modality of representational thinking, technology has been defined as a means to an end or a human activity. Heidegger counters that the *essence* of technology is something quite distinct from what we normally consider to be technology. He defines the essence of technology as a *bringing forth*, a way of allowing that which is not yet present to arrive into *presencing*. Heidegger recalls Aristotle's four causes of bringing forth a thing into presence: materiality, form, final use and effect. The Aristotelian causality, according to Heidegger, is superficial, as the model constructs the bringing forth of a thing so as to obtain results and effects: what the philosophers would call 'the productivist basis of the metaphysical tradition' (Fry 1993: 24). In contrast, Heidegger cites Plato's definition of *poiesis* as a *bringing forth*, as poetry, as art. In the *Symposium* (205b), Plato wrote that 'every occasion for whatever passes beyond the nonpresent and goes forward into presencing is poiesis, bringing forth' (quoted in Heidegger 1977: 293). The essence of technology, according to Heidegger's argument, is similar to art and poiesis, as an act of bringing forth the concealed to the unconcealed.

Heidegger constructs a very different model for modern technology. Modern technology does not enact a *bringing forth* of the *presencing* of the human or objects of nature, but rather operates as a *challenging*, which demands nature supply energy that can be extracted and stored. In this manner technology regenerates itself for itself through the fuel of nature.

> Such challenging happens in that the energy concealed in nature is unlocked, what is unlocked is transformed, what is transformed is stored up, what is stored up is, in turn, distributed, and what is distributed is switched about ever anew. Unlocking, transforming, storing, distributing, and switching about are ways of revealing. But the revealing never simply comes to an end. Neither does it run off into the indeterminate. The revealing reveals to itself its own manifoldly interlocking paths, through regulating their course.
>
> (Heidegger 1977: 298)

Heidegger terms this essence of modern technology *Gestell* or *enframing*. Energy in nature, in the process of enframing, is processed for the purpose of satisfying the revealing of technology. What transpires is an orbiting revealing of technology that perpetuates itself. In this model the real is subjugated to a *challenging forth* and *setting upon* by technology as a *standing reserve* for the revealing of technology. The only accessible real in technoculture is technological.

How does this model of technology inform the strategies of contemporary performance? Can one step out of the role of standing reserve? Can an *unconcealment* be possible in a simulated technoculture? My questioning is similar to that of Philip Auslander, who, in *Presence and Resistance* (1992), articulated the problems of transgressive or resistant action in postmodern culture, an argument which Baz Kershaw later strongly critiqued in *The Radical in Performance* (1999). Auslander questioned the possibilities of radical action along the lines of those propounded by Fredric Jameson in *Postmodernism: The cultural logic of late capitalism* (1991) noting the problems of aesthetically escaping the machinery of the hyper-commodification of capitalism. Kershaw argues for the necessity of maintaining the commitment to the possibilities for political action, and community-based theatre is one of the effective means of doing so. The theatre is surely at its best when it locates and addresses the local, as Brecht attempts in his *Lehrstücke*, or as Boal understands in his *Theatre of the Oppressed* (1985). The power of performance at the individual level maintains its unique effectiveness. Nevertheless, faced with the powers of late capitalism and globalism, performance can seem inadequate as a defense.

The questioning of technology posed, I will attempt to draw a provisional map of *televisual performance* in order to question how video technology plays itself out in performance. The history of video art and videated performance began with such video and performance artists as Nam June Paik and Wolf Vostell, who were innovators in the use of video in performance and art by the early 1960s. The introduction of Sony's *Portapak* video system in 1965 initiated the widespread practice of video art. Throughout the 1990s and early twenty-first century, video, performance and theatre artists such as Bill Viola, Laurie Anderson and *The Wooster Group* have furthered the aesthetics of video and performance through the digital processing of the videated image and the simultaneous generation of live and mediated images within performance. What can be seen in this work is, as *The Wooster Group* has claimed, 'a new theater language which redefines the traditional devices of storyline, character, and theme' (*Wooster Group* 1989: Programme Notes). I analyse this theatre language after first articulating the representational structures and ontological phenomena of the televisual.

The televisual has been theorized 'as a repository of our knowing and as memory [...] mark[ing] a key moment in the partial transference of metaphysics into techno-cultural systems' (Fry 1993: 12) conducting a 'reshaping of ways in which we see [...with] repercussions on the way that we think' (D'Arcy 1993: 104). Arguing along a similar line but challenging any theorization of the televisual, Fredric Jameson posits that television's 'exclusion of memory' and 'of critical distance' (1991: 71) results in a challenging of its theorization. In a similar vein as Paul Mann's declaration that 'the theory of the avant-garde is its death and the death of the avant-garde its theory' (1991: 3), Jameson claims that the theory of video is its closure of theory. If the televisual is the agent of enucleated memory, the suppressor of critical distance and the media machine of the undoing of presence and time, it surely does stand alone as the premiere contrivance of the postmodern art practice and the final solution of technocratic control in orgiastic commodity fetishism. Combine the claims of Fry, D'Arcy and Jameson, and the equation reads that the culture of the televisual is one in which the ways in which we think are increasingly televisual and that this thinking is without effective memory or critical distance.

Theorists such as Raymond Williams (1973, 1975) have modelled the uniqueness of television as a *whole* or *total flow*, which can only simulate the phenomenon of closure. The cycles of hour/half hour programming punctuated by even smaller segments of product marketing do not represent complete narratives. According to Frederic Jameson, television manipulates the material punctuation of traditional performance so as to give the simulation of beginning and end. Television's *fictive-fictive time*, its layers of channels and capacity for multiple viewings in real time (screen within a screen), multiple scrolling banners and frames, and the chance operations of the remote control device, constitute a sublime simulation: a simulation of simulations, a closing in of object and representation. Instead, by developing a structure of fictive-fictive time, television engenders an illusion of closure. The technique of fictive-fictive time is what can keep the attention of the viewer mesmerized for such long periods of time. It never actually concludes, so there is no satisfaction or even catharsis, to borrow Aristotle's troubled notion, as we might consider in a traditional theatre work. The object of desire recedes indefinitely on an endless loop. It is the troubling nature of the computer-generated and televisual flow that uniquely marks our contemporary media. The loop becomes the orbiting system that neither rises nor falls in action, but continues unabated in an infinite time register.

Jameson writes that video, and in particular what he calls *experimental art video*, has the capacity to represent the 'pure and random play of signifiers [...] now reference and reality disappear altogether, and even meaning' (1991: 96). Although video and television are unequalled in their capacity for depthless 'surrealism without the unconscious' (Jameson 1991: 67), the employment of video in performance can form a quite different function than that of the random play paradigm. The function is, as displayed in the American *liberation* of Kuwait in 1991, *Desert Storm*, a simulation machine of dreadful consequence.

As the so-called *100 Hour War* concluded, there was an unprecedented high approval rating from the American people to the exercise. Baudrillard (1995) and Virilio (2002) have offered analyses of how that Gulf War was packaged for the world spectator, and their readings reveal that the military–industrial complex of the time applied simulation techniques with great dexterity. The Pentagon producers of this 'Perfect descriptive machine, which provided all the signs of the real and short-circuit[ed] all its vicissitudes' (Baudrillard 1988: 167), appeared well versed in the strategic power of diffusing the real by installing its functional double. The orchestration of this war simulation followed several rules, rules of a game that theatre/performance artists have appropriated. These rules are:

(1) *Every action/image must be presented in its third order representation, preferably deterred by a mediatic intervention.* An example of this strategy was brilliantly realized in the installation of video cameras onto armed missiles. The distributed video images depicted unerring accuracy (e.g. the missile that descended a drainage pipe to reach its target) while deferring any rupture of the simulated real by the real itself (e.g. death and mutilation).

(2) *Every action/image encoded with the real must be deterred.* First-order representations, such as the direct results of a bomb on a human figure were censored or manipulated into a *less real* and thereby *more real* image for the spectator; do not show the body disabled, show the technology at work. The disenfranchisement of the media from the *real* war assured the strategists an ability to stage their simulation without fear of directorial interference and with the freedom to fulfil their goal of the substitution of the real for signs of the real. What transpired during the first Gulf War was

quite startling: the combatants, as well as the televisual spectator, were implicated and reconfigured within the simulation. Signs and images were loaded into the televisual warplanes by the Pentagon officials and dropped from the payload doors onto the global spectator, who watched the war unfold on CNN. The war hero/video technician had to infiltrate the spectator's consciousness via the cathode ray tube, supplying him with misinformation and terrorist tactics of mind control. Who was controlling whom? The simulation, by profiteering from the disappearance of the real, controls all within its occurrence.

The final pattern we can discern is perhaps the most telling technique of the televisual, and can tell us the most regarding how theatre and performance are altered by its inclusion: (3) *Confuse/Manipulate real time/simulation time*. The production of the simulated war occurred in the real time of the actual event, so that inquiries into the status of prior(ity) were deflected. A sign which is generated simultaneously with, or which even precedes, its referent further complicates the already problematized relation of sign to signifier, while opening up the files of origination and the issues of representation. The video performance exploits this same strategy of real time/simulated time simultaneity by displacing the human figure into different media. The same paradoxes of priority arise. As was suggested to me by Charles Lyons, we can easily posit the existence of a performer prior to the video image of that performer. But we can also surmise that the requirements of video editing, in the case of pre-recorded material, would necessitate that the image was prior to the performer *here and now*. If we include a live video camera in performance, the separation becomes more difficult. The power of simultaneous image generation begins the process of turning the simulation in on itself.

The distance (temporally) from the object to its representation is at its greatest in a work of plastic art, and at its least in its generation in the mind. As the sign and its referent approach each other's moment of generation, they begin to resemble each other to such an extent that there can be no critical distance. The *closing in* between the sign and referent displaces any phenomenon that is used to bridge the gap between them; phenomenon such as memory and critique as suggested by Jameson. There is no need for a channel or ideology through which to exchange information if there is no separation. When there is no distance to bridge, there can be no critique. This is the wickedness of the medium of video. This is why many contemporary performance, installation and video artists cannot let it go. Like the inversion of a tarot card's signification when placed upside down, so can video be transposed from an instrument of simulation and invisible ideological promulgation to a machine that runs the forced separation of object and representation, image and ideology.

There were two wars and two strategies employed in Desert Storm. The first was the expelling of the Iraqi troops from Kuwait. The second was the further simulation-indoctrination of the world spectator. The medium of this

Photocopy?

indoctrination was video. I will argue in Part II of this study that the era of simulation has ended, or at least has been extended or amended by the advent of embeddedness. Embeddedness, as exercised by the current (2006) war project of the US in Iraq and apparent in the use of embedded reporting, is a technique that seeks not to mask the real or to simulate an alternative reality, but works to infect information from within its construction, thereby controlling its production. The penultimate chapter of this book, *From Simulation to Embeddedness*, takes on this argument.

Via video, performance artists can orchestrate their work toward the questions of expression and representation, while developing the technique of simulation construction by subverting and contaminating the notion of character, acting and narrative. A videated performance operates through a gapping of the text and the human representative, through the distancing effects of technology. The technological signifier and human signifier's interplay can supply the performance with a fragmentation of here and not here, there and not there, and now and not now. What the televisual theatre displays is a schizophrenic distortion not only of time, but also of space and being. The technological signifier does not necessarily signify differently from the human signifier, but it does displace the spatial configuration both of the performance and of the subject and their respective texts. This process of fragmentation cannot take place in the traditional spatial/temporal model of the theatre that privileges the human signifier as the present, charismatic other. In this contemporary configuration, we witness the character-in-the-language-text, we see the character-in-the-spatial/temporal-performance-text, and we sense the character-in-the-electronic-space. The spacing and gapping that is created through this configuration sets up the interrogation of the subject constituted by text. The subject is not a whole; it is quite clearly a series of fragments. Priority, aura and authenticity are left tilted and skewed in the configuration of human subject in, around, outside and between the technological interventions of video.

The presence of the televisual in contemporary theatre has a similar effect. The televisual in performance, not unlike the Cubist rethinking of representational space on canvas, acts as an agent of transformation, altering the manner in which we represent and look at narrativity, subjectivity, spatiality and temporal images. The incorporation of the televisual in contemporary theater enacts a signifying *telepresence* that represents 'an experience of being present in remote locations' (Rheingold 1991: 158). Telepresence, or presence at a distance, is a term used in descriptions of virtual-environment technology to indicate the experience of the subject as being in two places simultaneously. Telepresence's real world applications include 'telepresence surgery [which] allows surgeons to combine robotic instruments with endoscopy [...] NASA uses slightly asynchronous transmissions to achieve telepresence outside terrestrial space' (Heim 1993: 158). Telepresence conferencing is now commonplace in business and academic applications. I-Chat AV on Mac OSX Panther offers four-way televisual chat sessions, and global events like *Live 8* beam simultaneous performances around the world. Performance that includes televisual technologies transposes the performing subject into an alterable digital space of *telepresence*. The actual/represented subject within the performance resides in both the cyber/virtual and the physical/real environments simultaneously. As I stated above, performance, in this configuration of technological interventions which disrupt the spatial and temporal texts, becomes what performance has never been: here and not here, now and not now simultaneously. The ontological nature of performance being in the now (the PLAY function) is altered through analog and linear technology (magnetic audio and video tape played on motor-driven cassettes) into a sequentially alterable but real-time dependent structure (the REVERSE, FAST FORWARD, PAUSE functions). Performance, through digital technologies, enters the simultaneous (INTERACTIVITY, RANDOM ACCESS) whereby the virtual image appears concurrently with or precedes the production of its referent. Performance, in the digital medium, has taken on the ontology of the technological. This theoretical concept was brilliantly engaged in *The Wooster Group's* performance work, *Frank Dell's Temptation of St. Antony* (1986).[7]

There has been a great deal, even something of a glut, of critical analyses of *The Wooster Group* over the last thirty years from such scholars as David Savran (1988), Philip Auslander (1992) and Michael Vanden Heuvel (1993), and even more recently the anthology *The Wooster Group and Its Traditions* (Callens 2004). The plethora of material on the company indicates both the wide ranging influence and genuine innovation of the company, but also suggests the paucity of a wider community of interesting aesthetic performance and theatre. *Frank Dell's The Temptation of St. Antony* is the third performance work in a trilogy by *The Wooster Group* called *The Road to Immortality*. The first two works are *Route 1 & 9* (1981) and *L.S.D. (... just the high points...)* (1985) with *Brace Up!* serving as the epilogue. *Frank Dell's Temptation of St. Antony* is a deconstructive response to Flaubert's dramatic poem *La Tentation de Saint Antoine*, which narrates St. Antony's spiritual journey into the desert. *The Wooster Group's* performance is a collision of a variety of texts including Flaubert's *La Tentation de Saint Antoine*; Ingmar Bergman's film *The Magician*; *The Road to Immortality*, which is a book concerning necromancy; and *Ladies and Gentlemen, Lenny Bruce* by Albert Goldman. According to the programme accompanying the 1990 mounting at the Museum of Contemporary Art in Los Angeles, California:

> Source texts are quoted, reworked, and juxtaposed with fragments of popular culture and social history as well as with events and situations, which emerge from personal or collective experience of group members. These various elements are fused into a theatrically cohesive collage score – the final text.
>
> (*Wooster Group* 1989: Programme Notes)

The Wooster Group's dramaturgical and performative strategies of appropriation and collage have more in common with video editing, both magnetic and digital, than with traditional theatre practice. The process of video editing is to create or collect source tapes and to reassemble segments of those tapes in a new order to create a *master*. The video editor creates a new original from the bits and pieces of the former originals, the source tapes. The source tapes for *The Wooster Group* are the series of chosen texts, personal narratives, and material culled from popular culture which are reordered, processed through extensive rehearsal, and edited into a new original.

When performed at the Performing Garage in NYC, the set for the *Frank Dell's The Temptation of St. Antony* was placed in a proscenium configuration and consisted of a large black platform about five feet in height that extended across a majority of the performing space. The platform, controlled by hydraulic lifts, could raise to a rake or flat wall with a large window and doors on either side. Fluorescent lights and huge industrial light bulbs were rigged from the ceiling in front of the platform and were raised and lowered via a motor-controlled pulley system. Video monitors were suspended from the ceiling and placed on the stage. Some of the audio and video equipment was located on the front of the set and was controlled by one of the performers. Ron Vawter, playing the role of Frank Dell, sitting on a stool, wearing a robe with suggestions of a faux Middle Easterner, spoke through a microphone. He had access to a video monitor and an electronic buzzer that he would ring to punctuate moments in the performance.

The first segment of *Frank Dell's The Temptation of St. Antony*, 'Episode 1: The Monologue', which takes place in 'a hotel room in Washington, D.C.', is given the following dual scene description in the programme:

> A Hotel Room in Washington, D.C.:
> In which Frank runs his tape, and takes a call from Cubby.
> and
> Sunset in the Desert:
> Enfeebled by prolonged fasting, the hermit finds himself unable to concentrate upon holy things. His thoughts wander: memories evoke regrets that his relaxed will can no longer suppress. His fancy leads him upon dangerous ground.
>
> (*Wooster Group* 1989: Programme Notes)

The live performers appear simultaneously on the five video monitors that surround the stage in a simulation of a cable-TV nude talk show with Vawter/Dell serving as the Host. The talk show is another appropriated text: in this case, an actual programme, *Interludes After Midnight*, that appeared on New York's public access cable station, Channel J. The show's original purpose seemed to be a creative excuse for appearing naked on TV. In *The Wooster Group*'s reworking of the talk show, the video's audio is supplied by Vawter. Live and on-stage and speaking into a microphone, Vawter/Dell creates a lip sync to his own visage on the video monitors and takes on the voices for all the guests on the talk show in a type of technological-ventriloquist act. He recites a conglomeration of Flaubert and Wooster Group rehearsal additions and it becomes apparent that he is assuming a distanced representation of St. Antony and that the figures in the talk show are taking on the signs of characters (Chimera, Devil, Sphinx, Hilarion) from *La Tentation de Saint Antoine*. Amidst the clutter of a stage exposed and opened with technology, which seems at times a materialist examination of theatrical image-manufacturing, along with the tacky, perverse and banal talk show, the choice of the metaphysical tale of St. Antony's spiritual battle in the desert is intriguing. Kitty Mrosovky in her introduction to her translation of *La Tentation de Saint Antoine* (the translation used by *The Wooster Group*), wrote that Flaubert, 'knew about psychic disturbance, because he was interested in religions and religious feeling, and because the desert saint's demonic illuminations could figure the arid tedium of life and the dangerously empty power of words' (Mrosovky 1980: 3). The juxtaposition of Flaubert's troubled metaphysics and the technological materialism both of *The Wooster Group's* staging and of the Channel J text allows the spectator to place the discourse of metaphysics in the technological, the technological into metaphysics and the body into both. On stage Frank speaks a portion of dialogue from the Devil in Flaubert's text concerning the immensity of the universe and God's place within it. He describes God as 'such and such a size'. Simultaneously, on the video, Vawter/Host is interviewing a naked woman as the camera pans down and zooms in to show her vagina. She turns to show her ass as Vawter/Frank and Vawter/Host repeat 'such and such a size' with a lascivious expression. Flaubert's hallucinations of the heavens and his philosophical inquiries are laced into the technological maze inhabited by comical nudes. Vawter/Dell reworks a speech from the Devil in Flaubert:

> Form is perhaps an error of your sense, and Substance an image in your mind. Unless – the world being a perpetual flux of things – appearance on the contrary were to be all that is truest, and illusion the one reality. But are you sure of seeing? Are you even sure of being alive? Perhaps there is nothing! Worship me, therefore! And curse the ghost you call God!
>
> (Flaubert 1980: 212)

The performance plays through technoculture's aforementioned witnessing of the 'partial transference of metaphysics into techno-cultural systems' (Fry 1993: 12) and the inevitable anxiety-turned-mania that has accompanied the transition. If there is no off-switch to the technological, as Avital Ronell suggests and if the call of technology has been placed and technoculture has answered, no one element of our existence will be untouched.

Many subjects of industrial countries now reside in a technological universe of *such and such a size* where it is common to question that 'perhaps there is nothing', but nonetheless obediently *stand by* as *standing reserve*.

The vertiginous dramaturgy of *The Wooster Group* is folded into another complication as Vawter/Dell occasionally asks to be reminded of his place in the text from his on-stage secretary, and directs the offstage video technician to rewind or fast forward the videotape so that he can rehearse certain sections of the 'talk show'. At one point when Sue, the secretary whose face is hidden behind a small folding curtain, is cueing Frank on his lines, she reads to him from *The Road to Immortality*. The book narrates the contact by Geraldine Cummins, through trance, to the deceased R.W.H. Meyers, the founder of the Society for Psychical Research. Lenny Bruce, we are told in the programme notes, had his secretary, Sue, read to him from *The Road to Immortality* during the last weeks of his life. The segment of text appropriated by *The Wooster Group* describes how the human body is always in a state of vibration, and the reality that is experienced by the subject is controlled by the vibratory rate of the body. Death, the text theorizes, is but a different rate of speed of the vibratory state. Change the speed, and change the reality. Vawter/Dell, taking some solace in this notion, tells the video technician to throw the tape into fast forward, thereby altering the reality of his subjectivity, cheating death or embracing it, one doesn't know. An ecstatic moment occurs on the stage, as the videated image races forward and the live image pulsates in the now. The vibratory rates of the two images are subsumed in each other in a reordering of performative time and space, resulting in a new metaphysics. The commingling of hallucination, materialism, spiritualism and perversion, played against the technological demands on the desiring body, disrupts a single reading of the performance, requiring the spectator to take on the new issues surrounding a mediated culture.

The density of the performance text of *Frank Dell's The Temptation of St. Antony* is exhausting. However, a quote from Flaubert included in the programme to the show provides a clue to the devising strategies of *The Wooster Group*:

> What strikes me as beautiful, what I would like to do, is a book about nothing, a book with no external tie, which would support itself by its internal force of style, a book which would have hardly any subject or at least where the subject would be almost invisible, if that can be so. The most beautiful works are those where there is least matter...Form, increasingly skilled, becomes attenuated; it gives up all liturgy, all rule, all measure; it abandons the epic for the novel, verse for prose; it no longer acknowledges any orthodoxy and is as free as the will that produces it.
>
> (*Wooster Group* 1989: Programme Note)

Analysis is rendered impotent in such a project where, like Joyce's recurrent acronym HCE everything is the same as nothing or, as in Beckett's *Godot*, in which nothing is everything. *The Wooster Group*'s project reaches just such a sublime aesthetic moment that reaches toward an *unconcealment* of the body in technology.

The Wooster Group makes use of video as an extension of the temporal and spatial configuration of the stage. The monitors hung across the stage allow the action of the performance to be cross-examined, pried open. *The Wooster Group* employs the film/video editing process not only in their devising but in the overall aesthetic as well. The filmic techniques of montage (the juxtaposition of images to represent an idea or narrative), dissolves (superimposing one piece of film over another), jump-cuts (editing within the same shot to create a shift in time or emotional value), and split edits (the audio for one shot overlaps the picture of another) are translated into the performance gestures of *The Wooster Group*.

Elizabeth LeCompte, director of *The Wooster Group*, has revolutionized theatre practice by incorporating the simplest techniques of video and film post-production; performance emulates the technological, and technology of the theatre is altered in the process. The collage techniques of Braque and Picasso are also echoed in the techniques of performance construction by *The Wooster Group*. The real objects of the base tray of cubist collage conduct two actions simultaneously: they represent something of an aspect of the total construction, as image; and they also present themselves in their presence as what they are as real objects. The performance actions of *The Wooster Group* often serve this same dual purpose. In neo-Brechtian fashion, the spectator is reminded of the fact that the actor is both performer and character, and that their actions are based in real-time. However, each element of the production is delivered up to the larger construction of the performance and the alterability of the videated image. In more recent work, such as *To You, The Birdie!* (2001) (Figure 2.1), the company continues the exploration of the videated body. The following statement appeared in the company's programme that accompanied the performance.

TO YOU, THE BIRDIE! allows us to further our exploration of the possibilities of 'dancing with technology' in three specific ways. We work with live feeds from on-stage cameras, which force the performer to simultaneously consider both the framed, mediated space of the monitor and the actual stage space simultaneously. We are also creating sequences that rely on the performer dancing a *pas de deux* with their own pre-recorded image, yielding movement that is psychologically evocative as well as physically captivating. A third approach involves the use of existing videotapes – including Marx Brothers films and dance pieces – on monitors visible only to the performers, who then translate physical actions and camera moves through their bodies onto the stage.

(*Wooster Group*, 2002: Programme Notes)

Figure 2.1 TO YOU, THE BIRDIE! (Phèdre), The Wooster Group, dir. E. LeCompte. Pictured (l–r): Frances McDormand, Kate Valk, and Suzzy Roche (on video). Photo: © Paula Court.

The Wooster Group's dancing with technology operates through three processes. The first process is to work with live feeds through cameras that record the actors' actions, with the signal being routed to on-stage monitors available for audience reception. As noted in the programme this requires the actor to be cognizant of both the televisual frame and the stage frame, which requires mediation between the different acting techniques required for each medium. A close-up on the television monitors requires that an actor be aware of the amplified or enlarged representations of their face, while on stage this same actor must consider how crucial it is that the theatre audience be able to read her stage face. This fluctuation of framing devices is not only an actor's challenge, but also an issue for the spectator, whose choices for viewing are at least doubled, if not further multiplied. An interesting matrix of tension exists between the actor's alternate techniques for live and mediated representations and the audience's various perspectives on those images.

The second dance with technology is referred to in *The Wooster Group*'s programme as a *pas de deux* between the actor and her pre-recorded video image. The claim is that the action yields an expression of particular psychological states and creates a charismatic physical exchange between live and technological representations. As I argued above, the confrontation of the subject's reflection by the subjection throws up for questioning the issues of priority (which came first), authenticity (which is the real) and psychic borders (where am I in the screen?). I refer the reader to Chapter 1 of this study, *The Screen Test of the Double*, for a detailed discussion of the event of a performing subject confronting her mediated self.

The third confrontation of performer and technology mentioned in the programme note to *To You, The Birdie!*, is an evocative exchange of video and filmic data displayed for the actor and conducting and directing their movements, but which are hidden from the audience. The performer becomes a medium through which technology reaches the audience. Agency and metaphysical presence reside in this formulation with the technological representations and the performers becoming like Shamans or translators, who speak the hidden knowledge to the spectator. If, as suggested, a Marx Brothers film is being played for the actors who are directed to reenact the physical antics of the film actors, the motivation and reasoning of these movements must remain strange and chaotic to an audience who has no manner of accessing the original technological representation. All the audience can observe are the performative results, and the motivating or initiatory material is unavailable. The metaphors that fly up from this technique are thick and suggest an uncomfortable position for the actor on a technological stage and, by extension, subjectivity in technoculture. The motivations for action initiated by technology remain hidden to the spectator and to the actor who is nonetheless compelled to repeat and reenact the patterns.

What one can read in *The Wooster Group's* performance is that the subject, displaced in video and performance simultaneously, is equally present in both. The live is not a privileged position and, in fact, the videated image, being alterable, contains the ability to oscillate realities within the technological and, thereby, retains an advantage over the temporal/spatially bound live subject. The interplay between the two performance modes of mediated and live creates a conflation of the mechanisms and the products of their respective image manufacturing. The mediated and the live are neither what they were, nor are they only one or the other. They have formed a discrete aesthetic form: the *tele-performative*, which presents performance at a distance, presence at a distance, a digitally malleable time and space. The structure of simultaneous live performance and prerecorded video creates a collision between the aesthetics of dematerialization (the live, the now) and the flow of the televisual (the reproducible) that challenges the autonomous nature of both.

I began this chapter by asking, through Heidegger's model, if, given the state of technoculture one could develop a *poiesis* capable of bringing forth that which lies concealed. The questions still to confront consider if the cultural logic of late capitalism, wherein critique and transgression are troubled in a fetishistic commodification, makes *unconcealment* impossible. Have the hyperreal states of simulation strategies and social dominations dealt by the apparatuses of Western technocracies (which, as Marcuse theorized, represent a decline in individual freedom and a new mechanics of conformity), created an endgame that only regenerates the eternal recurrence of the same thing wherein all is revealed in a shallow copy of depthlessness? Certainly the work of *The Wooster Group* confronts the ideological effects and cultural politics of mediatization by burying technology deep and immovably into the performance moment. *Frank Dell's The Temptation of St. Antony* collides the performative, the technological and the human, making nonsense of the notions of temporal linearity and spatial hierarchies of presence over absence. The performance becomes a non-representational thinking machine capable of critiquing the call of the technological and opening a moment for the revealing of the concealed nature of our culture.

I have sidestepped a discussion of what it is that might be concealed because an answer to such a question remains hidden in such a representational medium of theoretical discourse. I do not know; it remains desired, but out of reach; it remains unknown, impossible, cruel, Dionysian, unspoken and unspeakable. What is needed is a new theory that draws back the borders between theory and art and politics, subjectivity and objectivity, to be able to approach thinking beyond the known. But perhaps that is the work of art.

> The meaning pervading technology hides itself. But if we explicitly and continuously heed the fact that such hidden meaning touches us everywhere in the world of technology, we stand at once within the realm of that which hides itself from us, and hides itself just in approaching us. That which shows itself and at the same time withdraws is the essential trait of what we call the mystery. I call the comportment, which enables us to keep open to the meaning hidden in technology, *openness to the mystery*.
>
> (Heidegger quoted in Scheibler 1993: 126)

3 Posthuman and postorganic performance

The (dis)appearance of theatre in virtual spaces

Me*tem*psy*cho*sis: the supposed transmigration at death of the soul of a human being or animal into a new body of the same or a different species.

(Oxford American Dictionary)

The metempsychosis of performance through postorganic fields

In March of 1929 Bertolt Brecht, explaining how the traditional realist drama was inadequate as a representational device for the industrial age, wrote that 'Petroleum resists the five act structure'. He insisted that 'it is impossible to explain a present day character by features or a present day action by motives that would be adequate in our father's time' (Brecht 1964: 30). If you substitute the word *virtuality* for *petroleum* in the above sentence, you will understand the simple thesis of Part I of this book. A self-titled 'child of the scientific age', Brecht asked in *A Short Organum for the Theatre*, 'what ought our representations of men's life together look like?' (Brecht 1964: 185). The question still holds (sans the gender bias). As we consider performance in virtuality and the underlying ideology of the will to virtuality, what aesthetic performance gestures (if any) will seem appropriate to our current technological, digital and televisual culture?

What are the processes of performance and performativity in virtual domains? Before I outline my questioning, it is important to position the term performance in its material manifestation (I will discuss ontological matters later) and to isolate the areas of new media under consideration. My discussion of performance concerns itself with the category of aesthetic theatre that, according to Richard Schechner's useful 'Performance Time/Space/Event Chart' (1988: 252), includes both theatre and performance or live art. I will postpone until later chapters a discussion of the effects of technoculture on the larger models of performance and cultural phenomena. For now I forgo the areas of secular and sacred ritual, sports, and social drama, even though these categories of *restored behaviour* are being similarly affected in their convergence with the always-already mediated environment of technoculture. Acknowledging the severity of the infection brought on by the televisual and the virtual in all aspects of post-industrial culture, I will nonetheless confine my examinations to aesthetic theatre in this chapter. In subsequent chapters I will discuss contemporary cultural performance. It is important to remember that all that happens in the world can be rightly claimed to happen, to occur, to take place. It does not necessarily follow that all that happens or takes place is a performance. It is this little notion that has gotten lost in some performance studies models. An occurrence may exhibit elements of performativity without being a performance. Performance is the technology of repetition. Theatre is the doubling of that repetition that makes material the mystery that illuminates.

I wrote in the Oxford Encyclopedia of Theatre and Performance that:

> cyber-theatre, not unlike film and television, does not rely on the presence of a live actor or audience, and an argument can be made that many examples of cyber-theatre might be better described as interactive film/TV, installation art, new media art, or electronic communications. The theoretical question that is posed by these new forms is, is it necessary that some live element be present in the performance of cyber-theatre to make the genre distinction of theatre a useful model?
>
> (Causey 2003: 341)

This entry marks the variables and possibilities of cyber- or computer-aided theatre. The strategies include, *digital scenography*, which includes the use of 3-D projections, wherein live actors perform before an audience with special viewing glasses. Theatres working in this manner include San Francisco's *George Coates Theatre Works* and the *Institute for the Exploration of Virtual Realities* at the University of Kansas. *Televisual mise-en-scène* would include the use of a traditional theatre space supplemented with video monitors and projections of live and pre-recorded performers and images, such as in the work of *The Wooster Group* (US), Robert Lepage (Québec) and *dumb-type* (Japan). Mainstream theatres in London's West End and Broadway are likewise using video projections, most notably the designs of William Dudley for the National Theatre's production of Tom Stoppard's *Coast of Utopia* and Andrew Lloyd Webber's *The Woman in White*. *Telepresent performance*, facilitated through video conferencing and Internet access, denotes performance taking place in multiple locations and presented simultaneously in spaces both real and virtual.

Another possibility of computer-aided performance, a more practical term than cyber-theatre or postorganic performance, is to allow audiences *interactive access* to the performance with hypertextual, image and sound data banks, in which audience members are able to access and to direct the process of a performance. Perhaps the most promising potential computer-aided performance site would be a *smart environment* where objects, clothing and the environment itself, through sensor technology, respond to the presence of actors and spectators, triggering image and sound databanks for projections, or activating stage machinery in some manner.

Tracking technology is created with sensors attached to a performer's costume or body and fed to a computer that can process the information in real-time and animate a figure to be simultaneously projected upon the actor's body or stage screens. *Augmented reality* is used to allow audiences wearing special glasses or head mounted display (HMD) to see and hear visual and audio information, which is superimposed over a live perfor-mance. *Virtual reality* is the wearing of an HMD and navigation gloves to pass through virtual environments and interact with synthetic characters creating one's own virtual avatar. Finally there is *performance within virtual environments (MUDs, MOOs)*, which are electronic environments (MUDs, multi-user dungeons, and MOOs, multi-user dungeon object-oriented) wherein groups of individuals through Internet connections develop char-acters and scenarios, while forming virtual communities through impro-visatorial performance.

I concluded my entry in the encyclopedia by writing,

> the potential of cyber-theatre expands with the evolution of new elec-tronic communication technologies. Broadband communication through fiber-optic connections will allow for such developments as streaming video of live performances with simultaneous interactivity. The next stages of smart and virtual environments with robust interactivity will hold the possibility of creating a theatre not of actors and spectators but of individual interactivity in dramatic scenarios. Not unlike multimedia performance, which has developed into an element of popular entertainment, cyber-theatre, given its high costs of produc-tion, will likely find its most active proponents in the mass entertainments of sports, theme parks, and interactions with film and television. What is obvious is that the performativity of cyberspace is being explored and colonized. What is less apparent are how these experiments in theatre will alter our knowledge of performance, theatre, and art within and without the new technologies.
>
> (340)

As I suggested in the previous two chapters, it is, perhaps, the phenom-ena of the televisual and their *worlding of the world as picture* (to use Heidegger's model) that has most radically affected the ontology of performance. To reiterate my previous claim, the televisual, of which VR is the latest advancement, has become a primary repository for cultural memory, controlling patterns of knowledge acquisition and subject construction. Richard Dienst indicates the endgame of the televisual when he writes, 'television, then, is the perfect end point, more perfect and complex than either the Bomb or cinema, a pure will-to-vision that everywhere leaves things ready but unseen' (1994: 123). The trajectory of such theories of the televisual and the world picture leads to the suspicion that our notions of art and performance, our methods of thinking, are essentially now televisual. This is why Philip Auslander cautioned me that a term such as *televisual performance* is tautological. Performance, or perhaps more accurately, theatre, is now already televisual. The tendencies of televisual art and televisual thinking could be characterized as an incessant picturing that makes *everything* visible but nothing accessible – a simulation machine whose technological alchemy brings forth the creation of the signifier in advance of the signified, warping time, memory and critique. It is my impression that VR and the myriad of computer communication tools are merely extensions of the televisual world picture and carry that the same infections of the *plague of fantasies* as Žižek has argued (1997). The question that remains is whether the interactive properties of VR and their potential for the exploration both of social constructions and of the nature of the mind/body relation will transcend the tendencies of the televisual. Or is VR interactivity merely televisual multiple-choice that offers only the illusion of freedom and exploration? As Simon Penny put it, 'Virtual Reality [is] the completion of the enlightenment project' (1994: 231) through its insistence on sustaining the Cartesian mind/body duality, analytic geometry, and the self as steady and central. Or is it possible that VR technologies might offer new models of subjectivity, informed by post-structuralism and philosophies of discontinuity that can play into an undoing of the sense of a unified self (Nietzsche's *principium individuationis*)? In a very real sense, I am asking whether or not theatre folded in the virtual can continue, and perhaps accelerate the project of some radical philosophies and art practice that seek new models of subjectivity. I am referring to the strategies found in the cruelty of Artaud, the Dionysian of Nietzsche, the impossible of Bataille and the eros of de Sade, which all, more or less, seek to unwind the *universal lie* of the unity of self and the restrictions of identity. Or does the virtual only offer us what Žižek calls 'the unbearable closure of being' (1997: 127)?

The performance sites I am considering are located in the *virtual* territories of cyberspace created by the *concrete* technologies of computer networks interfaced with the human subject. It is, of course, the human–computer interface (HCI) that dictates the production and the aesthetics of virtual spaces. As technological advancements move us past the constrictors of keyboards, head-mounted displays and data-gloves toward more open, immersive spaces of ubiquitous computing, the interface will recede in a co-mingling of body and machine. The prosthetic body of future HCI will extend itself through the machine into distant and imaginary spaces and reordered time. It is at the moment when the subject is in a less mediated relation with technology that the notions of performance and performativity become the most useful epistemological models for understanding the process. It is interesting to note that most theory of new media and information arts are engaged through a discussion of the visual field. One example is *New Philosophies for New Media* (2004) by Mark Hansen, which draws on Bergson's models of the image and embodiment to understand processes of new media art production. The discussions are very useful but miss the essential relation of the body and machine *in performance*. I would argue that the image is now secondary to the presence of the space, the duration of the time, and the identity shifts of the subject in a new human–computer interface. Brenda Laurel's early *Computers as Theatre* (1992) is an exception to the dominance of visual critiques of new media, but makes a fatal error in using Aristotle's *Poetics* as a model for shaping narrative flow in interactive and virtual environments, thereby closing off any radical potential for virtual performance by relying on traditional narrative. I will discuss Laurel's thesis further below.

The questions explored in this chapter and in the practice of virtual or cyber-theatre are the following: How do the appearances of theatre *happen* in virtual spaces? What is the future of illusion in the technologies of the simulated real? What are the possibilities for performance aesthetics in the virtual domain? Can the fundamental and visceral property of the theatre, what Taduesz Kantor calls 'the revelatory message from the realm of death, the metaphysical shock' (Kantor 1993: 114), take place in virtual worlds? In a simulated state of hyperrealism, where is the taking place or appearing of the *sex and death of the flesh* that seems to have always phenomenologically marked performance? What is the ideology of the will to virtuality, the desire for disappearance in cyber-territories?

I will argue two issues: (1) Performance theory fails postorganic and posthuman performance. As I put forth in Chapters 1 and 2, I question the ontological claims made for performance, which regard the essence of performance as a non-repeatable phenomenon of the *now*. I call for an expanded performance theory that can address the issue of digital media, virtual reality, cyber-performance and theatre. What the mediated technologies afford performance theory is the opportunity to think against the grain of traditional performance ontology. (2) Postorganic performance fails performance theory. My concern is that postorganic performance, playing out the will to virtuality, may void itself of the capacity to realize the appearance of theatre, the presence of the flesh or as Levinas would have it, the face of the other. The trajectory of this chapter works from a call for a new perspective on the nature of performance so as to include the virtual, yet extends itself to a critique of that notion of postorganic performance.

The appearances of theatre and performance in the virtual spaces of computer networks establish a unique aesthetic object, a para-performative, tele-theatrical phenomenon wherein the immediacy of performance and the digital alterability of time, space and subjectivity overlap and are combined.

I suggest that there are two terms that can be useful in understanding the phenomena outlined: *postorganic* and/or *posthuman*. Postorganic is a term currently in use among cultural anthropologists to designate areas of research that explore the structural impact of digital technologies on contemporary social conditions. More than fifteen years ago, David Tomas wrote:

> [O]ne might envisage [...] the outlines of another postorganic form of anthropology developing in the context of cyberspace, an anthropology specifically engaged in addressing the problems of engineering cyberspatial forms of intelligence as opposed to the more conventional humanistic, more or less reflexive, study of premodernist, modernist, or postmodernist humankind.
>
> (1991: 33)

The adjective *postorganic*, for the purposes of my model for performance, reflects the transition from the privileging of presence, the authentic aura, the immediacy of the live to the exploration of issues surrounding the circulation of representations through a medium capable of temporal, spatial and subjective manipulation. The postorganic maps the stage that is revealed through the confrontation of the live performer with the various media of digital audio, video, film and the computer. In the model of postorganicism, performance is not what it was once theorized – a time-dependent disappearing act – for it no longer resides solely in the present moment of the theatre, screen or text. Auslander offers a useful critique of that model, which I quote below.

However, the term *posthuman* is likewise seductive, but no less troubling and faulty. Posthumanism, which is a different model than the posthuman, is an ongoing project initiated in the late 19th century. As a counter-argument to the notions of humanism – which tend to essentialize categories of gender and race, defer difference and construct a *family of man* as the centre of all things – strands of posthumanism have been promoted in the writings of Nietzsche, Freud and Marx. The scheme of dethroning a centralized *man* in favour of more marginalized concerns has continued in poststructuralist, feminist and postmodern thought. More recently, theorists have figured the model of the posthuman as an artefact of technoculture. The theory argues for a model of identity that is dramatically altered within technological cultures. The posthuman suggests that Western industrialized societies are experiencing a new phase of humanity 'wherein no essential differences between bodily existence and computer simulation, cybernetic mechanism and biological organism, robot teleology and human goals, exist [...] Embodiment is seen as an accident of history and consciousness is an evolutionary newcomer' (Hayles 1999). Both the body and its consciousness (no separation intended) and the spaces it inhabits are challenged and reconfigured. The technologies of scientific visualization of the body through magnetic resonance imaging, the territorializing of the body through genome mapping and genetic engineering, and the alteration of the body through aesthetic and sexual reassignment surgery and mechanical, electronic and biological prosthetics mark the speed of change in the ways the body is seen, controlled and constructed. Additionally, this posthuman body *lives* within new spaces of virtual environments and ubiquitous surveillance. This is something of an old story now, but the effects are only now beginning to be troubled over in the theatre.

I will use both posthuman and postorganic models, even though I realize the many problems of the terms and their need of correction. The ideas that our humanness has somehow disappeared or that our bodies are not of the same corruptible flesh as the animals and earthly environments that surround us are dangerous models. I use the terms to indicate the extensions and challenges to our bodies and selves brought on by the advances of new technologies. Answering the call of the technological has its ideological effects and ethical ramifications. An on-going concern is the giddy enthusiasm of technophiles for whom the technologies of digital culture are a displacement for thought, critique or action. The utopias of freed subjectivities and dispersed borders of cyberspace that many proponents of the info-age proclaim are often misguided fantasy, void of cultural or political critique, absent of accurate information concerning the actual possibilities of the new technologies, floating in a de-contextualized science fiction. The euphoria accompanying the development of computer communications and the toys of digital technology should not forgo an ideological critique and ethical consideration. The technologies of virtual realities, from avatar-assigned chat-rooms to interactive immersive virtual environments, can allow the performer/operator to explore a host of disembodied performance games and interactions that demonstrate 'the reconception of machine and organism as coded texts through which we engage in the play of writing and reading the world' (Haraway 1990: 194). Early celebrants of the power of the digital to expand consciousness included Sherry Turkle (1995) and Allucquere Rosanne Stone (1995), who saw in cyberspace an arena for the staging of transgender shifts, ethnic morphing, temporal and spatial reconfiguration, which could construct a cyborgian utopia that signalled the wholesale subversion of boundaries between man and animal and machine, wholeness and fragmentation, natural and artificial, origin and telos. Žižek questions these assumptions, writing:

> [...] the standard motif of 'postmodern' writers on cyberspace, from Stone to Turkle, is that cyberspace phenomena like MUD render the deconstructionist 'decentred subject' palpable in our everyday experience. The lesson is that one should endorse the 'dissemination' of the unique Self into a multiplicity of competing agents, into a 'collective mind', a plurality of self-images without a global coordinating centre, and disconnect from pathological trauma: playing Virtual Spaces enables

me to discover new aspects of 'me', a wealth of shifting identities, of masks without a 'real' person behind them, and thus to experience the ideological mechanism of the production of Self, the immanent violence and arbitrariness of this production/construction.

(Žižek 1997: 134)

In some ways I am trying to have it both ways. Or to be kind to my argument, I am trying to think dialectically. On the one hand, I use the scenario of a transitional phase for Western subjectivity in technoculture and rehearse, as Jacques Rancière cautions against 'the unsatisfactory mise-en-scène of the "end" and the "return" that persistently occupies the terrain of art, politics, and any other object of thought' (2004: 11). Along those lines I demonstrate a hope that new technologies might offer new ways of constructing subjectivity or of glimpsing or glancing beyond what is knowable. On the other hand, I am ready to critique aggressively those assumptions that would suggest that the phantasms of human consciousness that haunt our psyches can ever be erased, escaped or undone. I am resisting the fantasy that these new technologies can bring the *Real* to our consciousness, and I am more than willing to admit that the posthuman is/will be as overwhelmed by ignorance as is/was the human. 'Use your head, can't you, use your head. You're on earth, there's no cure for that!' (1986: 118) as Beckett puts it in *Endgame*.

The sticking point of this posthuman theorization of technology in regards to my thesis on performance is: if we are approaching the posthuman condition, will we need or desire the appearance of the flesh of the Other? Wouldn't a posthuman be at home in the simulacrum without referentials? It is the horror story that Žižek attempts to understand, as Simon Cooper has glossed:

> For Žižek the important distinction to be made with respect to cyber-environments and their real-world counterparts is not between reality and virtuality, but between appearance and simulacrum. He claims that 'what gets lost in today's digital *plague of simulations* is not the true form non-simulated real, but appearance itself'.
>
> (2002: 144)

Later in this study I will consider the notion of clouded appearances in virtuality and how that might undermine performativity in cyberspace. Here I take my cue from N. Katherine Hayles (1993), who steadfastly argues for the material base of all cyber-experiences and counters the theory of the obsolete body as practiced by body artists Orlan and Stelarc. They argue from different positions that technology has rendered the body limited and problematic, so it is safe to assume that the material body radically grounds all of cyber-culture despite the science fictions and facts of telepresent space and virtual timings. I am also supportive of a pragmatic model of theatre and performance that following Levinas would assume that face-to-face contact with the Other is always an essential component of human existence no matter how many phantasms we project upon that face. The notion of the posthuman, the postorganic, should not be construed as a totalizing paradigm that denies the authentic (mortal) nature of each operator.

Contemporary critical theory has critiqued the concept of *liveness* as an unmediated and present event. What we experience as *live* is always-already mediated. Herb Blau writes that 'there is nothing more illusory in performance than the illusion of the unmediated' (1987: 164). Philip Auslander, in critiquing the notion that performance is defined by its disappearance, writes:

> Disappearance, existence only in the present moment, is not, then, an ontological quality of live performance that distinguishes it from modes of technical reproduction. Both live performance and the performance of mediatization are predicated on disappearance: the televisual image is produced by an ongoing process in which scan lines replace one another, and it is always as absent as it is present; the use of recordings causes them to degenerate. In a very literal, material sense, televisual and other technical reproductions, like live performance, become themselves through disappearance.
>
> (1999: 45)

In developing my model of postorganic and posthuman performance I am not suggesting a *transfiguration* of performance, wherein the properties of liveness change significance so as to *symbolize* the regeneration of the simulations of technology. Instead I am suggesting a transubstantiation wherein the elements of the *now* are *changed* through the contemporary consecration of the new Eucharist, the linkage of human and machine. In the traditional Eucharist the elements of bread and wine are altered, mysteriously, to the flesh and blood of Christ, leaving only the accidents or appearances of bread and wine. The accidents of liveness, the appearances of the now, are all that remain in the passage of the ontology of the body of performance (now dead), driven into the body of technology. Nevertheless, I argue that theatre and performance can still appear in both live and virtual spaces (the same thing only different).

If my suspicions are accurate (that the theatre and performance in virtual environments are still theatre and performance) the question remains: are there any *universals of performance* that can be isolated? What are they and will they reoccur in virtuality? Blau, in the essay 'Universals of Performance; or Amortizing Play' from his 1987 *Eye of Prey* offers a useful analysis for thinking through these questions. Blau creates a sort of particle physics of performance which can help us think through some of the issues of virtual performance. His *universals* are areas of potentialities rather than a frame of ontological restrictions, and therefore are easily co-opted into my model of postorganic performance. Blau considers the *determining of time*, *consciousness of performance* and the *transformative nature of performance* as basic to all performance. Although time can be aggressively manipulated, the *marking of real time* through cyberspace is certainly possible. The human in the human–computer interface can only pretend to move outside time's relentless motion, but that has always been the case in performance. However, time and space can be dispersed, duplicated and simulated in virtuality, allowing for an expanded experience of what time and space are. *Consciousness of performance*, 'the marks of punctuation which are inflections of consciousness' (Blau 1987: 162), would seem to be able to operate similarly whether in virtual or real territories. The *transformative nature of performance*, the power to reorder all that enters its sphere (whether text, subjectivity or ideology), would also seem to remain intact in virtual environments. Given the digital flexibility of computer environments and the opportunities for shifts of all sorts, might transformation be the essence of the medium?

The most troubling notion of Blau's universals, in relation to my theory of the posthuman and the postorganic, is the *distancing effects of performance* (the splendid isolation of actor and audience) in the fleshlessness of the digital. In order to understand the operations of theatre in virtual spaces we need to understand what happens at the first appearance of theatre. Blau, as have many others, notes the *essential aloneness* and *the sense of removal or distance* at the appearance of theatre. On stage we watch someone dying. In the darkened house decomposing bodies wait for the arrival of the Other. Tadeusz Kantor wrote in his manifesto/essay *The Theatre of Death* that the 'first actor' brought with him 'the revelatory MESSAGE, which was transmitted from the realm of DEATH, [and] evoked in the VIEWERS [...] a metaphysical shock' (1993: 114).

Defining the ontology and marking the borders of theatre and performance by their invocations of death is a concept that requires amendment. Aleksandra Volska puts forward this thesis in an article from *Theatre Journal* (2005). I am not disputing the veracity of the claim that theatre gains much of its power from the spectre of death, but what is being left out of this model of death as the grounds upon which the stage is built is the presence of life. The much-quoted segment from Hegel's preface to the *Phenomenology of Spirit* is useful in understanding this correction.

> Lacking strength, Beauty hates the Understanding for asking of her what it cannot do. But the life of Spirit is not the life that shrinks from death and keeps itself untouched by devastation, but rather the life that endures it and maintains itself in it. It wins its truth only when in utter dismemberment it finds itself. This tarrying with the negative is the magic power that converts it into being.
>
> (19)

What is essential in Hegel's thought here is the idea of life that endures and maintains itself in the midst of devastation. It should be no mystery that our world is densely packed with presence of death. Life is the rare exception to the ubiquitous nature of death. The life that can stand and maintain its presence in the domain of death, which can tarry with the negative, is what transcends to spirit, to being. Learning from Hegel and the contemporary discourse of bio-politics (discussed in Part II), the presence of life on the stage surrounded by the operations of death is the central element of the theatre that demands our attention.

Nonetheless, Kantor understood that when a moment is metamorphosed from *not theatre* to *theatre*, there stands difference; there stands the shock of presence, the awareness of death, the lure of the flesh and the joy of time passing. Although I can easily discount the ontology of performance as being in the *now*, *present* and *live*, I hesitate at the lack of flesh, or difference in virtual performance. If all one can witness or perform in virtual environments is the scopic drive (the privileging of vision to the exclusion of other epistemological modalities) and the manic dance of picturing, where all presence is deferred to bodies in repose at keyboards or tragically isolated in a HMD interface, what have we left? Kantor, calling for a rediscovery of the art of the theatre, wrote,

> It is necessary to recover the primeval force of the shock taking place at the moment when opposite a man (the viewer) there stood for the first time a man (the actor) deceptively similar to us, yet at the same time infinitely foreign, beyond an impassable barrier.
>
> (1993: 114)

Simon Cooper, in *Technoculture and Critical Theory* (2002) writes of three modes of communication drawn from the work of Paul James. The three modes, *face-to-face*, *agency-extended*, and *disembodied*, can be grafted easily onto our thinking on performance. Face-to-face communication is traditional theatre or performance. The theatre and performance are built on the notion of one person or thing performing and one person watching in one space. Agency-extended communications are based in mediated representation, such as cinema and television. The agency-extended performance does not require a spectator, and the performer is no longer present, but only represented within the work. The virtual is the disembodied communication wherein we direct our machines to meet other prosthetic devices of the people with whom we wish to confer. There is agency in the disembodied communication, perhaps even more so than in the agency-extensions of film and television, but it is an agency that demands an absence. Virtual or disembodied communication can enjoy a face-to-face encounter through video conferencing, but it is still projected on to a screen, thereby missing the power of the local encounter.

The promise of interactivity in virtual environments is the breakdown of the isolation of the viewer and actor that can define the theatre. In a post-symbolic system as theorized by Jaron Lanier, there will be no need to watch Hamlet, since you can *be* Hamlet. Like the classic question of science fiction, 'am I real or am I a robot?', the issue turns from witnessing the other to being the other. What is theatre in such a field?

Let me articulate two opposing scenarios regarding a posthuman condition in technoculture. Each imagines the erasure and reconfiguration of subjectivity and identity. The first suggestion begins with Foucault's oft-quoted conclusion to *The Order of Things* that states,

> [...] Man is neither the oldest nor the most constant problem that has been posed for human knowledge. Take a relatively short chronological sample with a restricted geographical area, European culture since the sixteenth century, one can be certain that man is a recent invention within it. It is not around him and his secrets that knowledge prowled for so long in the darkness. In fact, among all the mutations that have affected the knowledge of things and their order, the knowledge of identities, differences, characters, equivalences, words, in short, in the midst of all the episodes of that profound history of the *Same*, only one, that which began a century and a half ago and is now perhaps drawing to a close, has made it possible for the figure of man to appear. And that appearance was not the liberations of an old anxiety, the transition into luminous consciousness of an age-old concern, the entry into objectivity of something that had long remained trapped within beliefs and philosophies: it was the effect of a change in the fundamental arrangements of knowledge. As the archaeology of our thought easily shows, man is an invention of recent date. And one perhaps nearing its end.
>
> (Foucault 1970: 386–7)

Perhaps the technologies of the virtual signal another 'fundamental arrangement of knowledge' and suggest another construction of the recent invention of Man (Foucault's erased face in the sand). As a result, the romantic notions of semblance, presence and the body will be lost. If man is un-invented, then so will the theatre be un-done as the site of Otherness, and the theatre will therefore remain impossible and unnecessary.

The second scenario requires speculating on the future of performative and virtual technologies. Perhaps advanced human–computer interfaces will take us past the isolated body typing at a keyboard and gazing into a screen toward an experience of total immersion that may, in its simulated state, not offer the *same* but signal a *difference*, a *distancing effect of performance* that accompany the appearance of the theatre. When placed in a liquid and transparent interface, what will the human face? The machine? The new human?

The theory and practice of the virtual

The developments in cyberspace, the technologies of virtual systems and their nascent aesthetics provide a series of challenges, which include the troubling ethical issues of access and control. The kind of theories employed to understand and to develop these new modes of aesthetic experience play a significant role in the conceptualization and implementation of digital art as it is today and will be in the future. The challenge is to appropriate or to develop analytic structures that will allow an understanding and discussion of these experiences and, at the same time, stimulate the development of expanded applications.

The appearance of performance within the virtual requires a theorizing that takes account of the performativity of cultural constructions. Within a virtual environment, the spectator is transposed into a digital space in which culturally based identities such as ethnicity, class and gender are volatile, not fixed categories. User/operators are free to perform via imagistic avatar icons or text-based identities with any identification they choose; gender, race and class, become performative differentiation, not fixed, hierarchical assignments within a social order. Certain theoretical strategies recognize that while sexual differentiation, genetic structure and age are biological phenomena, gender difference, ethnicity and class are cultural determinations that only appear natural because of the processes in which the ideological is absorbed into the perceptual. Because in the potentially open interactivity of cyber-performance categories of gender, race and class may be selected and transformed at will, we need theoretical structures that base themselves upon the performative nature of these schemes of differentiation.

In *The Order of Things* and more succinctly in *This Is Not A Pipe*, Foucault narrates a history of the sign from semblance (signifier is similar to the signified), to difference (signifier is contrasted to the signified) and simulation (the signifier and the signified lose their positions and hieratic relations). Although this genealogy of the sign is now canonical in poststructuralist thought, the biases of the designers of virtual environments have already demonstrated distinctly realist (semblance) tendencies. How are our notions of theatrical-dramatic performance redefined in a virtual staging?

Not unlike Racine and the neoclassical dramatists of the seventeenth century French theatre, some contemporary theorists working on models of human–computer interaction have drawn upon Aristotelian theories of drama to create a formalistic, scientific and irrefutable structure for uniformity (Laurel 1993). The interest in recuperating Aristotle, while avoiding more current thought on narrativity and performance, may be due to the fact that the *Poetics* posits the possibility of a comprehensive understanding of human action and the possibility of its representation, whereas poststructuralism and postmodernism supposes an unending play between possibilities that is not subject to the same kind of artificial collaboration and objective agreement. This is why one can position VR as an extension of the Cartesian model of space and subjectivity; why else a name like *virtual reality*? Non-affirmative sign systems forgo semblance and difference and work within the system of simulation wherein the sign is marked by its status as negotiable. In both theorizing and designing cyber-territories, it is desirable to approach these new fields from contemporary perspectives rather than by replicating baroque and classic sign systems.

Amid all the pronouncements of a human revolution of historical proportions, I think it is safe to say that we have not yet begun to think about virtuality. The joy that we encounter in the digital domain may have its dangers. The following is a quote from Baudrillard's *The Transparency of Evil*:

> If men create intelligent machines, or fantasize about them, it is either because they secretly despair of their own intelligence or because they are in danger of succumbing to the weight of a monstrous and useless intelligence which they seek to exorcise by transferring it to machines, where they can play with it and make fun of it. By entrusting this burdensome intelligence to machines we are released from any responsibility to knowledge, much as entrusting power to politicians allows us to disdain any aspiration of our own to power. It is not for nothing that they are described as 'virtual', for they put thought on hold indefinitely, tying its emergence to the achievement of a complete knowledge. The act of thinking itself is thus put off forever.
>
> (51–52)

I am not prepared to moralize an anti-technological prejudice to the degree that Baudrillard has. On the contrary, the advent of a digital art, a *postorganic* performance that will explore our notions of subjectivity, is to be welcomed. However, one hopes that cyberspatial technologies and their aesthetics and cultural applications will not be developed as better tools to get us to where we have already been faster. Discouragingly, Laurel's appropriated model has gained wide acceptance in the circles of human–computer interaction. In theorizing how artists might configure a virtual theater, L. Casey Larijani wrote that:

> Things like patterns of human behavior and emotional reactions must be defined according to professional standards to ensure continuity and consistency across disciplines. In the theater arts, especially, doing so will help establish 'givens' to underlie all productions.
>
> (1993: 123)

Herein we have the nightmare of the computer revolution: uniformity, conservatism, submission and control. The effective use of VR is contingent upon the discovery of VR's uniquely performative qualities, an environment that allows for 'a way of conceiving of political identities that simultaneously transgress boundaries and make possible unexpected and improbable unities' (Auslander, 116) and not a mimicry of the stage, tied as it is to a temporal and spatial paradigm of narrativity. Ken Pimentel and Kevin Teixeira suggest that VR will 'need to be familiar to the users [...] they can relax and participate [...] then users can bring to the world a sense of what their roles could be' (1994: 32). There is no change in such a thesis, merely the homeostasis of a new machine in a replicating culture.

If the goal is to create the ultimate arcade game or story-telling machine, then Aristotle's theory will suffice. However, if artists are interested in developing VR, as Heims has suggested, as a metaphysical laboratory for the exploration of our humanity, if they want to inaugurate a new aesthetics of the virtual, then they must advance new notions that critique Western narrativity and subjectivity, exposing their ideological bases and promoting social reconfigurations. Research should focus on how the performativity of the cyberspatial and virtual realities operate in and of themselves outside the models of theatrical and dramatic performance, and then extrapolate those data to challenge our notions of theatrical-dramatic performance, which we should then be able to redefine through our understanding of the liquid architecture of virtual stagings. The focus concerning virtual reality systems could be to develop a theory of virtuality outlining possible work within virtual environments as experimental laboratories for examining the fictive and real boundaries of cultural construction.

What is inherent in the medium of virtual environments is sensory immersion, remote presence and tele-operations. Laurel posits that the central challenge to the use of these capabilities is the implementation of 'designing and orchestrating action in virtual worlds' (188). I would challenge this notion by calling for aesthetic experimentation that attempts to harness the post-symbolic expertise of VR. Modernism rejected representation and instead staged the theatricality of theatre, produced paintings that represented the process of painting, and constructed dance that referenced nothing more nor less than the time and movement of dance. The postmodernism of VR should not return to aesthetic strategies of representation that modernism has already challenged but rather should explore new territory, focusing upon performing, not representing, constructing a reality whose virtuality will expand cognition of reality itself as an increasingly complex metaphor for what one experiences as the real, inaccessible as that real may be. The skill with which artists develop these aesthetic experiences will depend upon the profundity and complexity of the theorizing. The theory or theories most suitable are a kind of complex amalgamation, a pragmatic phenomenology that will not use the human consciousness as its model but rather a constructed virtual consciousness of significant freedom that, as human beings, we may inhabit temporarily and reify to some degree in experience upon return.

It is important to ground the headiness and enthusiasm, or dismay and critique, of the discussion surrounding virtual technologies. For many the immediate experience of donning an HMD and dataglove is deflation. The poor resolution of the LCDs, the awkwardness of the dataglove interface, makes one painfully aware that VR technologies are in a primitive stage of development, not unlike the magic lantern in the history of cinema. In addition, the interactivity of the unencumbered human mind and the text of *Hamlet*, for example, far exceed the multiple choice of interactive software. The theory has surpassed the realities, which may be the purpose of theory. In that sense VR theory has a unique opportunity to assist the agendas for VR experimentation.

Perry Hoberman, an artist working with virtual environments, developed a work titled *Bar Code Hotel* as part of the Art and Virtual Environments Project at the Banff Centre of the Arts in Canada in 1994. The work is now installed at ZKM, the Centre for Art and Technology, in Karlsruhe, Germany. *Bar Code Hotel*, avoiding the isolating HMD and data gloves of most virtual reality configurations, is an interactive installation. Hoberman uses the Universal Product Code (bar code) and laser pen (bar code reader), to which we have become accustomed in our supermarket check-outs, as interface.

> An entire room is covered with printed bar code symbols, creating an environment in which every surface becomes a responsive membrane, an immersive interface that can be used simultaneously by a number of people to control and respond to a projected real-time, computer generated stereoscopic, three-dimensional world.
>
> (Hoberman 1996: 289).

A guest entering the gallery space installed with *Bar Code Hotel* is given a pair of 3-D glasses. On one wall of the installation space is a video projection screen for the 3-D graphic. In front of the screen are tables on which bar codes are affixed to the surface. Additional bar codes are placed on hand-sized movable cubes and along the walls. Suspended from the ceiling are five cables that reach down to the tables and are connected to laser pens, accessible for the viewers to scan the codes. The bar codes on the cubes, when scanned by the laser pen, cause a computer generated object to appear on the projection screen. The objects include a bowling ball, camera, paper clip, hat, suitcase, glasses, scissors, light bulb and shoes. When scanned, the surface bar codes trigger specific modifications in the object, with such commands as *jitter, bounce, breathe, contract, expand* and *suicide*. Another category of bar codes control the interaction between the objects, with commands such as *avoid, chase* and *punch*. A set of bar codes is dedicated to the virtual environment that the objects inhabit, and control the *rooms, POV,* and the *sky* with commands such as *earthquake* and *loop the loop*. A final set of bar codes, inaccessible to the spectator/operator, and assumed to be inoperative, are placed high along the walls of the gallery space. They read, *think, remember, believe* and *accept*.

The objects in *Bar Code Hotel* are controlled by and are interactive with the spectator but are also autonomous.

> Between moments of human contact, when no bar codes are being scanned, the paper clip, for example will behave according to its own set of rules. Programmed to both act and react, objects appear to express behaviors, capabilities and personalities; they can be mutated, merged, killed or reborn.
>
> (Hoberman, Exhibition Notes)

The objects have individualized life spans and are responsive in anthropomorphic manners. As young objects they react speedily to commands, and as they age their response time is eroded. Each object does die, leaving a momentary ghost.

Having operated (or checked into) the *Bar Code Hotel*, I can attest to the delight in the interactive play of the 3-D objects. The work as an end in itself is impressive, but the future performative use of the technology is intriguing. The objects in *Bar Code Hotel* could be replaced with colours, sounds and abstractions that would allow configuring artworks. Replace the objects with representations of dancers and human figures with a variety of embedded texts, and one can begin to envision a truly interactive theatre.

Hoberman may have had something else in mind for his installation beyond an enthusiasm for technology. The object of *Bar Code Hotel* may reside in the inaccessible codes that would command us to think, remember, believe or accept, and which are placed out of reach of the spectator/operator. The operator can control the technological object to a somewhat limited degree, after waiting her turn for the laser pen. Like check-out clerks at the market, we are merely assigning a name or price to set the object in dance in the economy of representations. The capacity to think or remember or believe or even accept is out of reach. Hoberman, in *Bar Code Hotel*, avoids the mimetic replication of the surface real while offering a representation of Baudrillard's *fatal strategy* of the postmodern object emancipated from the subject.

The ideology of the virtual or speeding toward immobility

This section title is partially named *The ideology of the virtual*, but it could be transposed to *virtual ideology* or abbreviated to *The id of the virtual*. The former follows the transparency of ideology, ever-shifting, a roving opportunistic virus, probing, infecting, restructuring, unseen but material;

the latter acknowledges the fury and rage suppressed in the orderliness of tired and often unconscious politics, as well as the political unconscious now newly projected onto the vacuous screens of cyber-culture. To what end does the will to virtuality drive us? What is this desire for disappearance in cyber-territories? How is the *eros* and *thanatos* of performance re-inscribed through technology; the displaced body transposed, mutated; the wired flesh masturbating with one hand typing out *hot-chat* with the other; technoculture's desiring machines ecstatically racing in non-time to nowhere. If there is no off switch to the technological, as Avital Ronell has suggested; if, as Marshall McLuhan theorizes, we have become the sex organs for machines; if, as philosophized by Heidegger, the only *revealing* within technology is a *self-revealing* of technology for itself; if we have become contiguous with our machines, as Mazlish writes; if we have entered a postgendered world, as Haraway imagines; then in what manner, if any, can the art of technologized performance respond that will allow for critique, resistance and revealing of the ideology at work within this closed, homeostatic system?

In thinking on and in the virtual, I want to return to a classic work in modern drama. For the will to virtuality, the will to be replaced, duplicated, removed from the real and delivered up to fantasy, to smash the material and elevate interiority, to suppress the political and hold to the metaphysical, cycling out of the eternal recurrence of the same thing into a wired world where technology demands revealing, is not a computer-age compulsion alone, but a trans-historical phenomena. As Herb Blau reminds us, the battle over symbolic presence vs. real presence is not new. In calling on the ideas of Kantor, Genet and Pirandello to argue that the ideology of the virtual is tied to a falling into inauthenticity, an attempt to catapult over the shock of the body in performance toward a self-replicating absent body, I recognize that the journey away from the theatre's message of doubling, of cruelty, of absence, of death, toward technology has already taken place.

Speeding toward immobility comes closest to my perspective regarding the tendency toward virtualizing the real. It suggests through quoting Genet's *The Balcony*, that instead of the metaphysical shock from the realm of death in the theatre, we have created in the virtual a falling into inauthenticity wherein death is displaced, deferred indefinitely in favour of a painless, fleshless existence where the art process that runs from cruelty to absence to death concludes not with the 'excruciating magical relation to reality and danger' (Artaud 1958: 89), but is replaced with a *longing toward immobility*. The closure of representation sought after in the cruelty of art is replaced with replicating mirror images, eternal reflection, where the demarcation of the unknown is unknown, undesired, as all is Apollonian imagery that voids the Dionysian transition. The picture we have taken of the world of virtuality is a virtual world, revealed as a flat surface of depthless images circulating in an economy of late capital.

The Balcony by Jean Genet narrates the action of a fictional brothel where men play out the fantasies of power through the iconography of

Bishop, Judge, General and Chief of Police. An emissary from the aristocracy enlists the Madame and her johns to help quell a revolution that is underway in the city outside the brothel, by bringing their roles into the light of day. The play works like two mirrors held toward one another: no one – no thing – escapes the replicating scopic drive of the image-obsessed subject. I want to focus on the moment when the Gasman takes on the role of the Bishop and question how his sojourn into virtuality operates? It is the first speech of the play, spoken by the Gasman/Bishop as he is being dressed by a whore. It displays the map of both the path into virtuality and the process of radical art.

> In truth, the mark of a prelate is not mildness or unction, but the most rigorous intelligence. Our heart is our undoing. We think we are master of our kindness; we are the slave of a serene laxity. It is something quite other than intelligence that is involved ... (He hesitates) It may be *cruelty* and beyond that cruelty – and through it – a skillful; vigorous course towards *Absence*. Towards *Death*. God? (smiling) I can read your mind.
>
> (Genet 1991: 1)

It is the trajectory of desire from cruelty to absence to death that I want to discuss in relation to thinking through virtuality and performance. Genet, in *The Balcony*, defines the essences of art (coming to be) and performance (magical/ritualistic transformation) in the theatre, by way of a sadomasochistic religiosity, as a process through *cruelty*. The cruelty of *The Balcony* echoes both Artaud's paradigm of the Theatre of Cruelty and Kant's philosophy of sublimity: violence against the imagination and understanding, which demonstrates the limits of knowledge while unfolding the mind's capacity for the supersensible as the moment of the sublime appears. The sublime is not the beautiful, which exists as the harmonious appearance and recognition of object and subject. The beautiful comes to be when the faculties of cognition are experienced by the subject as similar to the attributes of the object. The sublime is the border at which point the unpresentable confounds the faculties of the mind, setting out the limits of knowledge while calling forth the unknown. The sublimity of performance and art within the theatre lies in their capacity to present the unpresentable in presentation itself, which is how Lyotard defined postmodernism (Lyotard 1984). Drawing from Derrida's analysis of Artaud's theory, the cruelty of the theatre is the moment of the collapse of the onto-theological structure of the stage (Derrida 1978). Text is no longer the legislative arm controlling desire. However, the virtual Bishop will miss the reordering of the body, of the mind, of consciousness and desire, in his fetishization of the object.

Genet extends his model of the borders of art and performance in the theatre beyond 'cruelty and through it, a skillful, vigorous course towards *absence*' (1). The moment of absence contains the wrapping of the subject into the image. In *The Balcony* the invention of subjectivity is represented as the fetishizing of the object, in this case, the Bishop's mitre. The subject, in order to define itself, stages its own disappearance by taking on the signs of identity, an act which mimics the simulation strategy of substituting the signs of the real for the real itself. It is here that we have the creation of the virtual through the desire to avoid (the fear of) the authentic, sexual, mortal human machine. The process of radical art, according to Genet, begins with cruelty (violence to the faculties of cognition) through absence (loss of subjectivity) toward death, the appearance of the border of art, performance and theatre: the unpresentable. Death is represented as the impossible, the falling into continuity (Bataille), the dissolution of borders (Nietzsche), a reordering of the psyche and the body (Artaud), or the sublime (Kant). It is this process that must be resisted at all costs in the establishment of the virtual.

As the Gasman/Bishop begins his aesthetic leap into the sublime, claiming to read the mind of God, he stops his revealing of the unknown and speaks to the mitre perched on his head. He addresses the virtual signs of identity:

> Mitre, bishop's bonnet, when my eyes close for the last time it is you that I shall see behind my eyelids, you, my beautiful gilded hat ... you, my handsome ornaments, copes, laces.
>
> (1995: 486)

The signs and simulation of God contained in the Bishop's bonnet, handsome ornaments, copes, laces are what hold the Gasman's fantasy. He will not complete the process into art through cruelty: the violence against rationality, the destruction of the conscious mind, the desire to undo that which structures and congeals, toward absence and the removal of the self into the images. Absent, he defers eternally death, the impossible, the falling into continuity, the dissolution of borders, the reordering of the psyche and the body, for his desire is to maintain his orbit in virtuality, masturbating, always watching the screen, which could be the cathode ray tube, but in this case is the mirror, for glimpses of the known, for dissolution into power, never death but always ecstatic image duplication and repeatability. The Bishop's moment of sustaining inauthenticity has become virtual culture's nightmare. Our world has been worlded as virtual, and we cannot change that.

Brief afterword

Žižek makes an alarming assertion in footnote 16 to his chapter 'Cyberspace, or, the Unbearable Closure of Being' in *The Plague of Fantasies*. He writes:

> [...] computerization undermines performativity. By claiming this, I am not resurrecting the myth of the good pre-computerized times when

words really counted. As Derrida – but also Lacan – emphasized again and again, the performative can always, for structural reasons, go wrong; it can arise only against the background of radical undecidability – the very fact that I have to rely on the other's word means that the other remains forever an enigma to me. What tends to get lost in virtual communities is this very abyss of the other, this very background of undecidability: in the 'wired universe', the very opaqueness of the other tends to evaporate. In this sense, the suspension of performativity in virtual communities is the very opposite of the suspension of performativity in the psychoanalytic cure, where I can tell my analyst anything, all my obscene fantasies about him, knowing that he will not be offended, that he will not 'take it personally'.

(1997: 166)

Žižek does not follow this assertion through in his essay, but it is striking enough in its claim to add further burdens upon thinking through performance and the performative in virtual environments. If the act of performance is undermined through computerization or virtual communications, then the process of what we think of theatre is likewise interrupted. The project of thinking theatre in virtuality may indeed prove to be unsatisfactory, but it is what we will have to address, those of us living within technoculture and concerned with live performance. The performative process in virtuality may indeed be a continuation of the revealing of inauthenticity to point of indifference, where all is visible but nothing available. Consequently, the process of redeeming the theatre in hyper-realism may seem impossible, but nevertheless it is, as Herb Blau reminded me, the nothing to be done that has to be done.

4 Perspectiva artificialis

The duplicitious geographies
of stage illusions, or
the not-so-splendid isolation
of the actor on the early modern
perspective stage and in the
historical avant-garde

The history of the theatre is the history of the transfiguration of the human form.

(Schlemmer 1961: 17)

The theatre is precisely that practice which calculates the place of things as they are observed: if I set the spectacle here, the spectator will see this; if I put it elsewhere, he will not, and I can avail myself of this masking effect and play on the illusion it provides. The stage is the line which stands across the path of the optic pencil, tracing at once the point at which it is brought to a stop and, as it were, the threshold of its ramification. Thus is founded – against music, against the text – *representation.*

(Barthes 1977: 69)

The history, philosophy, and ideology of perspective in art and architecture have been well rehearsed, but the phenomena of the body in performance within that artificial space have been under-theorized and under-historicized. There was a problem with perspective on the early modern stage: the actor's body refused to conform. The mathematical illusions of perspective were deflated with the appearance of the actor moving into the staged picture plane. The solution to the problem of the collision of the material presence of the actor and the fragility of the illusion created by the scenic apparatus was to locate the performer in a middle ground between the audience's gaze and the picture plane. It was at that position that the actor would not impede the illusion, but rather would appear to be *in the picture*, fully embedded in the frame. The nomadic space between the illusory stage and the one-point perspective, *vision in the first person*, was the province of the body on the early modern perspective stage. What the spectator might have willingly disbelieved was not that the stage represented a particular time, place or action, but rather that the body of the performer was resisting or challenging that illusory space and that space itself was being abstracted. One outcome of this positioning, or isolation of the performer, was to look past the body's corporeality and to redesign that body as image.

The performance work of the historical avant-garde demonstrated similar interests in suppressing or surpassing or supplementing the body in favour of plasticity and abstraction. From Edward Gordon Craig's *Übermarionette* to the Futurist Enrico Prampolini's *actor-gasses*; from Kasimir Malevich's and Pablo Picasso's costumes that abstracted and extended the actor's body toward a type of walking scenography; to Schlemmer's *Kunstfigur*, an artificial human figure; to the reconstruction of the proscenium arch and the privileging of stage picture in the work of Robert Wilson and Richard Foreman; the problem of the materiality of the body of the actor undermining the integrity of the picture plane found a solution: alter, deform or simply remove the body from the stage. These *not-so-splendid isolations* of the actor on the early modern perspective stage and in the historical avant-garde allow me an opportunity to attempt to historicize the conditions of subjectivity and bodily presence in computerized virtuality and techno-culture. I want to suggest that *the worlding of the world as picture* as Martin Heidegger put it, is not simply a problem of mediatization, but rather an ongoing project of Western culture. I realize that this line of argument might be read as an unsubstantiated conspiracy theory of bodily suppression by a controlling culture set on installing a new regime of the image and that accusation might be accurate. It is true that much theory and critique runs toward hysterical hyperbole to make its point. Žižek warns about the abuses of an all-too-easy critique of the Cartesian subject that dominates so much contemporary cultural theory and identity politics. I understand that the techniques of spectacle on the perspectival stage and in early avant-garde performances were motivated, inspired and over-determined by multiple impulses, historical circumstances and practical theatrical necessity, and were hardly a unified field of action bent on dominating the human spirit and bodily presence. However, the development of perspective and its subsequent usage on the stages of early modern Europe is a useful phenomenon to understand not only the struggle between the body and the will to virtuality, but also the drive to represent the world as malleable object and representation.

There has been much interesting research on the origins of perspective in recent years. One of the useful texts is Hubert Damisch's Lacanian reading of the phenomenon, *The Origin of Perspective* (1995). I will draw frequently from his argument to pursue my own.

Early modern scenographers had two options in attempting to create illusionistic perspective on the stage. The first was simply to use a painted backdrop. The earliest reported mention of an illusionistic décor painted and/or constructed in perspective is the performance of Ariosto's *Cassario* in Ferrara in 1508, with painted scenery by Pellegrino di San Daniele. The staging consisted 'of a *perspective* with various buildings, houses, churches, and towers surrounded by gardens' (Damisch 1995: 215). The second scenographic option was to create perspective scenery within the full cubic space of the stage, with duplicating forms of receding arches and wing-and-drop painted canvas or permanent structures, as one can observe in the *teatro olimpico* in Vincenza, Italy. Logically, these two options of backdrop and volumetric space are still our primary scenic choice, although virtual space in the form of video and computer projections offer a third way. It is interesting to note that the Futurist scenographer Enrico Prampolini, whose work is discussed later in this chapter, was already calling for the end of the painted stage in 1915. However, it is that very contribution of designing in three dimensions that is ascribed to Wagner, Appia and Craig, demonstrating again the weakness of some of our traditional Western theatre historical narratives and the use of hyperbole by certain artists.

The techniques of creating a perspective picture plane on a backdrop or within the space of the stage was achieved using the mathematical systems devised by such early innovators as Brunelleschi, Alberti and Vasari. Sebastiano Serlio's sixteenth century cross-section and floor plan of a perspectival theatre first appeared in Serlio's *Treatise on Architecture, Book II*, and describe 'the wooden theatre built by Serlio, in 1539, in the Palazzo Da Porto in Vicenza' (Damisch 1995: 391). The diagrams would seem to indicate that the raked stage, and even apron, were available as performance and scenic space. It also seems clear that the performer on the perspective stage was restricted either to the forestage or to the first wing section. If, perhaps, the actors were free to utilize the entire stage rake, the illusions of the perspective would be ruined. Again, the *teatro olimpico*, designed by Andrea Palladio in the sixteenth century, and the restrictive sightlines of its upstage perspective of the seven gates of Thebes, demonstrate the unlikely, even absurd performative uses of the perspective raked stage. The actor moving upstage grows visually larger in the foreshortened scenery. Nonetheless, no matter where the performer was positioned, it was only on the forestage where the actor would not interrupt the picture plane illusions. As I suggested above, it is at the moment of isolation between the picture plane and the auditorium that the body of the actor becomes part of the stage picture. If the actor moves into the picture plane, her materiality undermines the illusion. But it was, of course, not only the body of the actor that the early modern scenographer needed to manage in order to create the illusion or model of real space, but real space itself, which worked against the illusion and needed its own system of management.

Since the claims of a repressive aesthetic I am attempting cannot be materially proven, but only rationalized through theory, I am willing to submit another model that sees the meeting of the actor's body and the technique of perspective as an awkward, but novel and entertaining, spectacle. Perhaps the early modern audience simply enjoyed the ingenuity. Today we watch films whose green-screen and CGI technologies are easily discernible, but we are not concerned with some momentary glitch in verisimilitude. We willingly disbelieve, playing the game of the spectator, in order to enjoy the spectacle. Nor are we overly troubled by the multiplication of virtual actors on the screen, even though they do challenge the frame, and even the livelihood of the *live* actors. For that matter, even the necrophilia of virtually exhuming dead actors such as Fred Astaire or John Wayne to market vacuum cleaners and beer bears us little concern. Why should a theatre audience of the early modern period be otherwise alarmed? To answer my own question, the spectator may not think twice about the consequences during the performance, but the cultural effect is nonetheless engaged.

Yet another alternative reading of the perspective stage is to consider its reduction of the body to image, as a Nietzschean acknowledgment of the illusion of all appearance. The presence of the actor in the perspective theatre dramatizes the *mere appearance* of the scenery, the picture plane upon which the spectators have projected themselves, in conflict with the timely, spatial, abject nature of the body. That conflict is resonant with what I have argued is at issue in the meetings of bodily presence and virtual illusion. That conflict, like Nietzsche's *Apollonian/Dionysian* model, sets forth a world of appearances (the Apollonian) which, when understood and directed, can give way to a dispersal of the self within the regime of appearances in an ecstatic *truth* (Dionysian). To follow that line of thought would be to look upon the folding of the human into the picture plane of the stage not as an unwanted repression of identity and freedom, objectifying all as image, but rather as an act of liberation, allowing the body of the actor to play within the space of *mere appearance,* coming toward an understanding of the unreal status of the real and the meaningful depths of the surface. Isn't this notion explicatory of the mad element of thinking theoretically? Anything is possible in a theoretical frame, as Artaud demonstrated and Derrida disproved.

Nevertheless, let's assume for the sake of argument that the *project* (or to avoid intent on the part of the theatre artists, let us say *result*) of the early modern perspectival stage was to capture the world as picture. Heidegger's *The Age of the World Picture* (1977), to which I have turned several times, is another work like his *The Question Concerning Technology*, which is favoured by new media and technoculture theorists for its ability to articulate a fundamental affect of mediatization.

> The fundamental event of the modern age is the conquest of the world as picture. World picture [...] does not mean a picture of the world but the world conceived and grasped as picture [...] The world picture does not change from an earlier medieval one into a modern one, but rather

the fact that the world becomes picture at all is what distinguishes the essence of the modern age [...] The word 'picture' now means the structured image that is the creature of man's producing which represents and sets before. In such producing, man contends for the position in which he can be that particular being who gives the measure and draws up the guidelines for everything that is.

(1996: 56–9)

Heidegger's thesis argues that in picturing the world, we miss the *thingness of things* in an attempt to order all as representation and to establish our centrality and subjectivity. 'Am I right in the centre?' asks Hamm in Beckett's *Endgame*. 'I'd say so,' replies Clov. 'You'd say so! Put me right in the centre!' (Beckett 1964: 24). The world that is measured, literally and figuratively, in perspective theatre is a non-material abstraction wherein all space is measurable from any point by a definite system of coordinates, which reduces the unknown to the known and folds the body into image. In *Endgame*, again, Clov takes Hamm for a little turn in his chair. 'Right round the world! [*Clov pushes chair.*] Hug the walls, then back to the centre again. [*Clov pushes chair.*] I was right in the centre, wasn't I?' (23). Hamm's desire to be in the centre tells us much about the operations of subject construction on the perspectival stage. Beckett's stage design for *Endgame* has mirrored vanishing points through the two windows on the back wall. An infinity of greyness, the ominous void, recedes behind these open wounds, but before them Hamm still struggles to play the old games and to establish his presence through the old rituals, the old stories, and the 'old questions, the old answers, there's nothing like them', which are now degraded and being forgotten. Beckett lets us see the processes and absurdities of constructing and capturing identity, to be in the picture, to be in the centre.

> I feel a little too far to the left. [*Clov moves chair slightly.*] Now I feel a little too far to the right. [*Clov moves chair slightly.*] I feel a little too far forward [*Clov moves chair slightly.*] Now I feel a little too far back. [*Clov moves chair slightly.*]

(24)

The blind Hamm pictures himself, captures himself, and conceives of himself in the space. But Hamm cannot see, and therefore cannot tell his place. He must rely on Clov to picture him and to recall that picture in words. Hamm seeks the edge, the wall and its hollow bricks. Clov wheels Hamm to the wall and Hamm cries, 'Closer, Closer! Up against!' It is the edge of the void, the off-stage, that defines the area of the centre. If there is no void, there is no centre. Of course that contemplation of the void can only last so long. The void is too seductive, but also too ominous, for the comfort of the centre. To be in the middle of the picture is to be the vanishing point.

We look to a point in the visual field that is set before us. In each glance a proscenium arch, a frame, is constructed and a constantly shifting vanishing point appears, but that vanishing point lives up to its name as it vanishes in an infinite regression. What we look at disappears and is reconfigured as representation and picture. We see theatrically, but through a memory of what was just lost.

Gloucester in *King Lear* says to his disguised son, 'Set me where you stand' (IV, vi, 24). The lost and blinded father asks the masked, banished and betrayed son to position him where he can see again. Put me in the centre so that I might see and know again. Damisch works from Lacan to understand this process of subject construction in the visual field.

> This explains why, as Lacan observed, the geometral dimension allows for a glimpse of how the subject is caught, maneuvered, captured inside the field of vision, and how painting can deliberately exploit it to captivate the subject in a relation of desire, but one that remains enigmatic.
>
> (Damisch 1995: 46)

Damisch proposes that a painting, which I will extend to the theatrical *mise-en-scène*, presents or performs a seductive metaphor for the subject who sees a model of how her world is constructed. The actor on the perspective stage and the character in the modern drama undertake the establishment of a subject position, like an original GPS (geo-positioning system), in an otherwise distorted, disordered and chaotic environment.

The traditional narrative of the evolution of perspectival staging is derived primarily from George Kernodle's 1944 text, *From Art to Theatre: Form and Convention in the Renaissance*. He argues that in medieval art and staging a democratic ideology was at work, depicting a space constructed as a 'nucleus around which the characters or actors could be organized. In the perspective scene the character or actor was put in the centre, and the scenic elements were organized into a complex background which seemed to enclose that centre' (Kernodle 1944: 174). Now we might be able to apply a more severe critique of medieval staging practices of multiple frames, perspectives and spaces, seeing in them an ideological state apparatus of a Christian cosmology and an indoctrination to seeing God in all things. Kernodle asserts that early modern perspective was organized for an aristocratic spectatorship, and this argument continues to be generally accepted. However, this history disregards some of the critical issues of perspective in lieu of an easy liberal ideological agenda for some critics and historians on the one hand, and an easily disseminated *fact* for the classroom on the other.

In his *Treatise on Architecture*, Serlio points out in his diagram of a perspective stage that the nobility was seated in section 'F', and Damisch notes that this position is well below the location of the vanishing point at 'O'. The ideal location for the point of view is to be placed directly in line with the vanishing point. Damisch argues that the sustained popularity of perspectival staging suggests a more complex justification for its origins and growth.

Damisch disputes Kernodle's claim of perspective as aristocratic spectatorship. He writes,

> In theatre as in painting, then, it's up to the 'subject', even if it is the prince himself, to get its bearings within the configuration of the scene, as within that of a painting; and this, by means of an 'advance' requiring more than a century to reach fruition, and that without princes, dukes, cardinals, or kings deriving even the slightest benefit from it, aside from having their post designated in the centre of the auditorium; but this certainly didn't guarantee them the best perspective of the stage.
>
> (1995: 399)

Kernodle makes an interesting assertion, claiming not only that space is being rethought on the perspective stage, but that time is reordered as well. He writes, 'the perspective setting achieved its organization in space by attempting, for the first time in history, to rule out time' (1944: 175). Although Kernodle does not carry the idea through, he has pointed to a fundamental issue of perspectivalism. The challenging of chronological time through the invention of infinity can be read as a primary motivator in the foregrounding of the picture plane and is linked to the challenging of the material body of the performer. The marking of time, the consciousness of performance (Blau's *universals*), are central to our conceiving, processing and understanding performance. Undo time, and performance is undermined. Damisch writes, '*perspectiva artificialis* was preoccupied from the start by the question of infinity' (1995: xviii). The infinite regression of the vanishing point toward an infinity of perspectival illusion is descriptive of Hegel's dichotomy of good and bad infinity. Bad infinity can be diagrammed as a straight line that recedes and progresses infinitely. Good infinity, according to Hegel, is a circle, bounded but infinite, like Nietzsche's eternal recurrence, an infinite repetition of the same thing, only different. Perspective can be understood as being built on the infinite regression of the single point, a bad infinity, outside a contextualized time reference of history based in subjectivism and, like most spectacles, seductive and addictive.

What are the rules of perspective? Perspective is an invented convention for depicting three dimensions. The system is based in geometry wherein 'all space in the universe is abstract and measurable from any point by a definite system of coordinates' (Kernodle 1944: 178). The problem is that within this model, the subject is reduced to an eye and the eye to a point, as has been argued by Panofsky, as Damisch notes (45). The irony is that perspective as a technology of representation is designed to allow the positioning of the subject within an illusory space, yet the effect is that the subject is dissolved to a point within that space. *Perspectiva artificialis* was positioned against *perspectiva naturalis* by early modern scholars, in order to foreground the nature of perspective as a constructed, illusionistic and doubling technology of representation. Damisch argues that perspective does not mimic vision, but rather is a 'formal apparatus equivalent to that of the sentence, in that it assigns the subject a place within a previously established network that gives it meaning' (446). The three components of perspective are *point of view*, *vanishing point* and *distance point* roughly corresponding to *here*, *there* and *over there*, which lay out the geography of the stage. This mapping positions the subject within a known space, while allowing simultaneously for the abstraction of the body and the disappearance of the perceiving subject within that designed environment.

During the fifteenth century Filippo Brunelleschi conducted an experiment in perspective drawing. He painted an exact likeness of the Baptistery of Florence cathedral on a small wooden panel. The panel had an eyehole drilled into the centre. Facing the actual Baptistery, the viewer would hold the panel to her face, looking through the peephole, while positioning a mirror in which to look. The illusion was such that with the mirror held up or dropped down the same image appeared, a simulation created through the technology of perspective realized through the physics of the mirror. The subject placed behind the painted screen, whose vision is confined to a point, looks toward the mirror that disappears into a reflection of the real world. The world disappears into a reflection in the mirror of the panel that hides the subject and reduces it to a point. The performed experiment, like a theatrical whirligig from Genet, is a lesson in negativity. The experiment recalls Foucault's reading of the paintings *Ceci n'est pas une pipe* (1926) by Magritte, as well as *Las Meninas* (1656) by Velázquez and its pictorial depiction of the failings of representation and the rushing disappearances. The act of trying not to disappear by substantiating a subject's centrality in the picture, ironically, sets the machinery of perception so that the disappearance takes place. By being put in the centre one assures one's disappearance. The mirror in Brunelleschi's experiment rises like a curtain on the perspectival stage to reflect the screen that hides the subject and makes of the world a virtual double, a making of the world as picture.

Kernodle points to three principles of the perspective setting that deserve further consideration. First, he notes the *eyepoint* and *vanishing-point*, which we have already discussed. Second is the notion that all of the stage needs to be considered as one *picture plane*: 'All space should be considered as back of one picture plane and that that plane should be defined by a proscenium frame' (Kernodle 1944: 180). He notes how the early modern illusionistic stage was framed in three planes, organized through prosceniums to mark the forestage, the main stage, and the inner stage. The perspective stage was not complete until its boundaries were fully marked through 'the establishment of a single picture plane for the whole scene and the development of a formal proscenium arch and front curtain to define that picture plane' (188). If the entire world was a stage and the stage a picture, then a circular logic suggests the world was likewise being pictured or becoming part of the picture, and as a result would establish man's domain, control and centrality. Third, Kernodle writes of an obvious but intriguing technique of the perspective scenographer, namely, the *duplication of similar forms*. In order to create a sense of greater depth on the stage similar forms were repeated, such as the designs of the wings in successive diminishing frames toward the backdrop. The doubling, or duplication of similar forms, can certainly produce the depth suggested, not unlike current techniques in CGI that will duplicate a figure multiple times to create marching armies of hundreds of thousands as in *Troy* (Peterson 2004) or *Star Wars, Episode 1* (Lucas 1999). The spectacle of duplication of the perspective stage and current computer graphics imaging recall Genet's comments in *The Screens*, cited above, regarding the colonial power seeking hegemony through duplication. There is a unique power in the multiplication of an image. Consider the stagings of the Nazi rallies in which rows after rows of soldiers, flags and emblems were paraded, or even the rows of products in an American supermarket, there is a persuasive pull of the expansive and the multitudinous. Even the multiples of Andy Warhol, the endless replicating silk-screened images of Campbell's Soup cans or of Marilyn Monroe, work within this duplication and doubling technology. Even further, the desire for cloning might be recognized as the ultimate duplication.

Finally, regarding the proscenium, it is interesting to note the parlance for the frame that names the sides of the arch the *tormentors* and the top as the *teaser*. As I have heard Herb Blau wonder aloud, what is being tormented and teased? Is it the eye of the beholder, the body of the actor, or the space of the off-stage that marks area outside the theatre? Or is it the real standing just to the side of the picture frame or hidden within the image, the blind spot, which Lacan speaks of, without which vision is not possible. What is captured in the frame? What escapes? The subject is captured and the real escapes.

The historical avant-garde

The problem, or aesthetic challenge, of how to manage the body of the performer within the scenographic environment so that it conforms to the illusions of the stage has not been confined to early modernism. All theatres, in one way or another, confront an opportunity to play with the body on stage, to make of it an actuality and to exercise it as an illusion. However, there has been a long history of radical solutions to this dilemma, including the elimination of the actor altogether, to be replaced by theatrical automata or various technical, scenic or plastic objects.

The word *automata* derives from the Greek *automatos*, which means acting of one's own will, or self-moving. It is the source of the uncanniness that a machine would have a will of its own and its own animating force. This strangeness is what has drawn so many philosophers and artists to the automaton as a way to think toward the problem of life and being human. The practice of building automata began with *Hero of Alexandria* in ancient Egypt. Using hydraulic and pneumatic technologies, Hero was able to construct automated puppet theatres with moving figures, and even lighting and sound effects. Leonardo Da Vinci is credited with having designed the first humanoid automaton sometime around 1495, but his design was never realized (Vanderbilt 2004). Louis XIV had automata constructed by artisans in the mid seventeenth century. In the eighteenth century the famous automata of Jacques de Vaucanson of France were built, which included a mechanical digesting or defecating duck, a flute player and a pipe and drum player (ca. 1737). Wolfgang von Kempelen constructed his famous hoax chess player *The Turk* in 1769, more magic illusion or theatrical prank than actual machine. The Swiss Pierre Jaquet-Droz constructed between 1768 and 1774 automata including *The Writer*, *The Musician* and *The Draughtsman*, which were capable of writing set poems and drawing pictures.[8] Video of the automata of Jacquet-Droz in operation reveals an uncanny and haunting quality of the automata as their hollow eyes stare ahead as their *bodies perform*.[9] Likewise, reports of the breathing of Vaucanson's flute player and the swallowing of food by the Digesting Duck remarked on the unsettling quality of machine life or life as a machine (Wood, 22). It is this element of the puppet's performance of death in life and the linking of the human and machine that will reappear in the theatrical theory and practice of Edward Gordon Craig and Tadeusz Kantor discussed below.

Descartes, in *Treatise on Man* (1664), introduced a mechanistic philosophy that modelled the animal as a machine. The work began the modern debate regarding man as machine and argued that animals were essentially machines and that their interior structures could be substituted for machine parts. *L'Homme Machine* (1747) by Julien Offroy de la Mettrie further grounded the theory as a materialistic discourse that argued that 'life is a property of matter, not dependent on a separate entity called a soul' (Wood 2002: 12). The fascination with man-made and mechanical life continued into the early nineteenth century, as is apparent in the literature of the time, including the Homunculus creature in Goethe's *Faust* (1805), the short story *The Automata* (1814) by E.T.A. Hoffman and *Frankenstein* (1818) by Mary Shelley. It is no surprise that theatre artists and critics would similarly imagine the potential performativity of artificial life. In 1811, Heinrich von Kleist wrote in *On the Marionette Theater*:

> We see that in the organic world, as reflection grows darker and weaker, grace emerges more radiant and supreme. But just as two lines

intersecting on one side of a point, after their passage through infinity, suddenly reappear on the other side, or just as the image in a concave mirror, after moving out into the infinite suddenly becomes visible again, so too grace returns, when knowledge has, as it were, gone through an infinity: thus grace appears most purely in that human form which has either no consciousness at all or an infinite one – that is, in a puppet or a god.

(1994: 240)

Kleist's intriguing and esoteric passage, using mathematical, perceptual, and theological metaphors, seems to be describing the perspective stage discussed above, and sees a 'return of the repressed' in the figure of the totally full consciousness of the puppet or the god. Our grace, the grace of the human returns as a figure radically different from ourselves: the puppet. He suggests that the actor was inferior to the puppet, because 'puppets have the advantage of antigravity. They know nothing of the inertia of matter' (238). The problem of the actor, according to Kleist, is the materiality of the body, which is limited by the forces of nature and by its own strength, as well as by the nature of consciousness, which creates egocentric self-consciousness that undermines the free play of art and the theatre. Kleist's assertions are striking for their similarity to the body and new media artist *Stelarc*, who argues the body is now obsolete and requires digital and mechanical prostheses to meet its full potential.

The anti-actor prejudice runs through much of the historical avant-garde's performance theory and practice. Edward Gordon Craig, nearly one hundred years after Kleist, held the same concerns of the damaging effects to art by the actor. Craig in 'The Actor and the Übermarionette' published in his journal *The Mask* in 1908, quoted Eleanora Duse, who wrote that 'To save the theatre, it must be destroyed, it is necessary for all actors and actresses to die of plague ... for it is they who render art impossible' (Duse quoted in Craig 1983: 82). In that essay Craig wrote, 'The actor must go, and in his place comes the inanimate figure – the Übermarionette we may call him, until he won for himself a better name' (quoted in Bablet 1962: 105). However, according to Denis Bablet, it would be incorrect to read Craig's *Übermarionette* as an attack on the actor; it is an attempt at perfecting the art of the actor. Craig's battle does seem to be with realism and with egocentric actors, rather than with all actors per se. He suggests that through the *Übermarionette* one might supplement or reconfigure, not replace, the actor, to create what he called a *durable* theatre of *egoless* actors. Nonetheless, Bablet's attempt to convince readers that Craig was not out to ban the actor from the stage seems forced and apologetic because Craig's distrust and disdain for the actor is clear. He writes, 'Human facial expression is for the most part valueless' (quoted in Bablet 1962: 110). Craig's critique of the art of acting is tempered by his project of perfecting the art, and in this manner Bablet is correct.

The Übermarionette will not compete with life – rather it will go beyond it. Its ideal will not be the flesh and blood but rather the body in trance – it will aim to clothe itself with a death-like beauty while exhaling a living spirit. Several times in the course of this essay has a word or two about Death found its way on the paper – called there by the incessant clamouring of 'Life! Life! Life!', which the realists keep up.

(quoted in Bablet 1962: 109)

The linkage of the *Übermarionette* or mechanical life with the spectre of death goes to the root of why the objects exhibit such a powerful performative image. Tadeusz Kantor, in 1975, drew on Craig's *Übermarionette* for his manifesto *The Theatre of Death* to emphasize the power of the marionette, but chose to dissociate himself from Craig's 'renowned decisions on the fate of the actor' (1993: 113). Nonetheless, having misread something of what Craig was advocating, Kantor's ideas regarding the power of the mannequin, puppet or marionette is very similar to Craig's opinion.

MANNEQUINS also have their own version of TRANSGRESSION. The existence of these creatures, shaped in man's image, almost 'godlessly' in an illegal fashion, is the result of heretical dealings, a manifestation of the Dark. Nocturnal. Rebellious side of human activity. Of Crimes and Traces of Death as sources of recognition. The vague and inexplicable feeling that through this entity so similar to a living human being but deprived of consciousness and purpose there is transmitted us a terrifying message of Death and Nothingness.

(112)

The transgression of the puppet or mannequin is an obscene existence amplified through a mocking death-like figuration. Kantor, drawing from both Kleist's returning grace in the form of the puppet and the Übermarionette death aesthetics of Craig, promoted the use of the mannequins on the stage, not as a supplement to the actor, but rather as a *model* of the live actor, in order to achieve a clearer effect of death. In Kantor's theatre, it is the human-machine model that can trigger the uncanny experience of remember mortality. The live actor, in the models of Kliest, Craig and Kantor, is limited in its appeal as an art object and therefore needs supplementation by some other performing object, such as the mannequin or puppet.

Oskar Schlemmer, artist and director of the Theatre Workshop of the German art school and research centre the Bauhaus (1921–9), follows the same track as Kleist, Craig and Kantor, arguing for the power of the artificial to reveal artistic truths. He wrote in his diary in September of 1922,

The theatre, the world of appearances, is digging its own grave when it tries for verisimilitude; the same applies to the mime, who forgets that his chief characteristic is his artificiality. The medium of every art is artificial, and every art gains from recognition and acceptance of its medium.

(Schlemmer 1990: 126)

If the medium of every art is artificial, then what of the theatre, whose primary medium is the body of the actor? Schlemmer theorizes, like Craig and Kantor, a convergence of the artificial and the real in order to *play up* the appearance. Schlemmer suggests an applied awareness of the body as machine: 'Life has become so mechanized, thanks to machines and a technology which our sense cannot possibly ignore, that we are intensely aware of man as a machine and the body as a mechanism' (126). But he plays this awareness of the human as a machine against a desire for unmediated creativity and 'primordial impulses' (127).

Schlemmer created a series of dance theatre works performed through-out Germany and at the Bauhaus including *The Triadic Ballet*, *Space Dance*, *Form Dance* and *Gesture Dance*. Each of these works used stylized dance sequences with actors/dancers costumed in distorting outfits, working in 'conformity to organic or mechanical laws or they invalidate that conform-ity' (1961: 25). The costumes were realized as body stockings or leotards, padded to emphasize the hips and shoulders. Masks were worn to give a further abstract or machine-like quality. Similar to Beckett's *Quad*, the performance event was made up of deliberate actions that foregrounded the body marking various abstract patterns such as diagonals, squares or straight lines. In *Form Dance* spheres, wands or poles were used to high-light the abstracted and geometrical spaces. Schlemmer articulated well the problem I intended to voice above, namely the problem of the corporeal body in artificial space:

Man, the human organism, stands in the cubical, abstract space of the stage, Man and Space. Each has different laws of order. Whose shall prevail? Either abstract space is adapted in deference to natural man and transformed back into nature or the imitation of nature. This happens in the theatre of illusionistic realism. Or natural man, in defer-ence to abstract space, is recast to fit its mold. This happens on the abstract stage.

(1961: 22)

It is the abstract stage that interests Schlemmer and to that end he real-izes that it is costuming that can reconfigure the human body to function adequately within nonfigurative space. Schlemmer outlines four modes of the transformation of the human body in terms of stage costumes, including cubical, functional, motional and metaphysical, which lead to a performing body that is respectively ambulant architecture, technical organism, marionette and dematerialized form. Schlemmer is attempting, in my view, not to suppress the body, but to liberate the performing body in an abstract space, to rid the stage of naturalistic illusionism and, in its place, to establish an abstract stage that speaks spiritually and materialistically.

Schlemmer argues, like Brecht, that representations on the stage need to reflect accurately the historical, cultural and technological conditions of the time.

> Technology and invention which we can use to create altogether new hypotheses and which can thus engender, or at least give promise of, the boldest fantasies. The theater, which should be the image of our time and perhaps the one art form most peculiarly conditioned by it, must not ignore these signs.
>
> (1961: 17)

There is a utopian aspect that, unfortunately, is often attached to the inclusion of technology in art and culture. From the Futurist's dream of metallization of the body to the cyberculture's cult of a liberated wired world, technology is often unrealistically positioned as a panacea for the perceived weaknesses of system.

> In art, especially in painting, we are witnessing a search for the roots and sources of all creativity; this grows out of the bankruptcy brought on by excessive refinement. Modern artists long to recover the original, primordial impulses [...] Both these modes of consciousness – the sense of man as a machine and insight into the deepest wells of creativity – are symptoms of one and the same yearning. A yearning for synthesis dominates today's art and calls upon architecture to unite the disparate fields of endeavor. This yearning also reaches out for the theatre, because the theatre offers the promise of total art.
>
> (127)

Schlemmer's combining of the awareness of the human as a technological or machine entity and the desire or drive for the unknown or primordial domains of art and creativity is echoed in much of the work already mentioned of Kleist, Craig and Kantor. It is also very similar to the stated goals of some new media and cyber-performance artists who seek, through the human–computer interface, new epistemological models, new aesthetic practices and new models of subjectivity. However, at the base of this celebration of the artificial are the vestiges of an anti-biological or anti-corporeal prejudice that seeks to privilege the plastic, the artificial and the machine over the human. The Italian Futurists would take that prejudice to its extreme limit.

Various dramaturgical, scenic and theoretical innovations of the Italian Futurists (1909–44) help substantiate my claims regarding both the effectiveness and seduction of the performing machine object and the problems surrounding the alteration, deformation, reconfiguration, supplementation or elimination of the body from the plasticity and illusions of the stage. I will narrate a limited and non-chronological account of Futurist performance in order to fictionalize a project for the elimination of the body from the stage. The scenario I am reading into Futurist performance begins with the Futurist evenings, *Serate*, and cabaret performances that displayed the body-as-itself in direct face-to-face communication with the audience, while introducing new modes of identity through that performativity. Secondly, I look to several of the highly condensed, or syntheic, Futurist plays and performance, dance and theatre works that challenge verisimilitude in manners that called for the actor's body to be de-formed or re-visioned as machines through costuming or scenic interventions. Next, I consider the actor as a nonphysical presence in an *agency-extended* or *disembodied communication*, advocated in Futurist scenographer Enrico Prampolini's theory of *actor-gasses*. Finally, my narrative concludes with the complete absence of the body, or any recourse to anthropomorphizing, on the stage in Prampolini's *Magnetic Theatre* and Giacomo Balla's actorless *Fireworks*. The Futurist works I discuss were conceived and realized at different times and are not in a neat flow or chronology that my analysis constructs for them, that is, of the actor's path from presence to absence. Michael Kirby's essential study and anthology *Futurist Performance* (1971) supplies my main source of documentation as does the more recent and more complete *Italian Futurist Theatre* 1909–1944 (1998) by Günther Berghaus.

The Futurist *serate* were cabaret performances or *evenings* that began as poetry and manifesto readings. Marinetti's concept of poetry readings as *warlike declamation* is elucidated in his *Dynamic and Synoptic Declamation Manifesto* (1916). The performer is given instructions that require him to 'completely dehumanize his voice [...] his face' and 'electrify his voice', to 'gesticulate geometrically' and 'move to different parts of the room' and to 'make use of certain number of elementary instruments such as hammers, little wooden tables, automobile horns' (Marinetti 1991: 152). The notion of dehumanizing the voice and face while gesticulating geometrically is indicative of the Futurist move to present radically new identities through performance, which, at essence, was also crucial to many of the movements of the historical avant-garde. It was not enough to flood the museums or burn down the libraries; but the bourgeois models of subjectivity, even the human itself, needed to be undone. Marinetti, in the *Dynamic and Synoptic Declamation Manifesto*, called for a performative realization for his concept of *parole in liberta* (liberated language or speech). The performer would be 'precipitating new laws and creating unexpected new horizons in the words-interprets' (153).

The drive for the new that marked much of the historical avant-garde led the Futurist to rethink the human and its subject position, to imagine new models realized by new technologies. These models of heroic progress through liberation narratives, which have been critiqued in the historical avant-garde, also run through a good deal of the writings of cyber-performance advocates and theorists of technoculture. Technoculture apologists are following a similar path and may be subject to some of the same critiques made of the Futurists, namely utopian delusions coupled with male dominance, and an aggression that suggests fascist tendencies.

The Futurist plays, which began to appear in 1915, known as *sintesi* or synthetics, were generally very short vignettes. They followed the forms set out in the *Futurist Synthetic Theatre Manifesto* (1915) written by Marinetti, Emilio Settimelli and Bruno Corra, which states 'Synthetic. That is very brief. To compress into a few minutes, into a few words and gestures, innumerable situations, sensibilities, ideas, sensations, facts and symbols' (Kirby, 197). *La Pancia del Vaso* (The Paunch of the Vase), written in 1920 by Franceso Cangiullo, is a good example of the Futurist theatrical synthesis. Act I calls for a scientist to stare, with the 'eyes of an idiot', into a glass vase on a cluttered table for three minutes. Act II is a repetition of Act I. Such a laborious timing and repetition seems more like a Beckett or Robert Wilson extension, interruption and degradation of theatrical time than a Futurist ecstatic acceleration. Act III begins the same, but one minute into the action, the author, Cangiullo, enters the stage and splits the head of the scientist with a cudgel. Cangiullo exits and the scientist dictates a letter, stating all the punctuation marks, to a typist. The letter thanks Cangiullo for splitting his head and not the vase. Regarding this neo-absurdism, Michael Kirby noted that the Futurist *sintesi* prefigured Pirandello's and the Theatre of the Absurd's dramaturgical techniques of illogic. Unique and rarely emulated, the Futurists developed a dramaturgy of compression that would assume that everything could be said with just a gesture and demonstrated that it was useless to build an action, as in the psychological theatre of Chekhov and Stanislavsky, through a fictive real-time.

In one sense, it seems as if time is the primary worry of the Futurist playwright. When reading one of the Futurist plays, one can sense a frenetic pace, a falling forwards, a racing and a confidence of the new.

> (1) our frenzied passion for real swift, elegant, complicated, cynical, muscular, fugitive, Futurist life; (2) our very modern cerebral definition of art according to which no logic, no tradition, no aesthetic, no technique, no opportunity can be imposed on the artist's natural talent; he must be preoccupied only with creating synthetic expressions of cerebral energy that have THE ABSOLUTE VALUE OF NOVELTY.
>
> (Marinetti in Kirby, 201)

In a very real sense, the Futurists were imitating the speed of machine time, as in the work *Detonazione* (*Detonation*) by Francesco Cangiullo. Subtitled *A Synthesis of All Modern Theatre*, the *dramatis personae* consist of *A Bullet*.

The setting is a cold, deserted road at night. The action consists of a minute of silence followed by a gunshot and the drawing of the curtain. There it is, all presented in a synthetic moment.

Running through the plays is a nihilistic streak that seeks destruction of the past at all cost, and a war with the self and with the human. *Davanti all'Infinito* (*Faced with the Infinite*, 1915) by Bruno Corra and Emilio Settimelli, exhibits both the synthetic impulse and the nihilism that Renato Poggioli claims in *The Theory of the Avant-Garde* is an inherent trait in the avant-garde. A philosopher holds a revolver in one hand and a German newspaper in the other. He says, 'Faced with the infinite all things are equal', and he wonders that 'if after my usual breakfast, I should start reading *Berliner Tageblatt* or I should fire a revolver shot' (Corra in Kirby, 264). He fires the gun into himself and collapses. *Faced with the Infinite* is a short, shocking play that performs a suicidal desire to undo the past and burn down the self with intense speed. The anger extended to the audience as well. 'We Futurists, above all, teach authors to despise the audience' (Marinetti, 121). Futurism's agonism was universal and directed at themselves, the spectator, the world. The mood of a widespread hygienic programme to cleanse the world of its corruption is what many fear in the work of the Futurists, and most easily read it as fascist.

If we can read in the Futurist plays the displeasure of traditional models of identity and a clear anger at society there is also a large element of privileging plasticity, machinery and objecthood over the human. Marinetti's drama of objects, *Vengono* (*They Are Coming*, 1915), depicts furniture in an absurd confrontation with people. A Majordomo orders a group of servants to rearrange a table and chairs in a luxurious room. The Majordomo's language collapses into gibberish, and the armchairs march themselves out of the room as the servants cower in a corner. The structure of the play is that first there is a loss of language, and then a liberation of the object. Not unlike Baudrillard's *Fatal Strategy*, which posits that the 'era of the representational subject is past', causing the logic of the object to supersede the logic of the subject, and strikingly similar to Ionesco's *The Chairs*, *Vengono* presents a rebellion of the object no longer in representational control by the subject. Baudrillard writes, 'things have found a way to elude the dialectic of meaning, a dialectic which bored them' (185). Marinetti's march of furniture is a surrealist presentation of object liberation, a thinking outside a traditional subject position.

The modelling of new identities through performance, as seen in the Futurist cabaret and in the rejection of narrative and verisimilitude in the Futurist plays, began the work of challenging the actor's presence along with rational construction of reality from the theatre. The Futurist scenographers would finish the job. The Futurist scenographers were not interested in the two dimensionality of a painted stage of flats and backdrops, but chose instead to emphasize the full cubic space of the stage that included mechanical and mobile scenery. In their manifestos they called for the removal of the performer and the establishment of a purely artificial or even *postorganic* performance. The primary documents include the manifestos *Futurist Scenography* (1915) by Enrico Prampolini, *Notes on the Theatre* (1916) by Fortunato Depero, *For a New Theatre 'Electric-Vibrating-Luminous'* (1920) by Mauro Montalti, and the scenographic designs and mechanical and marionette stagings of Prampolini, Balla, Depero, Pannaggi and Clavel. The work called for, and realized, a *total theatre* that would eliminate the actor in a three-dimensional, electro-mechanical space that self-reflexively represented nothing more than its own non-objective theatricality.

Enrico Prampolini, one the more prolific of the Futurist scenographers and who designed over 130 productions, wrote the *Futurist Scenography* manifesto in 1915:

> The absolutely new character that our innovation will give the theatre is the abolition of the painted stage. The stage will no longer be a colored backdrop but a colorless electromechanical architecture, powerfully vitalized by chromatic emanations from a luminous source, produced by electric reflectors with multicolored panes of glass arranged, coordinated analogically with the psyche of each scenic action.
>
> (Prampolini quoted in Kirby, 204–205)

Although revolutionary in tone, Prampolini's declaration for the end of two-dimensionality had already been developed across the Continent by such innovators as Wagner, Appia and Craig. As Kirby notes, Prampolini's demand for a synchronous, harmonizing and unifying scenography that would coordinate 'analogically with the psyche of each scenic action', is an echo of such previous theories as Wagner's *Gesamtkunstwerk*, Appia's *rhythmic spaces* and Craig's *Übermarionette*. However, the vision of technological innovations such as a 'colourless electromechanical architecture' with 'chromatic emanations from a luminous source' is a remarkable vision of the potential of an advanced technological stage. Despite his theoretical objection to the painted drop, Prampolini's designs for Futurist *sintesi* were often just that. Granted, the designs carried the iconography of Cubist and Futurist fragmentation of vision. The early designs, nevertheless, remain rooted in a wing-and-drop configuration of two-dimensionality. One would need to look, as Kirby does, to Russian Constructivism, in such productions as Meyerhold's *The Magnanimous Cuckold* designed by Liuov Popova (1922), to find an actual *poly-dimensional, poly-expressive* theatre in action.

Prampolini's *Magnetic Theatre* (1925), a design left unrealized, is an example of a plastic, abstract and *postorganic* theatre. He wrote that the *Magnetic Theatre* would be:

> [...] made up of a mass of plastic constructions in action which rises from the centre of the theatrical hollow instead of the periphery of the

'scenic-arc' [...] to these plastic constructions, ascending, rotating and shifting movements are given, in accordance with necessity. The scenic action of the chromatic light, an essential element of interaction in creating the scenic personality of space, unfolds parallel to the scenic development of these moving constructions. Its function is to give spiritual life to the environment or setting, while measuring time in scenic space.

(Prampolini, quoted in Kirby 1971: 86)

The *Magnetic Theatre* sounds a lot like a contemporary smart environment of sensor-based computer actions of immersive projections and audioscapes. The scenographic design of the *Magnetic Theatre* is a theatre machine designed to operate under its own autonomous theatrical fuel. Prampolini wrote, 'I consider the actor as a useless element in theatrical action, and, moreover, dangerous to the future of theatre' (Kirby, 229). The *Magnetic Theatre* would eliminate the actor in a technologized space, which would represent nothing but its own non-objective theatricality. The *Magnetic Theatre* supplemented the actor with technology.

When the actor was present in Futurist performance, the figure was often de-centred, mechanized and altered through costumes, becoming an integrated element of the *mise-en-scène*, fully immersed or embedded in the picture. Depero's *Macchina del 3000* (1924) and Ivo Pannaggi's *Balletti Meccanici* (1919) depict the use of geometric machine forms to reconfigure the human body. The costuming for *Macchina del 3000* included the use of large cylindrical constructions that covered the performer's head, torso, arms and legs, creating the effect of humanoid machines, robots, or cyborgs, playing with the 'dreamt of metallization of the body' called for in Marinetti's founding manifesto. The extension of the body through the plastics of costume design was popular in avant-garde performance in Russia and Europe of the time. Kazimir Malevich's costumes and sets for *Victory over the Sun* in 1913 and Picasso's designs for Jean Cocteau's *Parade*, a ballet performed by Diaghilev's *Ballet Russe* in 1917, are exemplary. In each of these works the actor's form was radically reshaped toward geometric, cubistic and collage forms. The effect was to create a visual link with the actor and the stage space as Kirby claims. The Futurists' desire was formalistic in attempting to unify scenography, performer and text in a synchronous whole. Consider this costume description by Depero from one of his notebooks:

The framework will be made so as to open and close itself, that is to say, it must appear like a normal Futurist costume but the jacket opens by clicking one's heels; various movements with one's arms, hands, feet, legs, or raising one's hat, etc.... will open certain fanlike contrivances like tongs, etc.... simultaneously with luminous apparitions in bursts and rhythms of noiselike instruments.

(quoted in Kirby, 211)

The performer in Depero's design is walking scenography, a bodily theatre. Fortunato Depero's playscript *Colori* (*Colors* 1916) calls for a 'very empty cubic, blue room. No windows. No door frames' (Kirby, 278). Four abstract 'individualities', a grey ovoid, a red polyhedron, a white sharp point and a black multi-globe, are moved by invisible strings. The forms are assigned human voices: black is very profound, white is sharp, thin and brittle, grey is animal-like and red is roaring. Gibberish is spoken between the forms: 'TO COM momomoo dom pom grommo BLOMM uoco DLONN ... ZINN-FINN fin ui tli tli dlinn dlinntiflinni tli tli uuuuuuu' (278). The body has been erased further into simple forms and the power of the voice, language, is breaking down.

Prampolini theorizes going to another level of disappearance and abstraction declaring that the human body could be supplanted by the *actor-gas*:

> Vibrations, luminous forms [...] will wriggle and writhe dynamically, and these authentic actor-gases of an unknown theatre will have to replace living actors [...] These exhilarant, explosive gases will fill the audience with joy or terror, and the audience will perhaps become an actor itself as well.
>
> (Kirby, 206)

Prampolini is theorizing a postorganic stage. He did not, of course, have the technology to produce such a spectacle. Prampolini has theorized a reduction of the human form to an abstraction of gaseous existence. The last step in this admittedly counterfeit chronology is pure artificiality.

My final example of Futurist theatre is Giacomo Balla's designs for Stravinsky's *Feu d'Artifice* (*Fireworks* 1917), which was produced for the Ballet Russe at the Costanzi Theatre. The work was a scenographic realization of one of Balla's paintings. 'Balla built a complex of prismatic wooden shapes covered with canvas and painted. These were topped with smaller forms of translucent fabric which could be illuminated from inside' (Goldberg, 107–8). Balla designed a network of switches to control the lighting, which, while corresponding to the music, would alter the visual impact of stage. The performance lasted only five minutes and contained forty-nine light settings that included illuminating and darkening the auditorium, thereby implicating the audience in the performance. No longer is there a body in space, nor any reference to the human form.

Futurist performance enacted an attack on bourgeois models of identity and challenged the primacy of the actor on the stage. The strategy was first to change the structure of unified identities such as scene and playscripts, and then to alter the representations of the human form through supplemental costumes and scenic devices, and finally to remove the actor altogether in a postorganic plastic and technologically enhanced three-dimensional stage space.

Conclusion: the resistance to perspectivalism

The resistance to perspectivalism has been short-lived since the early modern period. If, as Blau has argued, theatre haunts all performance, then perhaps perspectivalism resides within all stage space. The proscenium is as much a part of the mechanics of consciousness as it is a technology of the stage representation. How can we see non-geometrically? If perspective is like a visual language, is it possible to see without it? Euro-American experimental theatre of the 1960s offered the most concentrated attack on perspective. Grotowski's *Polish Theatre Lab*, *The Living Theatre* of Julian Beck and Judith Malina, Joseph Chaikin's *Open Theatre*, Richard Schechner's *The Performance Group*, Blau's *Kraken* company, *The Manhattan Project*, Ariane Mnouchkine's *Théâtre du Soliel* and the directorial work of Andre Serban all looked to undo the restrictions of first-person spectatorship.

Richard Schechner was perhaps the most vocal of the 1960s avant-garde theatre artists regarding theatre spaces. He promoted the notion of an *Environmental Theatre*, the goals of which were to democratize performance space by allowing the spectator choice and variety in perspective and interaction or intervention in the performance action. The actor was to gain autonomy from the repressive forces of text, director and designer. Openness, exchange, presence, touch, communication, nakedness and liberation were the words commonly in use to describe the political or activist theatre of the time.

Schechner articulated an erotics of spatial confrontation and meetings. 'The fullness of space, the endless ways space can be transformed, articulated, animated – that is the basis of environmental theatre design' (Schechner 1). Schechner's radical egalitarianism argued that 'all spaces are actively involved in all the aspects of the performance [...] there is no dead space nor any end to space' (2). It is inspiring rhetoric that was part and parcel of the ethos of the 1960s. 'Move through the space, explore it in different ways. Feel it, look at it, speak to it, rub it, listen to it, make sounds with it, play music with it, embrace it, smell it, lick it, etc.' (12). But the utopianism, or more frequently, the eroticism or polymorphous perversity, is confronted by the spectre of the theatre frame, which continues its relentless appearance no matter which way one points, looks askance, or looks through a border or underneath a platform.

Jerzy Grotowski took the notion of reconfiguring the theatre in order to elicit cultural change to the ultimate lengths. He began this journey during his time with the *Polish Theatre Lab* using some of the first examples of multi-perspective stagings in non-traditional theatre sites, in which he sought an unmediated response from his actors. He carried this desire to challenge theatrical representation by removing all vestiges of theatrical presentation and by removing the borders of audience and actor toward the experience of an event, a meeting, a day, as he said, that is *holy*.

> Some words are dead, even though we are still using them. Among
> such words are: show, spectacle, theatre, audience, etc. But what is
> alive? Adventure and meeting: not just anyone; but that what we want
> to happen to would happen, and then, that it would also happen to
> others among us.
>
> (Grotowski in Wolford, 215)

Grotowski worked toward removing any perceived restrictions of the
stage, or the falsehoods of the theatre and illusion, in a liberative move toward
the essence of a face-to-face encounter as the grounds of a pure meeting.
Is it authentic, or another myth of participation or present un-mediated event?
Of course, the calls for authenticity and purity are disquieting, seeming
now utopian, fantastic and naïve. However, these were works created by
people of good faith whose desires were for a greater good and progress,
and they deserve recognition for that.

The sought-after freedoms of the *Environmental Theatre* came at a
cost. If the actor and audience alike were freed from a proscenium arch
and limiting imagistic representations, they were nonetheless victims of
audience members ill-prepared for, or taking advantage of, the participatory
scenes of nakedness, where community gave way to personal bias, egotism
and profligacy, which are the 'real stuff', the petty grounds of politics and
meeting. Schechner, commenting on the participation elements of *Dionysus
in 69*, wrote in a caption to a photo of the production, 'the performers are
the women in panties and halters. Everyone else is audience. After three
months the scene was dropped. Too often the performers – especially the
women – felt used, prostituted' (42). The problems of reaching the goals
of an anti-perspectival democratic spectatorship are well illustrated in that
quote.

What might be read as the last gasp of a historical, theatrical avant-
garde's final antithesis, the *Theatre of Images*, reintroduced the vanishing
points, points of views and distance points with a vengeance. The resemblance of Richard Foreman's and Robert Wilson's *mise-en-scène* to Serlio's
tragic and comic scenes is uncanny. The critique of the body's subjugated
position in the work of both Wilson and Foreman is not unfounded.
Consider the ubiquitous strings on Foreman's stage used to emphasize the
pictorial quality of the *Ontological* stage while bringing attention to the
very act of perception, of looking, and the relation of objects to each other
and to their environment. It was as if Foreman was recalling the proscenium
from its temporary banishment by the hippies, not to bring back the restrictions per se, but to enjoy the freedom and power of the limitations, to look
more closely to the material space of perception, to see things as they are:
not a utopian space of Environmentalism, which was to shape things as
they should be.

Or consider Robert Wilson's tortuous slow motion, in which time itself
became solidified as spatial phenomenon. The theatre, as a thing in and of

itself, was the object of Wilson's stage. Like Piet Mondrian's naturalistic trees that were abstracted to the formalism of *Broadway Boogie-Woogie*, the Bed in *Einstein on the Beach* was reduced to a simple band of light lying horizontally on the stage, rising vertically and levitating out of the fly space. The theatre was back – not that it had gone anywhere, but the theatre of off-stage, on-stage, of revealings and shadowing, of wings and drops, teasers and tormentors, was back – and the utopian space was seen or scene for what it was, a dream. The demands of consciousness, perception and the psyche brought the proscenium back to its problematic status.

The point I have tried to make in this chapter is that there has been a struggle between the material body and the desire for constructing stage illusions and perfecting the plastic arts of the theatre. The technologies of the virtual continue the process of picturing the world. Current advances in computerized scientific visualization afford unique visions of the body and of the world. Now that most everything can be transposed from analogue to digital and rendered geometrically, the process of perspectivalism accelerates.

The Visible Human Project® is an outgrowth of the National Library of Medicine. It is the creation of complete, anatomically detailed, three-dimensional representations of the normal male and female human bodies. A frozen male cadaver was sectioned at one-millimeter intervals, and a female was sectioned at one-third of a millimeter intervals. *Quicktime*® animations of 3-D fly-throughs of the cadavers are down loadable, affording unique perspectives on the human form. As Walter Benjamin argued, 'the enlargement of a snapshot does not simply render more precise what in any case was visible, though unclear; it reveals entirely new structural formations of the subject' (1968: 236). The visible human is such a snapshot, a picturing of interiority; a new structural formation of the subject from the inside out. What are we seeing? Finally, as we imbue our machines and weapons with the capacity for perspectival vision (e.g. smart bombs) – a smart perspectivalism if you will – the process of creating the world as picture takes a dangerous turn, or a tragic twist.

The desire to make of the theatre a machine of mathematical illusion, and later a machine of computerized virtuality, constitutes an ongoing process of the representation of the *ecstasy of immortality*. There is a thread in the history of western theatre wherein the representations of the stage call for the celebration of the illusions of the eternal at the expense of the authenticity of corporeality.

5 The ruins of illusion

Theatre in the rise of the virtual and the fall of illusion

In the ruin history has physically merged into the setting. And in this guise history does not assume the form of the process of an eternal life so much as that of irresistible decay.

> (Benjamin 1977: 177–8)

Theatre places us right at the heart of what is religious-political: in the heart of absence, in negativity, in nihilism as Nietzsche would say, therefore in the question of power. A theory of theatrical signs, a practice of theatrical signs (dramatic text, mise-en-scène, interpretation, architecture) is based on accepting the nihilism inherent in re-presentation. Not only accepting it: reinforcing it. For the sign, Peirce used to say, is something, which stands to somebody for something. To Hide, to Show: that is theatricality.

> (Lyotard 1976: 105)

[...] the theatre, a fraudulent institution that never pretends to be anything but fraudulent, an institution that calls forth what is not, that signifies absence, that transforms the literal into the metaphorical, that evacuates everything it represents.

> (Greenblatt 1988: 127)

Voice: Remember. This text is – as it were – inside out. That is, its presentation – to in a sense – make it clear – inside out. Because when you see the inside outside – the inside is clear, right?

> (Foreman 1976: 207)

Theatre's technologies of representation

I closed the last chapter with the quote from Walter Benjamin's canonical essay, 'The Work of Art in the Age of Mechanical Reproduction', that 'the enlargement of a snapshot does not simply render more precise what in any case was visible, though unclear: it reveals entirely new structural formations of the subject' (1968: 236). Theorists of cyberculture are making a similar claim that subjectivity in the space of technology is constructed differently. However, and this is a critical point, if an obvious one, the philosophical, political and aesthetic issues that arise from the interface of the human and its technologies of representation constitute a trans-historical event. Western dramas and theatre practices have worked through the problem incessantly. From *The Bacchae* by Euripides, which depicts the doubling technology of the mask of Dionysos and the tragic consequences of mis-seeing, to *Film* by Beckett, which demonstrates the failure and fear of the technologies of representation; from Shakespeare's *Coriolanus*, which narrates the fragmented subject undone by the politics of representation, to *The Screens* by Genet, a meditation on the terror of representation and the eternal recurrence of the screens as the material site (owned by the colonial other, operated by subjugated) upon which power projects a repressive virtual space; from the linguistic blood baths of Seneca, an ancient post-modern theatre of pastiche and schizophrenia, to *The Wooster Group*, whose deconstructions reveal the ideological substructures of theatre itself; the construction of identity and the manipulations of perception through their technologies of representation have been thoroughly interrogated. My point is to suggest that one history of the theatre could be a history of how to understand the theatre's own technologies of representation and their restructuring of subjectivity. What may be different in late twentieth century mediatized culture, and unforeseen by the theatre artists above, is the re-workings of the *powers of the false*, what I am calling the technologies of illusion, in response to the strategies and technologies of the virtual and the ideologies of the simulacrum.

I want to identify what might be perceived in contemporary performance as a *ruinous metaphysics* withdrawing toward and folding within material-ism, as a result of a relinquishing of art's powers of the false and the tech-nologies of illusion in response to the strategies of the virtual and the phenomena of simulation. I am attempting to isolate a strain of resistance in Western culture and aesthetics to the slow dissolve from illusion to the virtual. The argument of this chapter works from Hegel's critique of sense-certainty in the *Phenomenology of Spirit* (1807, 1977) and Giorgio Agamben's extension of that questioning in *Language and Death: the place of negativity* (1991), and considers how the theatre's structure is illuminated by that philosophy. I begin the line of reasoning by glossing Foucault's reading of Deleuze in *Theatrum Philosophicum*, which suggests that meta-physics is challenged in the event of the simulacrum, which sees the absence of the other, the recurrence of sameness and a loss of appearance and illusion.

I will attempt to ground this purely (and perhaps, maddeningly) theoret-ical model with an analysis of the most material of the theatrical arts, scenography. I contend that some contemporary scenographic practices and stagings can be interpreted as demonstrating this project for a *new metaphysics* projected on the flesh of the performer and on the remains of the stage, which plays among, or seeks refuge within, the ruins of illusion. I will look to the design work of *The Wooster Group*'s Jim Clayburgh as transparent industrial remains of a wasted theatricality, Richard Foreman's settings for his *Ontological-Hysteric Theatre* as re-inscriptions of the material stage upon which appear the phenomena of things in and of themselves, and Romeo Castellucci's ruinous and transparent sites of a new tragic consciousness for his company *Societas Raffaello Sanzio*. I am modelling a theatre that is grounded upon a metaphysics which exists upon the surface of things, an inside outside, in which events and phantasms reveal not only the falseness of appearances, but also the fact that the falseness is all there is. Nietzsche suggests (like Warhol after) that it is important to look no further than the surface, as it is there that the world (and its other) begins and ends.

Foucault in *Theatrum Philosophicum*, first published in English in 1977, writes,

> Illusion is certainly the source of every difficulty in metaphysics, but not because metaphysics, by its very nature, is doomed to illusion, but because for the longest time it has been haunted by illusion, and because in its fear of the simulacrum, it was forced to hunt down the illusory.
>
> (1997: 219)

Foucault's argument is different from mine, but helps to make my point. He is seeking a way through Deleuze to rethink metaphysics, or to be able to think metaphysically outside the problems of transcendentalism. He is seeking a way to think a material metaphysics, an incorporeal corporeality. In this manner he is working in a larger tradition of twentieth century philosophy that seeks to think being as *event*, not as transcendental other. In challenging traditional metaphysics, various philosophers such as Martin Heidegger, Slavoj Žižek, and Alain Badiou argue for a conception of being not as transcendental structure or objectivity, but as *event, act, happening, occurrence*. These notions of the event model a historicity of being, which suggests an engagement with truth as a decisive moment, a turning, a fundamental change or interruption to the *state of things as they are*. These occurrences of being are based on performative choices and chance similar to what, traditionally, one might think of as the essence of drama (e.g. *Antigone*). The event and performativity of being that these philosophical models propound can help expand our knowledge of how the theatre and drama function.

I am attempting to position the problem of the aesthetics and technologies of illusion within the theatre when confronted with the logic of the virtual. Foucault is stating that illusion acts as a resistance or a border in which metaphysics is challenged. In laying claim to transcendental signifiers,

metaphysics speaks of that which we cannot know. It works to think the impossible, which can lead to pure nonsense, to ill-saying what cannot be seen. However, every planned escape route from metaphysics establishes yet another metaphysics. There is always a leap of faith in any position taken up, meaning that any situation is indiscernible until it is named. The naming t is an article of faith based on a groundless belief. Alain Badiou's model of truth makes exactly that point. Foucault is attempting through his reading of Deleuze to uncover a metaphysics on the appearance of the material. In Foucault's model the problem is not illusion, but rather the simulacrum, which is often confused with illusion. In my argument I am linking the technologies of the virtual with the function of the simulacrum, which is a symbolic order without the underpinning or grounding of a Real. The simulacrum is pure surface behind which, or upon which, is concealed nothing. The virtual, or the simulacrum, is a supplement to the symbolic order, and therefore a cancellation or substitution, and thus severs the link with the Real. I am holding out a function for illusion – utopian perhaps, optimistic at least – that it offers an exchange with the Real that can be glimpsed through art.

Foucault's project is similar to Adorno's claim that metaphysics has merged with the historical. Adorno remarked on the slippage of meta-physics into the material in his *Lecture Fifteen on Metaphysics*.

> [T]he metaphysical principle of the injunction that 'Thou shalt not inflict pain' – and this injunction is a metaphysical principle pointing beyond mere facticity – can find its justification only in the recourse to material reality, to corporeal, physical reality, and not to its opposite pole, the pure idea. Metaphysics, I say, has slipped into the material existence.
>
> (2000: 117)

The slippage or re-appearance of metaphysics in material existence is precisely the phenomenon I am suggesting occurs in a technoculture infected with the virtual. I am further arguing that the phenomenon can be read as occurring in some contemporary theatre scenography.

Foucault's article, which is a gloss on Deleuze's *Logic of Sense* and *Difference and Repetition*, opposes the concepts of illusion and the simu-lacrum while suggesting a manner in which to think metaphysically. Foucault asserts that Deleuze created a metaphysical discourse that is,

> Freed from its original profundity as well as from a supreme being, but also one that conceives of the phantasm in its play of surfaces without the aid of models, a metaphysics where it is no longer a question of the One Good, but of the absence of God, and the epidermic play of perversity. A dead God and sodomy are the thresholds of the new metaphysical ellipse.
>
> (220)

Foucault's dead God, sodomy and a fleshy perversity may read as a rather outrageous Bataille-like pronouncement celebrating a new reign of unfettered freedom, and that may be true. If this is true, it points to a central problem of poststructuralist models of metaphysics, namely a calling upon a transcendental realm without a grounding or moral code to govern the freedom. Unrestrained freedom is what Hegel cautions against in his thinking on the reign of terror during the French Revolution. This *new* metaphysics of Foucault's Deleuzianism is one that sees the end of philosophies of representation 'of the original, the first time, imitation, faithfulness' (220). But this argument is part of the same story we have heard too much from postmodernism. It is still the basic reality/illusion dilemma of Plato and Pirandello. On a more useful level, Foucault is redrawing the metaphysical horizon through historical and material events. Foucault's reading of Deleuze argues that this metaphysical moment observes events that exhibit a non-corporeal materiality, the materiality of the immaterial, the presence of immanence, the physicality of the virtual, the plasticity of the unknown on the edge of the void, as Badiou recognizes in Beckett. The linkage of the material and the metaphysical is exactly where I think some of the most interesting scenographic designers in contemporary theatre practice are locating their work: at the edge of the void.

The binary that I am drawing from Foucault's thoughts is that of the illusory against, alongside or within the virtual. The mechanism of illusion, in my theoretical model, appears on the stage in culture and in consciousness, as the apparatus through which the double appears. This doubling is not an esoteric or metaphysical disappearance, but rather a simple pretending or presentation of being other than what is perceived. It is the double, as Artaud realized, that creates the negative that cancels out appearance, and can undermine, upset, undo our sense-certainty or perception of the real. The function of the double can be mapped, as Kant did in his *Critique of Judgment*, as either the beautiful, or the sublime. The beautiful, according to Kant, is the harmonizing of the mental process and the appearance of the object. This correspondence of subject and object might be understood as similar to the crude definition of truth as a correspondence of concept and occurrence between proposition and thing. However, the sublime (a doubling of the double?) upsets the capacity and limits of the mind, causing a collapse of sense-certainty and an experience of the super-sensible to occur. According to Nietzsche, the *mere appearance* of the world appears as illusion; but through the *powers of the false* of art and illusion, it is possible to glance upon the appearance the aura of the Real. Heidegger, in glossing the aesthetic philosophy of Nietzsche, attempted a 'characterization of Nietzsche's total conception of the essence of Art' (Heidegger 1979: 69). Heidegger concludes that for Nietzsche, 'Art is worth more than "the truth"' (75). 'Art, particularly in the narrow sense, is yes-saying to the sensuous to semblance, to what is not "the true world", or as Nietzsche says succinctly, to what is not "the truth"' (74). Illusion is the key to the map of understanding what is before us.

These are the basic teachings of the *Eleusian* mysteries. According to Giorgio Agamben, extending Hegel's precepts, it:

> [...] is nothing more than this: experiencing the negativity that is always already inherent in any meaning, in any *Meinung* of sense-certainty [...] Thus, the power of the negative that language guards within itself was learned in 'primary schools' of Eleusis. It is possible to 'take the *This*' only if one comes to realize that the significance of the *This* is, in reality *Not-this* that it contains; that is, an essential negativity.
>
> (1991: 13–14)

The foundational technology of representation of theatre is to present the *this* by displaying that which is *not-this*. This is the truth of the theatre: that it is always-already *not-this*, a negative, a double, fired by illusion. But further, it is a *not-this* that is simultaneously *being-there* and corporeally present. It is an incorporeal event, as Foucault through Deleuze would maintain. But the event of the theater is made corporeal by its falseness, fraudulence and duplicity, which are its shining graces. The truth can never enter the stage from the wings or drops, nor by way of the body in pain, as perhaps Chris Burden desired when he had himself shot in the arm by a rifle bullet at a gallery performance. Truth cannot penetrate the proscenium, it is the other to the stage and is therefore embedded in all that appears as *not-this*. What I am modelling is a recapitulation of Artaud's double, but the function of the double collapses in the event of the virtual. Everything *is* in cyberspace and thus nothing is ever *not-this*, not the double, not an illusion nor an appearance. This is a difficult claim to support, as at first glance the cyberspatial would appear to be nothing but appearance, to be nothing but nothing. In fact, it is an abrogation of illusory appearance and the presentation of a depthless surface in which all is available as virtuality. Žižek, as quoted above, argues that it is the loss of the symbolic order in the realm of the virtual that disengages any relation to the real.

In writing on the problem of *sense-certainty*, Hegel put forward that the '*Now* is just this: to be no more just when it is' (63).

> For he who is initiated into these Mysteries not only comes to doubt the being of sensuous things, but to despair of it; in part he brings about the nothingness of such things himself in his dealings with them, and in part he sees them reduce themselves to nothingness.
>
> (1977: 65)

The theatrical event: to be no more, just when it is. Is this not a most profound understanding of the theatre? As it is, there it is not, and there it is not as it is. To be no more, to disappear into its doubling, just as it commits to its being. But because it is *not-this*, it is also not *not-this*, which is a doubling that brings a materialization of the here and now. Not, not.

Who's there? Every thing. The theatre is an initiatory rite into the mysteries. However, most contemporary theatre practice wants to refuse its status as *not-this* in favour of a blatant *is*, in favour of reality over appearance, failing to learn from the mysteries.

Žižek figures that the problem is not a conflict between the virtual and the real but rather between appearance and the simulacrum. Earlier in the book I quoted Simon Cooper's gloss of Žižek's thought that 'what gets lost in today's digital "plague of simulation" is not the true form non-simulated real, but appearance itself' (144). What is being lost in the virtual is the phantasm of the other. According to Cooper, Žižek conceives cyberspace as a symbolic order that 'encapsulates a key direction contained within contemporary capitalist culture: an externalization of the subject's ego through technological means' (146). If, as Žižek implies, it is appearance that is being lost and not the true non-simulated real, then Nietzsche must be screaming or laughing in his grave. Appearance in Nietzschean terms (at least from *The Birth of Tragedy*) is what allows us to glimpse the real. Lost appearance is the loss of illusion, a primary *universal* of the theatre. Cooper writes, 'Žižek argues that cyberspace enacts a radical virtualization, not merely because it creates an artificial phenomenological space, but because 'the psychic investments that accompany it mean that cyberspace is in fact a symbolic order in the making' (146). The symbolic order of cyberspace is nothing more than a simulacrum, a nothing upon which rests nothing.

· I have made a case that the ontologies of the televisual and cyberspace have challenged the phenomena of the theatre. I am not insinuating that the theatre does not exist (not dead, just vanished, or just a ruin), although a fairly sound theoretical argument could be made for such a claim. I am attempting to look for a difference between theatre born of illusion – that which both conceals and momentarily unconceals that which is concealed – and theatre issuing from the virtual, born of the televisual, the essence of simulation wherein pure surface reflects everything as the same in a master projection of itself. What is the theatre of illusion? What is the theatre of the virtual? Are the powers of the false, the procedures of illusion and theatricality, the theatre machine, emptied out in the current rise of virtuality, of the televisual? Illusion has been the process by which one knows in the theatre. The theatre, through the theatrical machines of the mask, the stage and the curtain which goes up to reveal and down to hide, has been where and how the concealed is unconcealed. Nonetheless, the always-already doubled-over nature of the theatrical is such that illusion fails, and the unconcealed returns to its place of concealment, at which point the operation of illusion on the body of the stage begins again. 'Meaning is being concealed in the very act of uncovering it' (Blau 1990: 56–7). The virtual, issuing from the televisual and the cyberspatial, is the technology by which we know today. At the core of the experience of the virtual is an avoidance of those technologies of representation that excavate the double of the theatre and the mask, thereby denying the corporeal nature of the body and mind.

In short bursts, here is another way to make my point: the world appears in consciousness through a process of doubling operated by illusion. The theatre is (was) the place where the double is made material, engaged in and played through the technologies of illusion. Illusion necessitates the appearance of the double; it cannot function without that technology. The traditional theatre model: the double, accessed through illusion, gives way to an appearance of *truth*. The problem is that to experience the double is to be uncannily aware of death. The solution is to engage a discharging of the power of the double and of illusion, and thereby of the spectre of the corporeal body (death) through an engagement with the simulacrum. The simulacrum calls on the virtual to come forward. The televisual is the place where the simulacrum is made material and engaged in play through the technologies of the virtual. The problem: to experience the simulacrum is to be unaware of the corporeal nature of the body. The human is charged to 'please stand by', as death is disengaged in the simulacrum. Can the theatre continue to use the technologies of illusion to engage the double? Does the theatre need to employ the strategies of the virtual and the simulacrum in order to relocate the powers of illusion and the domain of the double?

My notion of theatre that *works* is a process wherein the double (the reverse negative of an impossible reality) appears through the machinery of illusion. My notion of theatre in a ruinous, defective mode is a process whereby the simulacrum, ordered by sameness and lacking all negativity, ambiguity or alterity, is constructed as virtual. The working theatre sets *mere appearance* and difference into play so that one might glance the interruption and eternal return of good infinity as the appearance of the Real through the illusion. The ruined theatre merely appears in a circulatory flow of immobility and in a chronological order of a bad infinity.

According to Nietzsche's metaphysical model put forth in *The Birth of Tragedy*, illusion gives way, or calls forth, through the Apollonian double of *mere appearance*, or the technologies of representation (the mask), an experience of the Dionysian (i.e. the Real). The *virtual* gives way, or calls forth, through televisual affirmative representations, an experience of the simulacrum's mere appearance of mere appearance. The double is uncovered through illusion, a Dionysian cessation of *principium individuationis*, an eternal return of a good infinity of theatre and death. The simulacrum is revealed through the virtual, the signs of the Real of solidified subjectivity and sense-certainty, the chronological progress of a bad infinity, of television and immobility. I hope not to fall into the trap of a 'video is evil, theatre is good' kind of binary. The TV might serve the moment of art in ways the theatre has lost, and the theatre may have collapsed into a televisual circulation. Perhaps the theatre I am thinking of is not isolated in one practice, but is instead a migratory phenomenon, capable of appearing in various guises and disguises.

If virtuality is the new ideological state apparatus and illusion has been relieved of its power to unconceal, then what are the excremental collective impulses, the orgiastic impulses, established in opposition to political, juridical and economic institutions now virtual? Are they to be found in an excavation of the ruins of illusion beneath the realm of the proscenium arch?

Three examples of contemporary scenography will help to ground my argument that the operations of illusion and the double are articulated on the stage through a recourse to transparency, a reduction of space to a ruinous metaphor and an echoing of a now-lost *untruthful* space of theatricality. First, I want to look at Jim Clayburgh's designs for *The Wooster Group*, including the pre-fab, metal, structural skeleton of a house in *Route 1 & 9* (1980) (Figure 5.1). Second, I want to consider the iconography of Richard Foreman's *Ontological-Hysteric Theatre*, paying particular attention to the strings, barriers and multiple frames that define the boundaries of his stage (Figure 5.2). Third, I will analyse the staging devices of Romeo Castellucci for *Societas Raffaello Sanzio*, including the desiccated bodies and debris-filled spaces of the performance of *Giulio Ceseare*, and the clearing of that space in the performance cycle *Tragedia Endogonidia*.

Jim Clayburgh is the primary scenographer of *The Wooster Group*, and his designs have greatly shaped the company's reputation. The exposed,

Figure 5.1 ROUTE 1&9, The Wooster Group, dir. E. LeCompte.
Pictured (l–r): Peyton Smith, Ron Vawter, Willem Dafoe and Kate Valk.
Photo: © Bob Van Dantzig.

industrial quality of Clayburgh's designs operates like Meyerhold's construc-
tivist theatre machines as part representational illusion, part machine. From
early in *The Wooster Group*'s history, Clayburgh has shaped a stage vision
that is both functional and demonstrative of the company's devising strategy and theatrical aesthetic: that of deconstruction, bricolage and appropriation. For *Route 1 & 9*, a reworking and ideological critique of Thornton
Wilder's classic American drama *Our Town*, *The Wooster Group*'s performance space, the Performance Garage, was stripped bare down to a black
floor and industrial white walls with exposed electrics and garage doors.
A railing, reminiscent of Richard Foreman's regular framing barrier between
audience and stage runs along the downstage border. White lines on the
floor echo the metal-framed house and ladder that stand to one side of the
stage. It is a skeletal form that stands in as a ruin of an American home,
perhaps like that of *Our Town*, but houses an obscene scene of unrelent-
ing blackface comedy. The metal-framed room is transparent, with a table
inside like that of the frame itself. Three tracks along the ceiling run perpen-
dicular to the audience from which are hung video monitors that slide
toward the audience via a pulley system. It is a negative space, primarily
black and white in makeup, costume, set, video imagery, and a negative
space in which the theatrical illusion has been cancelled and reconfigured
as violent eruption of repressed libidinous drives. Clayburgh's design is not
a representation of an American home, but rather a representation of a ruin,
or an x-ray of an American home. Clayburgh's scenography stands in as
a theatre for the presentation of a previous theatre, and for a time lost.

The Wooster Group's theatre of absence is further depicted with actors
appearing on the television screens. Their presence in many, if not all, of
the performances establishes an ethos of degradation and deficiency in a
technological ruin. The televisual actors fall under a separate ontological
regime, which is more absent than present, more image than substance.
Even the multiple uses of the industrial folding tables upon which are
placed the props and theatrical machinery in performances such as *L.S.D.
(just the high points)* are indicative of a post-illusory stage. The performers
sitting at the tables perform the actions with no recourse to illusion or traditional mimesis, but instead play through the loss of that aesthetic. Clayburgh's
mise-en-scène looks like a natural history museum, with the skeletal remains
of extinct creatures frozen in place. Yet through the remains appears a fitful
theatricality ready to dance.

Richard Foreman's stated concerns for the phenomenological basis of
theatre practice and spectatorship are evident in his design work. He emphasizes the frames, the always-already proscenium-arched theatre space, with
lines, strings and borders, drawing attention to the objects of the stage and
to the functions of the theatre itself. He wrote about his theatre designs:

> The sets are enclosed spaces, but in no sense should the audience feel
> it is peeking through an imaginary, transparent fourth wall. Instead, the

action of the play should bounce against the three walls of the stage, then flirt with the trick surface of a fourth wall that the audience is continually, vaguely, reminded of.

(1992: 58)

It is interesting that Foreman refers to the *fourth wall*, a concept not necessarily entertained in contemporary theatre practice and more an artifact of early naturalism and a target of the historical avant-garde. It indicates how, in some ways, Foreman's theatre space remains a traditional box theatre, not unlike how Beckett's dramas remain traditional narratives that use the form not only to deconstruct itself, but also to recognize the philosophical usability of the theatre. Foreman explains how he draws the attention of the spectator toward a phenomenological experience.

Often I introduce a railing, or some string, or even a wall of glass as an obstruction between the front row of the audience and playing space. These barriers reinforce aesthetic distance. I do not want the audience to be sucked into the resonating chamber of the stage. I want the spectator to keep his distance, precisely so that the action can bounce against that subtle fourth barrier.

(58)

Foreman is trying to sustain an aesthetic distance, a defamiliarization, by reinforcing the notion or phenomenon of a fourth wall. Foreman's theatrical or hysterical reverberation machines, as he calls them, present things viscerally as they are, but things are manically shifted and rearranged, in a futile attempt to avoid a disappearance or spectatorial lapse in awareness. The speed defeats the purpose as the work quickly jumps (unbalanced) into an impossible present moment. The illusions are amplified, a simulation of theatre is projected, and what remains are the remains. The strings are present to direct the eye and to slow down an empathetic response, but they also serve as a reminder of a previous regime when the eye did not need the support or direction. The strings are the shards of a theatre for which, at one time, the illusion was intact.

Foreman advises in his *Ontological-Hysteric Manifesto II* that it is important to '(1) Study all kinds of "FRAMING DEVICES" and (2) Study the superimposition of DIAGRAM upon reality' (143). Foreman's deconstructed proscenium arch splintered into multiple lines, strings, barriers, railings, frames, and borders forces an *intentional-perception*, but also functions as a ruinous illusory space. The Onotological-Hysteric stage works as a memory of a wilful suspension of disbelief, an illusion with a future. But the barrier that Foreman employs needs to remain transparent or porous to allow sight through and objects out. The half-hidden quality of a Foreman scenographic barrier operates a resistance, a force field, which repels the viewer and lets the theatrical action function as a radical otherness. The effect can be to

Figure 5.2 Zhomboid! The Ontological-Hysteric Theatre, dir. R. Foreman.
Pictured in foreground (l–r): Temple Crocker, Ben Horner and Stephanie
Silver. Photo: © Paula Court.

induce an active perception, such as is requested by the directorial voice-
over in Foreman's *Rhoda in Potatoland.*

> Compare. Her mind and our own mind. She is an actress in the play.
> But at this moment, her real mind is working just like your own real
> mind. (Pause.) Now there are spaces distributed amongst the audience
> but there are other spaces distributed over the stage. Find them. Find
> them. Try to find them.
>
> (1976: 210)

The audience's attention is directed to consider the imagined spaces of
the mental activities of the actors and the characters they play, and ultimately the audience members themselves. No willing suspension of disbelief to support illusion here, but instead an aggressive thinking through of
a new model of theatre built on the ruins of the older form. In *Rhoda in
Potatoland,* when the 'four big potatoes' appear, the text and voice suggest
that a new manner of understanding is possible. These overlapping frames
are like the overlapping bodies of knowledge alluded to in the final voice
of the play, which imply that what is left over is a *joie de vivre.*

But is it nonsense? You see, when I call upon my own knowledge, when I do that, it only shows me (my knowledge) the very tip of its wing. Is it therefore, as I had assumed, my knowledge? I do not possess it. In what sense then, do I call it my knowledge? It is a body of information to which I have occasional, peripheral access. As opposed to other bodies of knowledge. But are there bodies of knowledge? Of course not. There are a composite of partial accesses (other people, myself at different times) and the overlapping of these gives the illusion of a body. Knowledge. But what is it that is overlapping? A certain ... joie de vivre.

(1976: 223)

In what might be considered Foreman's classic period, during the second half of the 1970s, *The Ontological-Hysteric Theatre* was housed in a loft theatre on West Broadway. The theatre space was long, deep and narrow, being subject to the demands of the downtown NYC loft architecture, which was designed for light industrial function rather than for theatrical display. The audience was seated on risers at one end, with Foreman positioned at a control table in front of the stage. The tunnel effect of the cavernous space was like the receding proscenium arches in the duplication of similar forms in the early modern perspectival theatre. Kate Davy, in her introductory remarks to her edited collection of Foreman's plays and manifestos, quotes Foreman, 'Everything shakes. Is about to break apart. A post-Brechtian alienation technique of theatre, applied upon spiritual rather than social concerns' (1976: xvi). The shaking or de-familiarizing of the spiritual is what engages Foreman's theatre as a negative theatrical space wherein all that is not negates all that is, painfully, hysterically, here and now, as a ruin of illusion and a new body of knowledge.

Italy's *Socìetas Raffaello Sanzio* theatre company, under the direction of Romeo Castellucci, has in recent years staged a number of challenging performance works. The collective devised *Orestea (una commedia organica?)* in 1995 based on Aeschylus' *Oresteia*. Their 1997 *Giulio Cesare*, devised in part from William Shakespeare's *Julius Caesar*, was remarkable not only for its brilliant deconstruction of rhetoric and its dynamic use of stage imagery, but for the company's special performers with various conditions of anorexia, obesity and post-operative conditions (e.g. mastectomy, tracheotomy). *Socìetas Raffaello Sanzio*'s *Gensei: from the museum of sleep*, and the more recent performance cycle *Tragedia Endogonidia* will be discussed in later chapters.

In a discussion at Trinity College, Dublin, during the Dublin International Theatre Festival (2000), Castellucci noted three ways he approaches a text. He will burn it, evaporate it or absorb it. The idea is not to perform the text but to use it as a channel for exploration. In both *Orestea* and *Julio Cesare*, performers who are either dramatically emaciated or severely anorexic are placed amidst the ruins of a theatre in the case of *Cesare*, and in the detritus of what appears a type of medical facility in *Orestea*. The make-up and costumes echo or reflect the ruinous, damaged and misshapen anorexic bodies, standing as signs of the fragility of life, the thin red line of demise. If there is any illusion here, it is an illusion lost to the destructions of the real, a monument to a lost illusory surface. The exhausted bodies seem to be past an imitation or any pretense to mimicry. In *Julio Cesare*, two anorexic actors play through the scene of Brutus at the tomb of Cassius. In a ruined theatre, wearing fragments of torn armor and oversized boxing gloves, Cassius lies on the ground. He is covered by a likeness of a Magritte icono-graphic device, a black form resembling a cloud or ink spill, upon which is written the phrase '*ceci n'est pas un acteur*' in an obvious quote of Magritte's famous painting *Ceci n'est pas une pipe*. Clearly this performer is not an actor, as the body is reaching a troubling immobility from the ravages of the anorexia. The restless and dangerous nature of this perfor-mance moment generates the seclusion of a visceral reality in a scene of lost illusions. There are the wreckages of an older art: the ruined auditorium and the elements of Magritte in *Ceseare*, and Picasso (*Guernica*) in *Orestea*. Extreme bodies inhabit Castellucci's stage, and these real bodies act as signi-fiers for an impossible illusionism, a crippled doubling, that require a visceral corporeal marking. They make it real to make it misunderstood and thereby they double it and empty it of significance.

The scenographic work of Clayburgh, Foreman, and Castellucci, carry a transparent border, a porous barrier, which allows only some of what is available to be seen. It is as if the veil has been lifted but the traces remain and that which lies beneath is perceived through a glass, darkly. What is veiled on the stage is a ruin set upon a field of nothingness. I have argued for a lost illusion. Žižek sees the problem going a step further in a lost loca-tion of a place for things to *take place*.

> If, then, the problem of traditional (premodern) art was how to fill in the sublime Void of the Thing (the pure Place) with an adequately beautiful object – how to succeed in elevating an ordinary object to the dignity of Thing – the problem of modern art is, in a way, the oppo-site (and much more desperate) one: one can no longer count on the Void of the (Sacred) Place being there, offering itself to be occupied by human artifacts, so the task is to sustain the Place as such, to make sure that this Place itself will 'take place'.
>
> (2000: 26–27)

What I read into these designs of Clayburgh, Foreman and Castellucci, is the staging of a lost place (the theatre and its technologies of representa-tion, its machines of illusion), testifying that the lost place (the theatre) cannot create the required stage illusions (or apparitions) but occurs, takes place, as the remains, under-used and now use-less, but still painfully beau-tiful, hauntingly present.

6 The aesthetics of disappearance and the politics of visibility

The problem is that the theatre is often caught in the metaphysics of essences rather than paying heed to historical realities. The essence that concerns me here is of personal and collective identity, and the historical reality I am examining is the new social condition of subjectivity within technoculture. The critique and encouragement of the constructions of identity and the representation of the negotiations of subjectivity in various systems of power are tasks that the theatre neatly serves. Yet I seek to articulate a problem in the reliance on a *strategic essentialism* that concretizes the facticity of identity, while embracing a solipsistic realism. I am referring to Gayatri Spivak's model of strategic essentialism, which claims that it may be useful to draw upon essentialist notions in order to counteract certain intransigent political issues concerning identity, visibility and power. The problem, according to Spivak occurs when the strategy remains essentialist and forgoes a critique of its own position. I agree with Spivak, and I will suggest that a strategic essentialism is an understandable political strategy, but a problematic choice given the bio-politics of digital cultures in which virtual, televisual and mediated technologies challenge the subject forth toward a troubling dis-empowerment (as expendable data). Drawing upon a disparate series of dramatic, theoretical and performative examples, I hope to engage the problem of misusing strategic essentialism in the performance of identity and point to various useful alternatives of past and current theatre practices.

Two keynote addresses at the XIIIth World Congress of the International Federation of Theatre Research (Canterbury, 1998), by Erika Fischer-Lichte and Maria Shovtosa, are indicative of the problem I am pursuing. The speakers called for a return to the study and practice of theatre proper, back from the borders of performance studies. Each argued that the discourse of performance studies asserts that everything is performative. Each countered that if everything is performative, then nothing is performative, ergo, if everything is theatre then nothing is theatre. Basically the speakers were reiterating a semiotic precept that how we know something's identity is through difference, not sameness, and to some degree I agree with their concerns. Performance as an epistemological tool has been worn down. Furthermore, according to Guy DeBord's *situationist* model, these theatre researchers have it right; yet the option to return to things as they were, before the ignition of the televisual bomb and the encroachment of the ideology of the virtual, is not available. It is the extension of the televisual and information overload that has drawn so much attention to the phenomena of performance and performativity. No call from the podium for the simulacra of mediatized culture to cease and desist is going to alter the affects of the ontology of the televisual and the virtual on how we see performance, theatre and theatricality. The not-so-surprising tendency toward a bordered theatricality and critique of performativity as an ineffective epistemological model constitutes one flank in the defensive maneuverings by theatre scholars and practitioners against the perceived crisis of subjectivity in mediatized culture. The arguments appropriately indicate the growing concern within theatre scholarship that the analytical model of performance/performativity is too broad a concept to be an effective methodology.

Various contemporary theatre and performance artists in addressing the concerns of identity politics in a quest for representational visibility have staged a solipsistic return through realism. A historical sketch of Euro-American contemporary performance artists' and playwrights' reliance of the self as subject and theme can be drawn from the early body artists such as Chris Burden, Marina Abramovic and Gina Payne, through to the postmodern solo-theatre practitioners Spalding Gray, Tim Miller, Holly Hughes and Anna Deavere Smith. But perhaps it is not the particular artists that concern me, as all of these individuals mentioned have made great contributions to their art. My complaint resides rather with theatrical mimesis in general. Is it not true that the actor's presence is the constitutive moment of theatre? A debatable point, no doubt, but we can accept a strategic essentialism for the sake of argument. And does not that performing presence witnessed by another result in a habitual hermeneutic compulsion of the spectator to fill that appearance with a solidified identity? Often it is not easy to think in the theatre, as Brecht tried to correct, and more often than not the spectator will return to the safe and habitual harbour of projection and identification in a search for meaning. Even Beckett's masterful evasions of narrative logic and subject construction – in works such as *Not I*, *Rockabye*, and *Footfalls* – are themselves subject to the spectator's narratological drives.

The solidification, centrality and domination of the cultural critiques and empowerment strategies surrounding various models of subjectivity *have been* and are part of a much-needed and worthy process. Nonetheless they are now the norm and therefore the target for critique itself. I am suggesting, following Baudrillard's tortuous train of thought in *The Perfect Crime* (1996), that the anxiety engendered in the loss of the real in mediatized culture has resulted in some artists retreating from the borders of art and performance where subjectivity's visibility is always-already disappearing and taking up positions where the redeployment of the binary distinction between politics and classical representation is performed through a type of realism. The grounds of concern for digital culture's manipulations of the real, ubiquitous surveillance and challenges to subjectivity are legitimate. But I want to suggest that the strategy of re-engaging an essentialist position regarding identity is perhaps ineffective for resisting these issues. Against this phenomenon of the theatre's partial return to 'more traditional and reassuring perspectival or mimetic enclave(s)' (Jameson 1991: 54), I want to counter with examples of *techno-philosophical* theatres which question the conflicts between the ideological, political and aesthetic issues of the disappearing technologized body and the political visibility of the *lived body* in performance. I am designating theatres, as I have throughout this study (e.g. Beckett's later plays, *The Wooster Group*, *Ontological-Hysteric Theatre*, and *Societas Raffaello Sanzio*), that are (1) considering identity and metaphysics in the space and time of technology; (2) acknowledge the profound effects of the metaphysics of the televisual and the virtual on many means of communication; and (3) pursuing a question regarding the theatre itself and thereby the disciplines of representation and the problems of subjectivity.

In questioning identity or a reliance on traditional models of identity, I am not offering a critique of postcolonial discourse nor the importance of establishing identity and visibility for any particular oppressed or marginalized group or individual. Hegel, in the *Phenomenology of Spirit* wrote, 'Self-consciousness exists in and for itself when, and by the fact that, it so exists for another; that is, it exists only in being acknowledged' (1977: 111). The strategy of colonial power is to block the reciprocity of recognition and to disempower the other by looking through or past them as if they were invisible. That strategy posits an aesthetics of disappearance that demands resistance. The response is for the other to appear, but it must be an appearance that develops new models of identity that might break the cycles of corruption while avoiding a metaphysics of essence. The problem, in reiteration, is that the theatre is often trapped in a metaphysics of essences rather than of historical realities.

If the goal is visibility, then fine: stand up, be counted, marked and empowered. If the goal goes deeper toward a confrontation with empire, as Alain Badiou would suggest, then something rather impossible has to happen. Badiou writes in a short series of polemics called *Fifteen Theses on Contemporary Art*:

> 13. Today ART can only be made from the starting point of that which, as far as EMPIRE is concerned, doesn't exist. Through its abstraction, art renders this non-existence visible. This is what governs the formal principle of every art: the effort to render visible to everyone that which, for EMPIRE (and so by extension for everyone, though from a different point of view), doesn't exist.
>
> (2004: 86)

What is it that does not appear for empire? The *catch-22* of the situation is that we cannot know or seize it until it is brought forward or appears as a truth in art, science, love or politics. So says Badiou:

> 14. Since it is sure of its ability to control the entire domain of the visible and the audible via the laws governing commercial circulation and democratic communication, EMPIRE no longer censures anything. All art, and all thought, is ruined when we accept this permission to consume, to communicate and to enjoy. We should become the pitiless censors of ourselves.
>
> (2004: 86)

And, finally, Badiou cautions that if all one is capable of as an artist is the repetition of knowledge as opposed to the presentation of truth, then it is best to remain quiet:

> 15. IT IS BETTER TO DO NOTHING than to contribute to the invention of formal ways of rendering visible that which EMPIRE already recognizes as existent.
>
> (2004: 86)

I quote Badiou's admonition to suggest that simply stating identity which is clearly visible, if not privileged, to empire, is to miss an important opportunity. That said, I want to distance myself from a dismissal of the postcolonial or marginalized problem. I am trying to articulate a different concern, which is finding a theatre that can come to terms with the radical new identities within technological and digital culture without reverting to older models of identity boundaries. In fact, my argument would not be with postcolonial discourse, upon whose sophistication I build elements of my own argument. Consider Frantz Fanon's comment, which Homi Bhabha quotes in *The Location of Culture*: 'The Negro is not. Any more than the white' (Bhabha 1994: 41). This is a provocative comment that underscores Fanon's work, which 'splits between a Hegelian-Marxist dialectic, a phenomenological affirmation of Self and Other and a psychoanalytic ambivalence of the Unconscious' (Bhabha 1994: 41). This rhetorical strategy disallows an unproblematized relation to identity, while maintaining the goals of revolutionary change:

> That familiar alignment of colonial subjects – Black/White, Self/Other – is disturbed with one brief pause and the traditional grounds of racial identity are dispersed, whenever they are found to rest in the narcissistic myths of negritude or white cultural supremacy.
>
> (40)

Bhabha's deliberating on Fanon's work critiques the easy binaries of identity politics for a more nuanced approach to subjectivity. The linkage of identity, nationalism and fascism is a troubling pattern. The identity of America was shocked into attention on September 11, which gave rise to fervent nationalism, which in turn led to government action that can be read as fascistic (e.g. the Patriot Act, extraordinary rendition and torture). Irish identity is brutally oppressed in Northern Ireland, which leads to a fervent nationalism, which delivers a fascistic terrorism and the pattern repeats. Nonetheless, and for valid reasons, personal identity needs a marker, a voice and agency. If one's goal in performance theory is a crude politics or social advocacy, power shifts rather than power interruptions, then my argument is of no weight. Political advocacy will often seek success by any means necessary including not thinking the problem.

The argument against my questioning of identity and visability is brought into sharp focus in an article brought to my attention by Professor Gay Gibson Cima of Georgetown University titled 'The Postmodernist Turn in Anthropology: Cautions from a Feminist Perspective' (1989). The authors convincingly argue that the devaluation of the subject by Western white males has been generated as a strategy to neutralize the empowered subjectivities of marginalized people. Suspicions of the reader of this chapter may be raised in that I have named African-American, queer and female artists in my challenge. I would hasten to add that I am attempting to foreground an *alternative* theatre, NOT to impugn the value of performance work for which the construction of identity is critical. However, given the phenomena of the human immersed in technology and the strategies of simulation, the returnings to a traditional subject position are impossible and, if possible, unfortunate, as they represent an avoidance as things as they are and thereby postpone any type of genuine resistance. The slippage of subjectivity in the space of technology is at issue in Sue-Ellen Case's book, *Domain-matrix*. Professor Case writes:

> The immediate problem is how, or where, to begin to write the conjunction performing and lesbian in this time of slippage and upheaval, when: medical technologies are redefining basic definitions of gender assignment, even the deep structures of corporeality itself, in genetic codes; a sexually-transmitted pandemic is loose in the world, taking (safe) sexual practices out into more virtual, abstract realms; political categories such as race or sexual preference are scrutinized at the deepest level as unstable, and even the seismology of such instability doubts its own methods.
>
> (1996: 1)

The world that Case describes is all that is the case in the West. The move toward a *posthuman* construction of subjectivity has been taking place, and the motors of science and capitalism are certain to accelerate the process at any cost. I wonder if within this *posthuman* moment – instead of a theatre immersed in the politics of visibility and identity, which inevitably calls on affirmative representations in a bid to rebuild a unified subject – what might be imagined as an aesthetics of disappearance,[10] at the border of theatre where at play is the cessation of the *principium individuationis* in the space of technology.[11] Practically speaking, how can we know the world that has been worlded as virtual through a theatre that operates with the technologies of a past age?

The process of reducing, reading and articulating the world through a model of *identity* is considered in Deleuze's *Difference and Repetition*. He argues that it is a problem that is both methodological and ontological. Melissa McMahon, glossing Deleuze's argument, writes that 'the function of the concept of identity [...] is essentially that of "managing" difference' (2005: 43). It is a transcendental illusion 'which systematically subordinates the concepts of difference and repetition to that of identity' (42). Deleuze's project is to grasp things in their being and not simply to categorize while eliding difference. But this tendency is not easily overcome:

> The illusion is 'transcendental' (the term comes from Kant) in so far as it is not simply an historical accident that can be corrected with the right information, but forms a necessary and inevitable part of the operation of thought, and thus requires a perpetual work of critique.
>
> (McMahon 2005: 42)

For all the talk and drive for difference and celebrating marginality, could it be that many of the operations of identity politics and critique are essentially excluding difference? And if this modelling of identity through sameness is a necessary and inevitable part of the operation of thought, is it an impossible charge to ask of the thinking subject to re-order its biases? What drives the desire for a recuperation of traditional subjectivity at the moment when identity and the body are being challenged, mapped, commodified and colonized through scientific visualizations, genetic engineering and body modifications should not be overlooked. My assertion is that the demand for a solidified subject position is a retrograde motion in space (a slowing down to make things visible) to counteract the speed of the time of technology (making things disappear).[12]

A philosophical alternative

Brecht, describing his model of Epic Theatre, wrote, 'the theatre becomes a place for philosophers, and for such philosophers as not only wish to explain the world but wish to change it' (1964: 80). Yet according to Lyotard:

> [...] philosophers ask questions without answers, questions that have to remain unanswered to deserve being called philosophical [...] answered questions are only technical matters.
>
> (1988: 8)

One of the unanswerable questions of philosophical thinking regards the process of 'grasping things in their utter *thisness*' (McMahon 2005: 43), which is partially what Deleuze sought in suggesting a new way of thinking the unthinkable horizon of thought.

> How could thought avoid going that far, how could it avoid thinking that which is most opposed to thought? With the identical, we think with all our force, but without producing the least thought: with the different, by contrast, do we not have the highest thought, but also that which cannot be thought.
>
> (Deleuze quoted in McMahon 2005: 48)

The *thingness* or *thisness* of the theatre, the riddle of the ontology of theatre, has not been solved. Hopefully, it never will be resolved, for it is this impossible thought, this site of theatre's aporia, that seduces us to return continually to the event *for to begin yet again*, waiting for the occurrence of the same thing, only different. The un-answerability of the theatre is what makes it an ideal philosophical space ready to ground the main questions of philosophy: being, truth, and the subject. Asking answerable questions, posing solvable problems in the material and visible world, is the difficult work of the engineer in decidability and the politician in representation. The contemporary theatre is engaged primarily in questions of politics and psychology, which choose a moral position and discard philosophical problems. The cultural critics that dominate new theatre practice and theory pose not only answerable questions, but also morally and ethically simplistic ones. Nonetheless, there are many exceptions to this problem, including the *Wooster Group's* use of black-face, pornography and appropriated texts, Suzan-Lori Parks deconstructions of *blackness*, or *Societas Raffaello Sanzio's* challenging representations of the disabled body. Additionally, it is important to acknowledge the many fine examples of philosophical reflection in current theatre practice, including the plays of Howard Barker and Michael Frayn. I admit to using my own strategic essentialism to chastise the theatre for its psychologism and moralism. Perhaps the position I am taking is weakened by this admission and/or slips too close to a simple polemic, or at the least the area in which I stand is reduced, but I still hope to argue that much of contemporary theatre seems unavailable to work through the difficult issues of identity and subjectivity in digital culture, choosing instead to reenact well-worn essentialisms.

Lyotard theorizes in his book *The Inhuman* that painting has become impossible in the light of photography, that literature has become impossible as a result of journalism. This has not been an aesthetic issue alone, but symptomatic of capitalism. The world needs journalism, needs photography, but has no need for writing or painting. Yet within the impossibilities of painting and writing is the birth of philosophy through these media and a question regarding their essence and ontology. What is painting? What is writing? The failed systems become insanely self-reflexive, philosophical, reordered as the site of art production. Now at the point where theatre has become impossible, or at least challenged, as a result of the simulation strategies of the virtual and the televisual, is the moment where a philosophical (failed) theatre can take hold to offer a *thinking through* of the forms of theatrical production? What is theatre? What are its borders? The process of a philosophical theatre is to avoid the answerable questions regarding the politics of the visible, while approaching the unanswerable issues of the aesthetics of disappearance and the sublimity of the unpresentable.

Coriolanus, Film, Ontological-Hysteric theatre, and *Socìetas Raffaello Sanzio*

Next consider the trajectory of these citations from the dramatic literature, theatre theory and performance practice of Shakespeare, Beckett, Richard Foreman's *Ontological-Hysteric Theatre* and Romeo Castellucci's *Socìetas Raffaello Sanzio.* I use them to highlight the problems of performing identity politics and suggest how some theatre artists continue to work toward the theatre's potential for openness to the mystery of transformative ritual or perhaps, more importantly, theatre's capacity for rigorous, singular thinking, despite its place in the simulacrum of digital culture. I will trace a historical trajectory from early modern to high modern drama to postmodern performance, so as to foreground the ongoing crisis of subjectivity and representation while critiquing the essentialism of identity politics in performance. From Shakespeare's *Coriolanus,* I borrow the notion of the inevitability of cultural fragmentation and the need to seek and sacrifice representations of unity (scapegoats) in order to establish visibility and power no matter who or what is sacrificed. From Beckett's dramatic and media works, including *Endgame* and *Film* (a work I discussed above), I use the dramatized dissolution of self through an attempted escape from the technologies of vision, perception and representation to rid ourselves of ourselves through the act of seeing ourselves. From Richard Foreman's *Ontological-Hysteric Manifesto I* (1972), I take a model for a philosophical and phenomenological theatre involved in the struggle of making things appear not as representations, but rather as they are. And finally, drawing from the work of director Romeo Castellucci and his theatre collective *Socìetas Raffaello Sanzio,* I suggest, following the theory of Giorgio Agamben, that the virtualizing of the bare life of the subjects of the biopolitics of digital and techno culture is one of the central issues confronting contemporary performance. Castellucci's work indicates the importance of not drawing solely upon past models of subjectivity, but also taking account of the new position of being in virtual, mediatized and technologized domains.

Coriolanus

Shakespeare's *Coriolanus* (1608) is considered one of the great dramatic works on the problems of representative politics, of republicanism at odds with aristocratic rule. It is also a magnificent treatise on metaphysics made material by their historical circumstances. The drama opens as the ancient city of Rome is in upheaval, and its mutinous citizens demand that their bellies be fed and their voices be heard. They resent the senators for their power. They mark Caius Marcius (later Coriolanus) as chief enemy of the people. In order to have 'corn at our own price' (I, i, 10), the First Citizen suggests they kill Caius Marcius. Menenius Agrippa, a senator trusted by the people, counsels the mob through a parable:

> Menenius
> There was a time when all the body's members
> Rebell'd against the belly, thus accused it:
> That only like a gulf it did remain
> I' the midst o' the body, idle and unactive,
> Still cupboarding the viand, never bearing
> Like labour with the rest, where the other instruments
> Did see and hear, devise, instruct, walk, feel,
> And, mutually participate, did minister
> Unto the appetite and affection common
> Of the whole body.
>
> (I, i, 94–103)

A class system, divided as always by wealth and labour, exists in this metaphor of the body. The stomach receives the resources earned by the other body parts, but does not share the work load. However, the belly sees it otherwise and responds:

> Note me this, good friend;
> Your most grave belly was deliberate,
> Not rash like his accusers, and thus answer'd:
> 'True is it, my incorporate friends,' quoth he,
> 'That I receive the general food at first,
> Which you do live upon; and fit it is,
> Because I am the store-house and the shop
> Of the whole body: but, if you do remember,
> I send it through the rivers of your blood,
> Even to the court, the heart, to the seat o' the brain;
> And, through the cranks and offices of man,
> The strongest nerves and small inferior veins
> From me receive that natural competency
> Whereby they live: and though that all at once.
>
> (I, i, 126–139)

The analogy of the body parts to the body politic suggests that the structure of any social and political organization is founded on fragmentation and injustice. The belly receives the food first, as would the ruling class and the richest of the state, but through the beneficence of the belly and the state, the supplies are distributed to the other organs and people. The system is integrated but not necessarily fair. All social systems, except theoretical utopias, are systemically unfair. Each fragment serves the other, but some fragments accrue more wealth, goods and services than others. The system is inherently and necessarily unequal and alienating.

To appease the rabble, the people are granted 'Five tribunes to defend their vulgar wisdoms' (I, i, 215). Coriolanus, a warrior of Rome and member of the ruling class, has been marked through war, and his mother Volumnia counts the wounds on her son's body to confirm his suitability, his visibility, to act as representative for the people. As Coriolanus parades back into Rome after battle, Menenius, Volumnia and his wife Virgilia watch and count.

Menenius
Is he not wounded? He was wont to come home wounded.

Virgilia
O, no, no, no.

Volumnia
O, he is wounded; I thank the gods for't.

Menenius
So do I too, if it be not too much: brings a' victory in his pocket? The wounds become him. Where is he wounded?

(II, i, 117–122)

Volumnia
I' the shoulder and i' the left arm there will be large cicatrices to show the people, when he shall stand for his place. He received in the repulse of Tarquin seven hurts i' the body.

Menenius
One i' the neck, and two i' the thigh, – there's nine that I know.

Volumnia
He had, before this last expedition, twenty-five wounds upon him.

Menenius
Now it's twenty-seven: every gash was an enemy's grave.
(*A shout and flourish.*) Hark! the trumpets.

Volumnia
These are the ushers of Marcius: before him he carries noise, and
behind him he leaves tears: Death, that dark spirit, in 's nervy arm doth
lie; Which, being advanced, declines, and then men die.

(II, i, 146–60)

The visible wounds mark Coriolanus as suitable to lead and to appear or
act as a representative and as a representation. The corporeal evidence (the
material signifier, the material substantiation) needed to perform representation is revealed in the realm of sacrifice and pain, with the trace of
violence, the trail of blood and the reality of death. These phenomena,
metaphysical markers and remembrances located within the wounds of
Coriolanus's body are the chosen supplements for the voice of the people.
The wounds are the negotiation point between the polis and their representative. *The wounds become him* and they are the identifiable signs of his
identity and by extension the identity of the people who wish his representation. And as this radically visible figure moves through the city it is the
spectre of death that is felt. The wounds are traces of those left dead or
subjugated. The wounds give presence and identity to Coriolanus because
they are the traces of the fallen, the channels of death.

The sighting of Coriolanus's identity becomes the site for a power struggle
for representation. The markers of identity are nothing without the acknowl-
edgement of the people, as the people are nothing-ed, or *monster'd*, without the leader's organizing principle in which differences are elided. The
citizens debate the ethics and politics of lending their voices to Coriolanus,
to give their identity away. Should they deny the gift, they remain unmarked
and un-represented.

Third Citizen
We have power in ourselves to do it, but it is a power that we have
no power to do; for if he show us his wounds and tell us his deeds,
we are to put our tongues into those wounds and speak for them;
so, if he tell us his noble deeds, we must also tell him our noble
acceptance of them. Ingratitude is monstrous, and for the multitude
to be ingrateful, were to make a monster of the multitude: of the
which we being members, should bring ourselves to be monstrous
members.

(II, iii, 3–13)

The speech reads like a whirligig concept of Genet in which the seduction of representation lies in its cyclical nature. If Coriolanus shows his
wounds to the people, they must lend their voices to speak for his wounds,
as Coriolanus must agree to speak for them. The power lies neither
with the citizens nor Coriolanus, but in their negotiations. If Coriolanus
exposes his wounds, they are obliged to speak for them. The people speak

through his wounds and the sound that is heard is ambiguous. Whose voice is being heard? They have no choice, as the Third Citizen warns, lest they become monstrous, remaining fragmented. In this drama neither the people nor Coriolanus are served, as the wounds of Coriolanus consume the voice of the people and Coriolanus remains mute among the babble of voices. It is a power negotiation in the form of an orgy of communication, with many tongues inserted into his multiple wounds, representing the representative politics, to put it crudely, as a cunnilingus polling process or a voting booth rimming. It is a sexual advance from the people that places Coriolanus in an exposed role that he rejects. Like a back-alley tryst, Coriolanus must be confronted by the citizens and willfully expose his wounds. But he desires to maintain his own autonomy, his own fragmentation and isolation, and loathes the idea of making something out his own nothings.

> Coriolanus
> I had rather have one scratch my head i' the sun
> When the alarum were struck than idly sit
> To hear my nothings monster'd.

(II, ii, 75–76)

Although nominated to consul, he resists making his identity visible, or *having his nothings monster'd*. He is repulsed by the required performance as an accurate representation and begins his own disappearing act aided by the machinations of his enemies and his banishment from Rome. He seeks the enemies of his homeland, the Volsces. His memory fades: 'like a dull actor now I have forgot my part' (V, iii, 40), and he seeks his erotic disappearance in the arms of the enemy, finally calling for his own slaughter: 'cut me to pieces' (V, vi, 15). The state begins fragmented: Coriolanus is scapegoated as representation to unify difference, yet he cannot bear the weight of that collective desire. He calls down his own *sparagmos* thus fulfilling the scapegoat mission of unifying (re-membering) through a dis-membering sacrifice. It is here that the thinking of the play melds the political with the metaphysical, and a decidedly new event happens to the character. The play reasons up to this point that with an assertion of identity comes a will to power at the expense of the other. However, the play performs a drama of the conflict and asks: how can one promote identity, gain power, but not lose the other in the process? Certainly, a pragmatic response to this problem is that the assertion of identity is a necessary element in a communicative exchange. Any loss of alterity is made up in the process of building social exchange, communication and consensus; that is, an acceptable loss for a sizeable gain. But the play lets go of that pragmatism in what Levinas might call the *phenomenology of eros*. It is Coriolanus's retreat from representation, his desire to vanish, to disappear in the arms of the enemy, that speaks to my thesis. Levinas models this movement as a metaphysical desire for the *invisible*:

> The metaphysical desire tends toward something else entirely, toward the absolutely other [...] The metaphysical desire does not long to return, for it is desire for a land not of our birth, for a land foreign to every nature, which has not been our fatherland and to which we shall never betake ourselves.
>
> (1969: 33–4)

The forsaken return to homeland toward the absolutely other defines Coriolanus's drive. It isn't anguish but a lustful summoning of a self-evisceration in radical alterity, the longing to be undone, unreclaimed, irredeemable. Trying not to reargue the premise of the infamously titled MLA conference presentation, 'Putting the Anus back in Coriolanus', the confrontation with the other draws Coriolanus into an erotic exchange with his enemy Aufidius, who states that:

> And I have nightly since
> Dreamt of encounters 'twixt thyself and me;
> We have been down together in my sleep,
> Unbuckling helms, fisting each other's throat,
> And waked half dead with nothing.
>
> (IV, vii, 127–31)

Love aims at the other, is how Levinas understands it. But Coriolanus's drama works toward a love that has as much in common with sado-masochistic eroticism or the practices of *cutting* that seek a border zone of the self. The liberation narrative of sadomasochistic practices is that through pain, violence and radical subjugation, one can discover the self, or the pitiful nothingness that is the ground of that self.

> We are here before a new category: before what is behind the gates of being, before the less than nothing that eros tears from its negativity and profanes. It is a question of a nothingness distinct from the nothingness of anxiety: the nothingness of the future buried in the secrecy of the less than nothing.
>
> (266)

Levinas's prose poetry, his philosophical question, is strongly suggestive of Coriolanus's drive to be cut to pieces in the camp of the enemy, to enter behind the gates of being and tear from its negativity, to profane the nothingness. In the end, as we learn from Beckett and Shakespeare, the nothing comes from nothing.

Beckett

If *Coriolanus* can be read as marking the problems of political, personal and aesthetic representation and the inevitability of fragmentation in social systems that result in a need within those structures to seek out representations of unity, Samuel Beckett's *Film*, a short film featuring Buster Keaton (which I discussed in some detail above), goes a step further, evaluating the technologies of perception and representation as a process of tragic, and thus comic, self-delusion. However, most of Beckett's prose work and much of his drama including *Not I, That Time* and the later TV plays, and even the earlier *Endgame* and *Happy Days* – for that matter, his entire oeuvre – can stand as examples of a critique of romantic and metaphysical constructions of identity, subjectivity and consciousness. Considering the problems of subjectivity in the work of Beckett is a well established path in Beckett studies and much has been written on the topic including Daniel Katz's *Saying I No More: Subjectivity and Consciousness in the Prose of Samuel Beckett* (1999) and Alain Badiou's *Dissymetries: on Beckett* (2002). Katz writes, 'But if "I" and its "voice" are both eliminated, language and speech are allowed to continue' (1999: 2). Katz suggests that in the prose work of Beckett the illusions of 'I' and 'voice' are shattered, and what remains are the ruins of their technologies, language and speech. Although Katz warns against too easy a leap from the notions of Beckett's prose to the actualities of Beckett's theatre, an accounting of subjectivity and consciousness is a clear and primary motivator in his plays. The incessant negatives of Beckett's prose and drama, pushing all toward the void, challenge all that exists. This is exemplified in the excerpt from *Texts for Nothing* quoted in both Katz and Badiou: 'Where would I go, if I could go, who would I be, if I could be, what would I say, if I had a voice, who says this, saying it's me? Answer simply, someone answer simply' (Beckett quoted in Katz 1999: 1). Beckett's simple answer is: you don't know who is saying what it is you are saying, you were never there (as Hamm realizes). Beckett presents us with a more complex question than I have been pursuing here. It is not merely a question of a kind of postmodern pop-psychology, a Zen-lite ridding the self of the self, but rather that the self was never there. Consider the anguish of Hamm in *Endgame*, who realizes toward the end of the play what is at the root of his disturbed questioning: 'What's happening? What's happening?' 'You know what it is? I was never there. Absent always. It all happened without me. I don't know what's happened. Do you know what's happened?' (1986: 128). It is a call to think historically: 'Use your head, can't you! What has happened?' (128). And when Clov does think or remembers what has happened, he recalls an injustice when Hamm refused Mother Pegg oil for her lamp, and she died 'of darkness.'

Beckett's millet grains of the old Greek (Zeno) represent the paradox that nothing exists at all, that 'time was never and time is finished' (133), that time never existed; but if you must hold on to the illusion of time, then time is finished. Beckett continually negates all that is, to the point of reaching the edge of the void, and it is at the edge, at the wall, that the void, the ominous void of the 'other hell' that Hamm desires begins. 'Closer. Closer. Up against.' (104). But Hamm's courage fails, and he must return to the centre, or rather demand that Clov roll him back to the centre. *Endgame*'s brutal logic and inexhaustible negatives stand against the celebrated loss of self I seem to have been advocating; 'Infinite emptiness will be all around you. All the resurrected dead of all the ages wouldn't fill it' (109). Of course (or is it perhaps) Beckett is here considering death, not the loss of self or identity, but is there a difference?

The quote from Chapter 1, 'How can we rid ourselves of ourselves and demolish ourselves?' (1986: 66) is the way Deleuze reads Beckett's *Film*. Like Coriolanus's longing to vanish in the face of the other, or the contemporary performer challenged by the mediated representations of the self in virtual environments, Beckett's screenplay/film implies that to see one's self is to demolish one's self in an autopsy of perception. The eye (I) is blinded. As Peggy Phelan suggests in *Unmarked*, what we see of the visible is locked to the matrix of surveillance, fetishism, appropriation and violence (1993).

Deleuze, in *Cinema I* and *II*, narrates a history of the image in film that passes from the movement-image to the time-image. The movement-image consists of descriptions which assume the independence of the object of discourse, its chronological progression and the principles, which determine the order of the real. The unreal (dreams, memory, the imaginary) exist as contrast. In the model of the movement-image, the imaginary and the real operate as oppositions, each substantiating the other's presence: 'Narration is truthful, developed organically, according to legal connections in space and chronological relations in time' (1986: 133). The time-image consists of descriptions that replace their object, substitute, actuate, eliminate and are subsumed by other descriptions, and bring about 'the coalescence of an actual image and its virtual image' (127), in which narration is falsifying, operating in 'a chronic non-chronological time which produces movements necessarily "abnormal", essentially false' (129). The actual is cut off from its 'motor linkage' and the real is cut off from its 'legal connections'. According to Deleuze, *Film* 'elaborates a system of simple cinematographic conventions' (1986: 66) to represent the process of extinguishing the three varieties of the movement-image: action, perception, affection. The subject *O*, who is object to the perceiving self, moves through a cityscape trailed by the camera (action-image). In his room he perceives subjectively while the camera does so objectively (perception-image). Finally, the affection-image occurs as the self comes face-to-face with itself. The three varieties of the movement image are passed through and closed, but to what end? Deleuze answers, it is 'Death, immobility, blackness' (68). But this is only a subjective end, Deleuze writes:

It is only a means in relation to a more profound end. It is a question of attaining once more the world before man, before our own dawn, the position where movement was, on the contrary, under the regime of universal variation, and where light, always propagating itself had no need to be revealed.

(68)

Deleuze here speaks of a pure immanence. It is, as Žižek has noted, not a question of virtual reality for Deleuze but of the reality of the virtual, of all that that has not happened or taken place, but which can or might occur. Deleuze's metaphysical claims are perhaps hard to follow or to accept, but what is important in his reading of *Film* in regards to my thesis is the quest for disappearance, which I hope to make clearer through the theory of Richard Foreman below. What drove much of Deleuze's work was as Žižek notes not the crass technology of virtual reality but the reality of the virtual, pure immanence, life as becoming, not being. *Film* points toward that Otherness. The film *Film* represents the approach of the other side of representation (Artaud's cruelty or Genet's screens) as a quest for otherness. The goal is attained not through consolidation of identity, but through a loss of subjectivity. When *E* meets *O*, the rocking stops.

The Ontological-Hysteric Theatre

Coriolanus proposes that the representational model is flawed, as it stages the sacrifice of the self in an attempted unification of the un-unifiable; as all begins and remains fragmented, unity is a cruel fiction. The hero seeks his own destruction to avoid the burden of representation, but falls toward the erotics of folding into otherness and ripping oneself to the edge of the void and through the screen that represents it. *Film* narrates the impossible escape plan from perception and representation, while suggesting the territory of the unpresentable by seeing what it is to see, and thereby positing the myths and borders of subjectivity. If, in my theoretical narrative, *Coriolanus* and *Film* stand in as cautionary metaphors for the reliance of traditional representations and the error of relying on the metaphysics of essence of identity, then Richard Foreman's thirty-year project, the *Ontological-Hysteric Theatre*, demonstrates a philosophical alternative to grounding a theatre on identity. Foreman in *Ontological-Hysteric Manifesto I* (April 1972), writes: 'Art = make there assert self, not turn into project that absorbs there' (1976: 67). To assert the *there* is to actualize a material *here and now*, a *thisness* of the theatre. Foreman's interest in the phenomenologists Husserl, Scheler and Heidegger is evident in his stagings, which involve a *mise-en-scène* wherein objects are essential components. In an interview Foreman stated, 'I'd call it a phenomenological orientation, because I was also reading Husserl, Max Scheler, Heidegger, and so on, and focusing on the essence of the objects I bracketed onstage for repetitive iteration' (1992: 80). Speaking of his early work, he said regarding the objects on his stage that 'they were simple objects in static situations, phenomenologically bracketed off from contaminating contingency, so that the lamp on the table said only, "I am a lamp. I go on. I go off. Don't try to do anything with me that you should not do with a lamp"' (81). In *Hotel China* and the later works, he stated that he became interested in the 'psychic significance of objects' (81) in 'a world ruled by objects' (82). His work travelled from the phenomena of the object to the psychic matrixes of consciousness that set the objects in play, which in turn play upon the subject's perception and emotions.

Foreman writes, 'Art: not concerned with essence but with THING used in such a way that it vanishes and what is left is suspension' (1976: 69). This idea drives to the heart of my discussion. Foreman is considering that an object when approaching itself, its *thingness*, approaches its disappearance, its suspension, its present absence. When the *this* appears as the *not-this*, which I discussed above in the *Ruins of Illusion*, it affords a unique moment in theatricality in which the negative becomes the grounds for its own disappearance. 'What interests me is my own disappearance', as Foreman says it in his play *Blvd de Paris*.

Foreman's staging and dramaturgy are structured as levels or spatial configurations of autonomous garments set into reverberating motion by theatrical hysteria, driven by the engines of an ontological drama. No one element holds dominion, and each element is set off and sets off the other, just like in real life. *Coriolanus*, *Film* and the *Ontological-Hysteric Theatre* represent three models of the aesthetics of disappearance, which seek to undo the illusions of subjectivity while giving rise to otherness.

Socìetas Raffaello Sanzio

My final piece of evidence is the performance work of Romeo Castellucci's *Socìetas Raffaello Sanzio*, which I introduced in an earlier chapter and through which I represent a second strategy (to Foreman's phenomenological stage) around the trap of staging a solipsistic turns to essentialism and identity. My thesis concerning the work of *SRS* as the staging of *bare life* will bridge the two sections of the study. *Socìetas Raffaello Sanzio* is a contemporary Italian collective formed in 1989 and their best-known works, *Giulio Cesare* (1997), *Genesi: From the Museum of Sleep* (1999) and the performance cycle, *Tragedia Endogonidia (2003–5)* have toured throughout Europe and the Americas. The work of *Socìetas Raffaello Sanzio* combines the use of complex imagery and dense audio scores, in linguistically minimal works devised from deconstructed classic texts with what the director Castellucci calls the 'dis-human': actors' bodies altered by disease and surgical interventions, animals, children and performing objects. I will discuss *Genesi* in detail in Chapter 9 and analyse *Tragedia Endogonidia* in Chapter 10. In Part II of this study I discuss *Socìetas Raffaello Sanzio* in some detail paying particular attention to the effects of the supplements of the performing machine, animal and child.

The narratives of Castellucci's *Genesi: From the Museum of Sleep* draw from the histories and mythologies of Adam and Eve's expulsion from the garden and the advent of nuclear catastrophe (First Act), the Holocaust (Second Act) and Cain's murder of Abel (Third Act). In the Second Act of *Genesi*, entitled *Auschwitz*, with secondary titles of *Genetics of the Non-Man* and *The Body without Organs*, a group of children of various ages (Castellucci's own offspring), dressed in white (gowns, rabbit suit and tuxedo) on a white stage screened by a white scrim, perform a series of simple and harrowing actions (e.g. murder) with a toy train, a mechanical milking machine and a hydraulically convulsing chair. An embryo in a large specimen jar is placed downstage, and various body organs hung from wires are lowered from the fly-space during the scene. The recorded audio track shifts from a sleepy, off-stage dance hall music to the original 1947 recording of Antonin Artaud radio play, *Pour en finir avec le Jugement de Dieu* (To Have Done with the Judgement of God). The concluding image of the section of the children drenched in an actual shower leaves no doubt as to signs of the Holocaust. The use of children with performing objects develops two interesting stage strategies. First, the children and machines work outside a traditional model of mimetic acting in what Michael Kirby identified as matrixed performance.[11] They instead perform non-matrixed tasks. The de-familiarization of non-matrixed tasks by the child performer sets off an uncanny and unsettling echo to the memory of the events. Secondly, the use of children (non-Jew? non-German?) presenting signs of the Holocaust indicates a wider association for the historical context, implicating everyone in the horror.

Giorgio Agamben, in his book *Homo Sacer*, devises a useful theoretical model for thinking through the issues of Castellucci's staging as well as my thesis regarding the problems of the subject in the bio-politics of digital culture and the admonition against essentialist models of identity. Agamben, extending Foucault's unfinished work on bio-politics, maps the history of the sacred human (*homo sacer*) in order to understand the possibility of the extermination camps of Nazism. The sacred human is one who is both un-sacrificeable and for whom there is no law against killing, who exists 'at the intersection of the capacity to be killed but not sacrificed, outside human and divine law' (1998: 73). Agamben states that the sacred human is the result of both totalitarian and advanced democracies' politicization of life, wherein the subject's *bare life* is the central, expendable commodity, and the locus of power of the state. Agamben writes, 'If today there is no longer any one clear figure of the sacred man, it is perhaps because we are all virtually *homines sacri*' (115). The west is experiencing the maturing of the 'genetics of the non-man'.

As the shower runs over the children in the closing moments of the Second Act of *Genesi*, Artaud's voice is heard in a loop ranting, 'I am not raving. I'm not mad.' Yet it is the next line of the radio play that seems to have the most resonance with Castellucci's performance: 'I'm telling you that microbes have been reinvented in order to impose a new idea of god' (1995: 305–6). Castellucci is confronting two epoch-marking events in *Genesi*. In the First Act, the performance considers the splitting of the atom as a new resource for destruction unparalleled in history. In the Second Act, the performance works from the idea that the construction and operation of the extermination camps places the human body as a resource for the production of corpses. Echoing Artaud's disturbing voice exposing the new image of God, Castellucci is choreographing the twentieth century's reordering of the life of the human toward political commodity and the restraining of nature toward destruction.

My link from Agamben to my thesis is twofold and leads to an abrupt conclusion, which opens the way to Part II of this study. Firstly, Castellucci stages the *bare life* of the sacred human through the non-matrixed performance of children whose re-enactment of the Holocaust indicates the current un-sacrificeable and expendable status of the subjects of late-capitalist and bio-political systems. Secondly, digital culture sees the deployment of advanced technologies to manipulate further the subject's *bare life* toward a virtual position. The operation of subjectivity constructed through immersion in the domain of the virtual is not yet understood, but it offers unique problems and opportunities for oppressive control and philosophies of discontinuity. If the theatre hopes to resist or to support these projects, it will have to be able to confront the field of the virtual, not through essentialized constructions of failed subjectivities and antiquated technologies, but rather through a strategic manipulation of the virtual, turning the system against itself.

The last segment of the Second Act (Auschwitz) of *Genesi* is named 'Milk from Nadir'. Nadir is the lowest point, the time of greatest depression or adversity. Perhaps, in this time when the West is confronted with the long-repressed demands of the other, there will be an opportunity to draw milk from nadir.

Part II

Embeddedness (after)

The performance of 'bare life' and the bio-politics of digital culture

7 Stealing from God

The crisis of creation in Socìetas Raffaello Sanzio's *Genesi* and Eduardo Kac's *Genesis*

I'm telling you that microbes have been reinvented in order to impose a new idea of god.

(Artaud 1995: 305–6)

The only *Genesi* I can conceive is starting from an idea of crisis of creation: I can only preserve and capture those images that I have always thought could be of interest to someone like God.

(Castellucci 1999)

Transgenic art, I propose, is a new art form based on the use of genetic engineering techniques to transfer synthetic genes to an organism or to transfer natural genetic material from one species into another, to create unique living beings.

(Kac 2002)

The dis-human, the dis-real and the posthuman

The scope of the sheer possibilities of contemporary science and technology is staggering, even sublime. The performance work *Genesi: From the Museum of Sleep* (1999), discussed in the previous chapter, directed by Romeo Castellucci for his company, *Socìetas Raffaello Sanzio*, explores a perceived crisis of creation, brought on by the scientific revolutions of genetics and nuclear physics and by the singular event of the Holocaust. In this chapter, *Genesi* is analysed against Eduardo Kac's theory and practice of transgenic art in general and against his art installation *Genesis* in particular. Kac's art controversially combines genetic engineering of animal and plant life, new media for telepresent interactivity and robotics in both virtual and actual installations. Castellucci and Kac relate not only in their concerns regarding science and technology, but also in their interdisciplinary strategies, which include combining aspects of theatre, visual art, sculpture and technology. Castellucci and Kac engage the risks inherent in the destruction possible through creation (both aesthetic and scientific) and isolate manners in which contemporary constructions of the human are challenged. The works signal an awareness of the constantly shifting boundaries and borders of aesthetic genres and the developing convergence of the disciplines of science and art.

Discussed in Part I of this study, Italy's *Societas Raffaello Sanzio* theatre company, under the direction of Romeo Castellucci, has in recent years staged a number of challenging performance works. Their 1997 *Giulio Cesare*, based in part on William Shakespeare's *Julius Caesar*, was remarkable not only for its brilliant deconstruction of rhetoric and its dynamic use of stage imagery, but also for the company's special performers with various conditions of anorexia, obesity and post-operative tracheotomy. *Societas Raffaello Sanzio*'s more recent performance cycle *Tragedia Endogonidia* will be discussed in a later chapter. Here I will focus on *Genesi: From the Museum of Sleep*, first presented in 1999. The work is a dense, highly visual, sonically fierce and linguistically minimal staging that explores the phenomenon of creation in myth and science. The work abstractly represents Madame Curie's discovery of radium against Eve's expulsion from the Garden of Eden, the Holocaust against children at play, and Cain and Abel against each other. *Genesi*, like Hegel's model of thought as a series of violent acts, each thesis attacking the preceding and giving rise to a third, enacts a world where within each creative action lies a potential or virtual ruinous possibility or inevitability. Castellucci writes in the programme notes to *Genesi* 'Genesis scares me more than the Apocalypse. Here it's the terror of sheer possibility' (1999). Castellucci's *Genesi* carries a warning, as the possibilities performed arrive through the discovery of radium, which leads to the birth of modern physics and contributes to the development of nuclear technologies. More disturbing is the suggestion that humankind's own genesis, at its most 'extreme and inconceivable consequence', reaches its logical and tragic culmination in the Nazi 'evisceration chamber' of Auschwitz. Creation, in Castellucci's *Genesi*, carries with it the deadly force of annihilation.

Eduardo Kac, an installation artist and Associate Professor of Art and Technology at the School of the Art Institute of Chicago, has developed a form of art he calls *transgenic*, which involves the use of genetic engineering on animal and plant life. A recent work of Kac's, *Genesis* (Figure 7.1) illustrates the challenges and opportunities that exist in the development of new life forms through genetic engineering.

The key element of Kac's *Genesis* is an 'artist's gene'. The synthetic gene was created by:

> [...] translating a sentence from the biblical book of *Genesis* into Morse Code, and converting the Morse Code into DNA base pairs according to a conversion principle specially developed by the artist for this work.
>
> (Kac 2006)

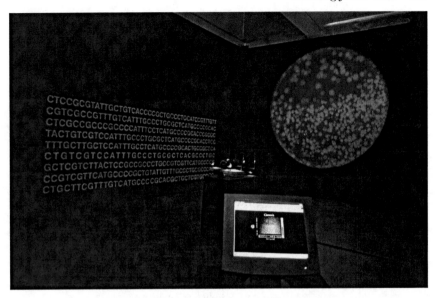

Figure 7.1 Genesis (1999), Eduardo Kac. An interactive installation using video
projection, telepresent computer connection for web interaction,
synthetic gene in *E. coli* bacteria and ultraviolet light.
Photo: Otto Saxinger. Courtesy Eduardo Kac.

The text from *Genesis* that Kac transposed reads: 'Let man have dominion over the fish of the sea, and over the fowl of the air, and over every
living thing that moves upon the earth'. The Genesis gene was introduced
into *E. coli* bacteria, placed in a Petri dish under a UV light and video-
projected on a gallery wall. Web-users were able to switch on an ultraviolet light in the gallery, stimulating real, biological mutations in the bacteria.
In turn, the biological mutations *rewrote* the Biblical sentence by altering
the Morse Code sequence. Spectatorship becomes active participation as
the web-user, with a click of the mouse, activates the installation's ultraviolet light and creates real change in the bacteria, which in turn creates
biological mutations in the DNA structure, thereby rewriting the sentence
of *Genesis*.

Kac's *Genesis*, in a troublingly specific and material manner, demonstrates the capabilities of human creation through genetic engineering. The
'terror of sheer possibility' that Castellucci stages is brought to a material
reality in Kac's interactive installation. Kac has taken his *transgenic art* a
step further by *creating* a rabbit that glows green when placed under
florescent lighting. Kac created, or designed the *GPF Bunny*, or Alba, as the
work is called, through similar genetic engineering as that of *Genesis*
(Figure 7.2).

Figure 7.2 GFP Bunny (2000), Eduardo Kac. Genetically altered rabbit which, when exposed to ultraviolet light, glows green.
Photo: Chrystelle Fontaine. Courtesy Eduardo Kac.

Kac's use of advanced media, telepresent interactivity and experimental bio-science to create new organisms vividly repositions performance spectatorship within a virtual environment, while challenging the ethical borders of bio-science and medicine. What are the possible results of such action? Who can take responsibility for the results? Is this not the introduction of the terror of unlimited possibilities in a crisis of creation? These problems are not confined to the science or theatre lab. The challenges of increased creative possibilities multiply in technologized cultures where the combination of information technologies, virtual environments, genetic engineering and medical advances offer new constructions of identity and space. Life and art become one in genetic engineering.

Two theoretical concepts can help sort out the problems arising from these works. *Posthuman subjectivity*, which I discussed in Chapter 3, is a notion developed in the advent of information technologies, virtual cultures of cyberspace, surgical alterations of the body (sex change, artificial limbs and organs, computer implants) and new scientific visualizations. Theorists such as N. Katherine Hayles (1999) argue that the posthuman is a new phase of humanity wherein no essential differences between bodily existence and computer simulation, cybernetic mechanism and biological organism, robot teleology and human goals, exist. Kac's *transgenic art* is symptomatic of the posthuman. *Transgenic art* exercises the artist's ability not simply to create the object of art, but actually to create the subject within art. The boundaries of art and science are traversed with unsettling ethical dilemmas. Who has the right to create new life? Who takes responsibility for the results? What are the final results?

The second concept that can help unpack these works is that of the *dis-human* and the *dis-real*, a theoretical and performative strategy employed by Castellucci. The aesthetic of the dis-human and dis-real acts as an erasure of traditional constructions of human-ness and identification on stage. The stage of the dis-human incorporates non-human performers such as machines and animals, as well as non-traditional performers such as children and disabled adults. The supplements of the performing machine, animal, child and the 'disabled/perfect' actor establish an aesthetic that resists acting, metaphor and narrative in favour of performance/enactment, metonymy and image. Each of the elements of machine, animal, child and disabled adult supplies a unique presence which circumvents an imitative illusion. A strangeness pervades the performance of authenticity in Castellucci's *mise-en-scène*. Both theories, the posthuman of Eduardo Kac's *transgenic art* and the *dis-human/dis-real* of Castellucci's theatre, suggest new ways of perceiving contemporary subjectivity within the space of advanced scientific and visualization technologies.

The concepts of the posthuman and the dis-human are not entirely dissimilar models. The posthuman constructs a subjectivity that does not differentiate between machine and human, which, in turn, creates a new type of human subjectivity. In posthuman thought, human consciousness is extended, altered and transfigured by technology. Kac's installation places the spectator within an ethical problem, gives her power to take an action, and presents the choice as to whether or not to continue. The sentence that Kac appropriates from *Genesis*, 'Let man have dominion...', remains now ironic, its ideology of human-centrism apparent. The human, armed with the power to rewrite nature from the inside out, finds itself rewritten and, in a very real sense, posthuman. Since the human is intimately immersed within nature, since the human essentially is nature, and since there is no separation between human and nature, when nature is rewritten so is the human reconfigured.

Castellucci's use of the performative strategy of the dis-human and dis-real suggests a no less disturbing place for the human. The dis-human returns to a corporeal presence via new constructions of staged subjectivity. Both the dis-human and the posthuman view contemporary models of subjectivity within technologized cultures as a significant historical shift. In the aftermath of the creation of nuclear warfare, genetic engineering and final solutions, we arrive at what Castellucci calls the 'genetics of the non-man', as mentioned in the previous chapter. He argues this 'new man' is a horrible inversion of Artaud's dreamt-of *body without organs*. Artaud's *body without organs* is a transgressive and liberative action that rejects subjectivism and limitation within a socio-political structure. The genetics of the non-man is a concept similar to Agamben's *homo sacer*, a bare life that is unsacrificeable but is expendable or killable. The body in *Genesi* is often displayed as a dismembered object, with body parts displayed in the museum boxes and internal organs flown in from the fly space to hover over the stage. The body without organs (or the body with externalized organs in *Genesi*) is an object subjected to the controlling function of science, art and religion.

I am suggesting that the anxiety and crisis of creation, brought on by the cultural effects of the scientific revolutions of biology and physics, has led both Castellucci and Kac to engage in a performance of the posthuman. Kac's *Genesis* and Castellucci's *Genesi* engage the risks inherent in the devastation possible through creation (both aesthetic and scientific) and isolate manners in which contemporary constructions of the human are challenged.

The not-being of the dis-human

Genesi is structured in three acts: *At The Beginning, Auschwitz* and *Cain and Abel. Act I: At The Beginning*, begins in the laboratory of Madame Curie where Lucifer 'in layman clothes' speaks 'Torah's Hebrew and repeats the same words of God' (Castellucci 1999). Curie's discovery of radium, according to Castellucci:

> [...] is the only substance in the world that emits light. A light that gets into the bones. It's from radium (the discovery of which marks the beginning of modern physics) that you increasingly sink into the core of things until you break it.
>
> (1999)

'Sinking in the core of things' seems to be a recurring strategy in Castellucci's *mise-en-scène* as the works aim for the essence of a narrative (e.g. the notion of rhetorical strategies in *Julio Cesare*, creation in *Gensei*, tragedy in *Tragedia Endogonidia*).

The image of the power of radium to see through things extends throughout the stage, which in *Act I: At the Beginning* takes on the iconography of the x-ray. The stage is shrouded in a downstage black scrim and darkness covers the space. At times in *Genesi*, like a *museum of sleep*, museum display boxes and tables containing stuffed animals and body parts are suspended from the fly space or rolled across the floor. At various moments in the performance, a glass box or aquarium descends from the fly space. It contains six rods immersed in water. Slowly, the water begins to bubble or boil as the sound score by the remarkable Scott Gibbons roars and shakes the foundation of the theatre. The danger is apparent. Later, Adam, wearing only dark trunks, his head in a black leather S&M mask, is revealed within one of the display boxes. The performer, Moukhtar Goussengadjiev, is a contortionist who twists his body into severe and unsettling positions. In a smaller box next to Adam's is the skinned head of a dead animal that I presumed to be a cow. A large vice slowly crushes down on the skull of the cow, causing the bones to crack and the eyes to distend. The grotesque stage-poetry of this moment brings a visceral corporeality to the stage. The body of the animal mutilated in the vice, as the limbs of Adam are bent and distorted, brings a cruel theatricality and presence that spirals the Biblical notion of creation (Adam's rib) toward a violence that bleeds and exists within pain.

Eve appears through the actions of a naked older woman who, in *real life* has undergone the removal of her left breast. Her body and muscle tone have slackened and reveal her age. Representing Eve through an older body which carries the marking of disease brings a sense of a recurring history, even a ruinous element, to the scene. Eve is naked save a white skullcap, and she stands next to a small wooden spinning wheel. As the wheel spins, Eve pulls at the strings that run across the stage to a large cylindrical frame of perhaps 100 spools of string that Castellucci names *Macchina Tessile*. The cylinder spins back and forth, and the individual spools turn as well. The machine remains in a shaky motion like some type of life force whose threads issue from a single source but move out in multiple patterns. The threads run from Eve to the world as the result of the expulsion from paradise. She is projecting herself through a *thrownness* into the field of possibilities, echoing with anxiety in a historicity of being in time. Eve, pulling at the strings, jerks into a posture of astonishment or horror with her hands thrown back. She walks upstage in movements choreographed to resemble Masaccio's fifteenth-century frescoes in the Cappella Brancacci, of the expulsion of Adam and Eve from the Garden of Eden. Eve lies on the stage and body organs with hanging arteries fly in and hover over her body and finally rest upon her. An alligator in a museum display case hung at the top of the proscenium is illuminated, and the stage below Eve begins to swell upwards. The effect is captivating and disturbing as stage-poetry, theatre as theatre, no more or less. Meanings elide, evade, appear and merge in a labyrinth of images that are evocative and draw the spectator in.

Eve's actions are performed rather than acted, eternalized rather than psychologized. As I mentioned earlier Michael Kirby's distinction between *matrixed* acting and *non-matrixed* acting is a useful model for considering the performance strategies of *Genesi*. The technique plays counter to the *actual* of her aging and post-operative body. The collision of *actual* and *assumed* gestures creates a gap that forces the mythological (Eve's expulsion) and the lived, diseased body in one gesture. The effect is a stage presence of profound duality. Castellucci's stage is a space of *not-being* (seeming) that regurgitates spasmatically the presence of being (not seeming), foregrounding the lived body in mythological space. Castellucci writes:

> Lucifer is the angel of art, because he wishes to go back to the father but cannot do it. He is the remotest and most confined in the possibility of not-being. Only in not-being can he think of re-creation in the art.
> (1999)

The presence of the not-being of the dis-human becomes the essence of Castellucci's art. Paraphrasing Heidegger's thesis on Nietzschean aesthetics, the *not-being* of the *dis-human* is worth more than the truth of the being of the human. In this model, each leads to the other. Either/or art begins with the not-being of the dis-human, which leads to a revealing of the beingness of the human or visa versa. Therefore, in an argument taking its cue from Pirandello, traditional stage mimesis of psychological realism, and the imitation of the real lead to more illusion; illusion in the guise of the not-being of the dis-human leads to a glimpse of the truth, which steps aside, evades and evaporates upon arrival.

The complexity of signs in many of the scenes of *Genesi* works against interpretation and rational analysis, relying on a performative effect to drive the narrative. In Act I, between Lucifer's chants in the lab of Madame Curie and the entrance of Adam and expulsion of Eve, a reel-to-reel tape-recorder descends from the fly space. The machine is pictured in *Epitaph*, a book of photos of many of the SRS productions. The caption under the picture is '*la voce di Dio*' (voice of God). The tape is stretched across the stage to a naked black man wearing a gold skullcap. He is captioned in *Epitaph* as *Dio Nero* (Black God). He is lying down with his head toward the audience. Sitting up after blowing a cloud of white dust into the air, he pulls the tape, causing the recorded sounds (distorted popping) of the magnetic tape to play. Next to him is a pile of dirt in which three carrots are placed and whose tops protrude. Dio Nero rises and on his right foot is a white sock. He covers himself in white dust as upstage a robed man, an Archangel, spins rapidly on a wheeled platform. Behind him a video projection of an animated, black-and-white torso spins in the opposite direction. A large metal hoop flies in between the figures. A museum display box of golden lungs appears to be breathing. A suspended sword (Damocles?) bursts into flames. A third man with long hair and beard, wearing a white robe, slowly presents a white mask under the foot of the black man. The robed man removes the sock from the black man's foot and retrieves the claw of a large bird. The scene is a matrix of mythological powers that set into action the events that will give rise to a troubled history, to the multitudinous happenings of the world from the beginning (as the title goes). Make sense who may, as these mysteries inspire an interpretive contemplation of evasive meanings.

Many of the props in *Genesi* reappear. The sock and claw are handled by Lucifer and hidden in his jacket as he stands beneath the small nuclear reactor in Act I, played with by the children in Act II, and passed between Cain and Abel. Castellucci refers to the object as the *uterus-sock*, which can obviously be read as a localized and transitory site of creation. Yet it is the men who manipulate the emblem as it is transferred from the sock of Dio Nero to the Archangel to Lucifer to the child in the scene of the Holocaust to Cain. The sock is controlled not by Madame Curie, but by Lucifer, not by Eve, but by Adam. The sock is taken from the black man, an Orpheus who controls the mechanized music, and circulated amongst the white men. I think it would be a mistake to read this series of images in too specific a set of identity politics or in terms of race and gender. Although the action can be interpreted in such a manner, the signs are clearly over-determined, registering on multiple levels.

The act of constructing and deconstructing the world on the stage is enacted with a ferocity and deliberate passion. Castellucci writes:

> This Genesis is not only the biblical one, but it is also the one which gives birth (on stage) to my rhetoric pretension to remake the world. It puts the most vulgar part of myself on stage: the artist, the one who wants to steal the last Sephiroth from God: the most important one. The open secret is this: stealing from God.
>
> (1999)

Lucifer, the angel of art, isolated in not-being, can only recreate through stolen images of a distorted creation. The artist only knows the not-being which gives rise to art. The appropriated uterus-sock gives only the remains of a lost being to serve as a symbol for an unattainable otherness.

Act II: Auschwitz uses the signs of the Holocaust, such as a train, yellow star and showers, performed by children whose actions belie the horror of the reality they represent. It is through the stage use of the dis-human and the dis-real that the *real* itself can be fully brought to presence. The stage for this section of the performance is covered in white canvas, and a white scrim runs across the downstage proscenium. Across the back of the stage is another white scrim upon which is the phrase 'I SLEEP' in red paint, hand-written and backwards. A very large chandelier hangs low near centre-stage. Various objects are placed on stage that resemble or suggest medical apparatus: a specimen jar in which is placed a human embryo, a large clear cross that fills with red liquid, and IV bags hung from hospital rolling frames. At one point a young boy, wrapped in a white sheet from the waist down and whose face is covered with white cloth, kicks at the downstage scrim and beats at it with the aforementioned dismembered talons of a large bird of prey. As mentioned in Chapter 6, the 1947 recording of Antonin Artaud's radio play *To Have Done with the Judgment of God* plays. Another child sits downstage right with the same white attire, while beating a white metal drum or canister in rhythm to the recording of Artaud's screaming and primitive drumming. Suddenly the music shifts to a distant ballroom band echoing as the chandelier illuminates and begins to swing across the stage. Four more children, all dressed in white, that have been standing at the back of the stage near the lettering of *I SLEEP*, walk forward. One is dressed in a suit with a top hat, the other as a rabbit and two others in robes with white head wraps. The boy downstage places the talons in a white sock. The child in the rabbit suit stands on a white desk table, holding the ends of a milking machine to his chest as the machine slowly cycles and pumps. Life here is a resource to be harvested as standing reserve for the machine. The chandelier is now a shower spraying water down upon the stage. The children shower in the flow, and calmly embrace each other for short moments.

Castellucci writes about the troubling use of the Holocaust in a performance work:

> I wonder whether it is immoral. I wonder which degree of purity I might reach to get close to this horror, so difficult to be included among events, which are thoroughly human. I think the challenge lies in being able to say it. Actually, being willing to say it, going beyond that limit of un-utterance, which tragically confuses the respect for the impossibility of saying it fully, with a silence that only the dead may keep without ambiguity.
>
> (1999)

Castellucci does speak the un-utterance, while acknowledging the impossibility of saying or presenting Auschwitz fully. Adorno, in a lecture on metaphysics in July of 1965, commented that 'It is therefore impossible, I would say, to insist after Auschwitz on the presence of a positive meaning or purpose in being' (2000: 101). It is the negation of purposefulness of being that might take us to a meaning within *Genesi*. Additionally, the inclusion of the original radio broadcast of Artaud's *To Have Done with the Judgment of God* tells us a lot about what Castellucci is doing in this scene. If only the title of Artaud's work is confronted one gets the message. But *having done with the judgment of God* carries mixed messages. It may seem like liberation and a release from the taxations of an onto-theological stage for a historical avant-garde, but for those implicated, stained, destroyed within the events of the Holocaust, from which no one escapes, to have done with the judgement of God holds a terror of being beyond good and evil.

The beyond, or the before or after, of good and evil is where Castellucci positions his performance, and where Artaud developed his radiophonic 'research on fecality'. The third section of Artaud's radio play is subtitled *Research on Fecality*, and it considers the phenomena of human waste, excess and shit, as a defining marker in the construction of subjectivity. 'There where it smells of shit/it smells of being' (291). It is the remains of the excess and waste that tempt the subject toward being and are constitutive of their presence. Artaud ends his work with a vision of his own *sparagmos* and a new body formed, creating him as 'unforgettable':

Who am I?
Where do I come from?
I am Antonin Artaud
and if I say it
as I know how to say it

immediately
you will see my present body
fly into pieces
and under ten thousand
notorious aspects
a new body
will be assembled
in which you will never again
be able
to forget me.

(323)

He names himself, Antonin Artaud, saying it in only the way he knows how to say it. Artaud is trying to say that to see onself is to 'fly to pieces', to have done with the judgement of God, the barriers, the limitations and to play God. He wants to embrace the full power and the horror of creation and its foundational destruction. Nothing is created without something being destroyed. Artaud rehearses his dismemberment and reconfiguration and draws attention to the manners in which the body as organ like Coriolanus's fragments, is challenged forth as representation and limitation. Castellucci's stage plays through this idea.

As noted throughout this study to the point of becoming something of a *slogan* or mantra of the argument, Heidegger, in explaining Nietzsche's views on art, wrote that 'Art is worth more than "the truth"' (1977: 75), which is to argue that truth is always veiled and concealed. Art, through a strategy of the dis-real, comes upon truth. Castellucci's use of children in simple and calm play within a *mise-en-scène* of white is that dis-human representation of the horror. He writes, 'I must disguise the horror with a lamb's skin. Only in this way it can penetrate into your house. It's the title of this act [Auschwitz] which imposes it to me. Sorry' (1999). *Genesei*, in attempting to come to terms with both the reality of the Holocaust and the critical problems of representing the Holocaust, creates a stage that evokes the horror through dis-real performing supplements. The negative formulations of the *dis-real* and the *dis-human* are similar to Hegel's critique of sense-certainty and the notion of *not-this*, which I discussed above. It is through the creation of a negative on the stage that Castellucci reaches a visceral moment of the *here and now*.

The last components of Castellucci's stage that I want to bring to attention are the performing objects that appear through the performance. The objects in *Genesei* include: a small glass reactor, perhaps constructed from an aquarium, its radioactive rods distended into water as it hovers above the stage in Act I; a hydraulic hand with ink pen that jerks and shutters on the side of the stage; the skull crusher vice; the string tree; a bouncing chair; a milking machine; the tape-recorder; and a small robot audience member who stands and applauds like a wind-up toy monkey with cymbals.

The machines' dynamic presence tends to provoke a tension between and suggests an intimate link among the objects and the humans with which they perform. Adam appears in the same display box as the stuffed animals, Eve holds onto the strings as if for emotional support, and the director/ writer himself seems supplemented by the hydraulic writing hand that writes its illegible messages on the floor of the stage. Even the audience is implicated in the convergence of human and machine with the presentation of the small spectator robot that is placed on a pedestal, outside the stage, looking toward the performance. The transference of attributes between machine and human performers insinuates that the dis-human is very close, in theory, to the posthuman that models subjectivity in an intimate relation between machine and human.

The presence of the machines brings an uncanny charge to the stage, as they are always-already *in performance*. The human performer walks on and off the stage, begins and ends a performance, but the performing machine or object is always *on*. The timelessness of the machine, the inexhaustible performativity of the object, summons forth a revealing of the timed nature and fatigued performance of the human. Mortality is brought back to the stage through the immortal nature of the machine.

The stage of Romeo Castellucci and *Societas Raffaello Sanzio* evokes a materiality through the misdirection of the dis-human supplementary performance of machines, animals, children and disabled/actors in mytho- logical space. The installation work and *transgenic art* of Eduardo Kac explores the borders of biological science and new manners of spectatorship in virtual environments, which both reflect on the contemporary construction of the posthuman. Together, the artworks present visions of failed models of human subjectivity that threaten to continually return if different systems of subjectivity are not engaged.

The ethics and anxiety of being (with) monsters and machines

Eduardo Kac defines *transgenic art*:

> Transgenic art, I propose, is a new art form based on the use of genetic engineering techniques to transfer synthetic genes to an organism or to transfer natural genetic material from one species into another, to create unique living beings. Molecular genetics allows the artist to engineer the plant and animal genome and create new life forms. The nature of this new art is defined not only by the birth and growth of a new plant or animal but above all by the nature of the relationship between artist, public, and transgenic organism. Organisms created in the context of transgenic art can be taken home by the public to be

grown in the backyard or raised as human companions. With at least one endangered species becoming extinct every day, I suggest that artists can contribute to increase global biodiversity by inventing new life forms.

(Kac 1998)

Can you break all Ten Commandments in one sentence? Can you break them all in one act? The work of Eduardo Kac seems intent on trying. 'I will covet God's capacity to create life and doubt his existence, but lie about it, and will therefore steal his glory, placing science, technology and art before *him*, killing life to create more; and here is where it gets difficult: 'I will do all this on Sunday after sleeping with my neighbour's spouse, leaving the windows open so as to mock my parents mercilessly'. Obviously, I am being facetious, but Kac's comments contained above seem designed and determined to create a certain amount of anxiety in the reader. 'Inventing new life forms' or genetically modifying life as it exists has led to much debate and concern. Genetically modified plants and animals are now commonplace and part of the world's food chain; however, the consequences of this are far from certain. Therefore, the public debate regarding the ethics and environmental safety of genetic modification is ongoing. Thus, the importance of Kac's work is that he brings these advanced technologies to the active participation of a general public. Otherwise, these processes may have remained hidden in research and industrial laboratories. As mentioned above, Kac has genetically altered rabbits, fish, mice, bacteria and plant-life so that they generate green fluorescent protein, which causes the entities to glow green when placed under UV light. These animals, bacteria and plants are placed in installations where they sometimes interact with machines known as *bio-bots*, and where local and telepresent spectators can interact with or alter them in some manner.

I will pursue four components of Kac's transgenic art: aestheticizing the life of plants and animals, the ethics of genetic engineering, the ethics of robotics and the construction of virtual spectatorship. In order to consider the first issue regarding the aesthecizing life forms, I look at Kac's work within the context of twentieth-century art practices of conceptualism and installation. It is with these two modes of art production that Kac's work shares many similarities. I will pose some very basic questions about how Kac's transgenic and interactive work operates in the tradition of modern art. Additionally, I will begin an inquiry into the philosophical and ethical issues that Eduardo Kac's art raises; namely, the elimination of the borders between art and life, virtual and embodied spectatorship, aesthetic genetic-engineering, the ethics of robotics and the responsibilities of the artist to the art of monsters and machines.

The re-materialisation of the art object: from conceptualism to installation to biologically based work

Although Eduardo Kac's transgenic art is establishing new frontiers of art practice that challenge the boundaries of biology, robotics and aesthetics, the manner in which the artworks generate meaning and construct specta-torship are similar to the practices of much conceptual and installation art of the twentieth century. In conceptual art, idea and process are promoted over representation and object through a dematerialization of the art object. Kac's work may only be partially satisfying as art object, but it certainly is over-burdened by interest as concept, driving as it does to the crises of modern science and individual sovereignty. Installation art follows a simi-lar concern but emphasizes a contextualized space for the performance of the dematerialization. Much of Kac's work appears as installations, but, again, as art they are merely utilitarian, functioning as support to the conceptual premises. To paraphrase Duchamp, the art of the future is that at which the artist points, and Kac is a very good pointer. While the goals of transgenic art, conceptualism and installations share certain concerns, the biological and mechanical certainty of objecthood in Kac's work represents a radical re-materialization of the art object: a re-materialization with certain problems.

Art critic Lucy Lippard modelled the trajectory of modernist art as a process of the dematerialization of the art object (1973). From abstraction to action painting; from Happenings to conceptualism, installations, video and performance; the effect has been to challenge the representational element and objecthood in art in favour of its conceptualization and process. The deconstruction of the object and its location in space and time in the paintings of the Futurists and Cubists in the early twentieth century was an important development in confronting the problem of representa-tion within the discourse of art. Multiple planes of space and accelerated depictions of time reordered the ways in which both the object and the subject were constructed as coherent and chronological phenomena. Of course, the techniques of abstraction were being introduced even earlier with Impressionism, Fauvism and Expressionism. During the post-World War II era, the process of challenging art's reliance on representation and objecthood was pursued in the action paintings of Jackson Pollock, where the trace of the artist's gesture was as critical as its painterly accident on the canvas. Further, the incorporation of performance in art practice by artists working in Happenings presented the penultimate attack on the object. At the point that performance superceded objecthood in the production of art, conceptualism and installation were established as central modalities of art production. Nonetheless, as an anonymous editor for *Crossings: Electronic Journal of Art and Technology* reminded me, it is important to remember that, like all historical outlines, Lippard's model is necessarily reductive and fails to address the multiple critiques (language, technology, politics, etc.) inherent in conceptualism in favour of a privileging of the crisis of representation.

The rise of performance as a critical shift from modernism to post-modernism is another way of understanding Kac's work. Nick Kaye in *Postmodernism and Performance* (1994), constructs his main thesis and defines modernism by glossing the modernist art theory of Clement Greenberg and Michael Fried. Greenberg's 'After Abstract Expressionism' (1962) and Fried's 'Art and Objecthood' (1967) are, according to Kaye, the signal texts of the period and helped to form the theoretical basis for American modernism. Greenberg argues, in a para-Hegelian manner, that the history and progress of modern art is a march toward a purifying and divesting of all extraneous material, culminating in art being realized as a wholly manifest, self-sufficient object. Kaye quotes Greenberg's theory that the modernist project in art is to demonstrate that many of the 'conventions of the art of painting' are 'dispensable, unessential' (25). Greenberg's model of art historicity champions the works of Noland, Morris, and Olitksi, as they represent the modernist ideal of a totally autonomous art with colour fields seeped into the fabric of a dematerialized canvas, the coalescing of literalism and illusionism. Greenberg, in 'Modernist Painting', writes:

> The essence of Modernism lies, as I see it, in the use of the characteristic methods of a discipline to criticize the discipline itself – not in order to subvert it, but to entrench it more firmly in its are of competence.
> (Greenberg quoted in Kaye 1994: 101)

The transitional stage between Greenberg's defense of Field Painting and Fried's attack on Minimalism is only briefly mentioned by Kaye, but constitutes a critical moment in the history he narrates. In answer to the call for an autonomous art, and maintaining that the canvas was inherently representational, artists such as Donald Judd and Robert Morris furthered the quest for an essential art form through minimalist sculpture. The artists created, through the absence of connecting parts, artificial colour or representation, Minimalist sculptures that were realized as pure objects of indivisible wholeness. The 'literalness' of Minimalist sculpture was to supplant the illusionism of the canvas. The objecthood of the object (the thingness of the thing in Heideggerian terms) became the object of art. However, Michael Fried spotted a problem in the work of the Minimalist. He argued that the Minimalist objects supplanted their objecthood by foregrounding the space that they occupied and the duration of the experience of observation, requiring (calling upon) and amplifying the spectator's perspective of that object. In short, the Minimalist object was theatrical and, therefore, not art.

Fried writes in 'Art and Objecthood', 'Art degenerates as it approaches the condition of theatre' (1968: 141). According to Fried, the theatrical is incapable of generating the modernist ideal of the wholly manifest thing-in-itself due to its movement in time, its audience, its maintenance of the subjective/objective paradigm of performance. The synthesis of the literal and the illusionistic – demonstrated in the work of Noland, Olitski and Stella – is the height of Modernist art. According to Fried, the experience of witnessing the paintings of Olitski or Noland or the sculpture of Anthony Caro has NO duration 'because at every moment the work itself is wholly manifest' (145). The proper Modernist goal is an instantaneousness and presentness (as opposed to a theatrical presence) leading to the breakdown of the subjectivity of the spectator and the objectivity of the object of art. Fried's theory attempts to challenge the theatre and performance as non-art. Greenberg and Fried's argument hinges on the contradiction that the destiny of Modern art is to arrive at its objecthood, unencumbered or sullied with a multi-disciplinarian or theatrical approach. However, the Minimalist art objects are counter-revolutionary to this goal because their physicality shifts focus to their situation, their duration of experience, their presence as opposed to their *presentness.*

If one accepts Greenberg and Fried's model of modernism, then performance's innate disruption of the autonomous art work (performance is by necessity multi-disciplinary), its spatial and temporal specificity, its very 'messiness', or as Kaye more eloquently puts it, performance's 'evasion of stable parameters, meanings and identities' (35), makes performance the postmodern gesture of resistance.

Certainly, Kaye is not the first to make this claim for performance's stature in postmodernity. Henry M. Sayre in *The Object of Performance* (a book to which Kaye is seemingly indebted) quotes from a catalogue for an exhibition of contemporary sculpture at the Hirshhorn Museum (1982) written by Howard Fox, which states:

> Theatricality may be considered that propensity in the visual arts for a work to reveal itself within the mind of the beholder as something other than what it is known empirically to be. This is precisely antithetical to the Modern ideal of the wholly manifest, self-sufficient object; and theatricality may be the single most pervasive property of post-Modernism.
>
> (Fox quoted in Sayre 1989: 9)

Quite apart from the modernist desire to create the thing-in-itself, the desire for the de-materialization of the art object has run concurrently and in some cases, prefigured the modernist attempts reflecting Lyotard's suggestion that the postmodern is, in fact, pre-modern. It is more than mere anomaly that the history of Euro-American avant-garde carries with it a series of performative experiments: Symbolist and Expressionists theatre, the Futurist *serate* and Dadaist *soiree*, Surrealist drama, Happenings and performance art. My point is that performance's qualifications as postmodern or anti-modern have been well established. Greenberg and Fried's problematic notions of authenticity, purity, essence, all reside in a historical, foundationalist and essentialist discourse that has been thoroughly discounted from a postmodern position and critiqued as irrelevant in a contemporary model of art. Succinctly and reductively defined, conceptual art, through its insistence on idea and process over object, offers a critique of art production and institutions of the culture industry that evaluate and market the art product. The spectator's commodity fetishism is likewise challenged in the conceptual art that forgoes artifact. Simultaneously, conceptual works pose philosophical questions regarding the nature of art. When John Baldassari, in *I Am Making Art* (1971), stands before a video camera making simple gestures while repeating the phrase 'I am making art' for twenty minutes, the viewer is invited to dialogue with the work about the veracity of his statement. The statement raises the question as to whether or not he is creating art, which requires a definition of art, which requires some philosophical reflection. The loss of the object opens a space for thought.

Installations found favour with those artists during the 1950s and 1960s who wished to structure a context in which their concepts could be played out. Distinct from sculpture or theatre, installation art offers a presentation of conceptual matter that remains outside simple objecthood. The work of installation represents the staging of an art concept through the creation of a spatial context. The saleable and knowable object is still disenfranchized from the art moment, as the environment of an installation is a presence always-already in the process of dematerialization, given its performance in a timed manner. In the last two decades artists' use of video and interactive installations has risen dramatically, indicating an interest in establishing a performative space for the virtual environments of electronic communications.

Eduardo Kac's *transgenic art* carries with it the remembrance and the results of the temporary disappearance of the art object into concept and the performance of that loss in installation, as well as the return of the theatrical in art production. This may seem a strained relation to model, as the objects of transgenic art are biological and mechanical. The art object is very much there. Yet this is the very point I wish to make. The biological subjects and performing machines of Kac's *transgenic art* are constructed as idea and placed within installations for philosophical reflection, making performances of their existence. Therein lies the rub: animal bodies and machine bodies revealed not within their own destiny but altered within and serving, unknowingly, an aesthetic discourse. In an interview included on the *Eighth Day* website, Kac states that:

> A lot of the art I make is both an attempt for me to grapple with an issue, to try to develop an understanding for myself and create a context, not in which I convey my understanding to the public but always create a context in which the public can develop his or her own understanding, their own understanding of an issue.
>
> (Kac 2006)

The context here is a life in a state of becoming, whose potential is captured within an aesthetic. What is at issue in transgenic art is an aesthetic of conceptualism housed in installation, which is built on the bodies of altered animals and articulated through machines. The animals and machines are fuel for the art engine. This is not necessarily a bad thing. Kac himself is keenly aware of the responsibilities demanded of his creations:

> There is no transgenic art without a firm commitment to and responsibility for the new life form thus created. Ethical concerns are paramount in any artwork, and they become more crucial than ever in the context of bio art. From the perspective of interspecies communication, transgenic art calls for a dialogical relationship between artist, creature/artwork, and those who come in contact with it.
>
> (Kac 2006)

Given the volatile nature of his art, Kac strives to foreground the ethical ramifications of the process. I am not trying to decide if he is right or wrong. His explorations of biological and mechanical transgressions give us a remarkable path to think through the current revolutions of science that are unmaking and redoing our bodies, subjectivity and identity.

Animal aesthetics

Regarding the process of aesthetic genetic engineering, Kac writes, 'Every living organism has a genetic code that can be manipulated, and the recombinant DNA can be passed on to the next generations' (1998). The manipulation of the genetic code and its passing down through generations is the problem. As represented in popular films such as *Jurassic Park* (1993) and *The Island* (2005), it is the chaos, the uncontrollability of life, the unknown outcomes, which are cause for concern. A recombinant DNA home-kit for the artist, like the invention of Sony's *Powerpak*, promises (threatens) great shifts in creation of art. A valid question to ask is: is this is a useful domain for art? Is an aesthetic model or frame appropriate in designing new life? In the next chapter, I look in detail at the problem of aestheticizing politics, which, in many ways, is essentially the same problem exhibited in Kac's work, and it cannot be easily dismissed. Can one promote a free, open, reciprocal and balanced relation with objects under one's genetic modification? Botanists and gardeners breed plants and create new species. Farmers use GM plants. Pet owners breed animals to promote special features and now even have the option to clone their animal companions. Parents have the opportunity to pre-screen embryos for disease or sexual identification. Is this a difference in kind or difference in degree to Kac's development of transgenic art? At what point do we regard the process of intervention in *natural life* as a step too far? Or are we already there in terms of human/machine control of nature and the creation of life? If there is no off-switch to the technological, then it is unlikely we could find one to the technological interventions in life creation. If there is no stopping it the question still holds: is art an effective means of promoting a free, open, reciprocal, ethical relation of the human/machine/new life form matrix? The usefulness of Kac's work is that it allows, or requires, that we question that position.

The problem of conflating art and life has a rich theoretical history. In the eighteenth century, Denis Diderot wrote in his *Encyclopedia* that 'In the arts of imitation the truth is nothing, verisimilitude everything, and not only does one not ask them to be real, one does not even want the pretence to be the exact resemblance' (1974: 289). As I stated earlier, Heidegger, in outlining the aesthetics of Nietzsche, suggested that 'Art is worth more than "the truth"' (1979: 75). What all three philosophers are stating is that the convergence of art and life is a corruption of both phenomena. If you believe that art is life and life art, then you do not understand either one. The lies that form art, the dissimulation that constructs its beingness, the illusions that build its world, mysteriously open to an appearance of the truth. Nietzsche would argue that the real, or the *truth*, simply leads to more illusions. Aesthetics, as an autonomous activity, shows us the truth of life. Life has a tendency to be devalued when it stands in for the goals of art. Heidegger's notion of truth is useful, in that it considers the idea not as a correspondence of word and thing or signifier and signified, but rather what he calls 'a comportment to letting things be'. If art seeks a truth, then perhaps questions need to be ethical, then aesthetic.

The posthuman spectator

The spectator in Kac's interactive and transgenic art is positioned, in part, as a disembodied participant. Entry to the work is either through physical presence in a gallery space or through virtual participation online. Kac describes how telepresence offers interaction with his work *Uirapuru* (1999):

> 'Uirapuru' merges virtual reality with telepresence through the internet. Virtual reality offers participants a purely digital space that can be experienced visually and in which one can be active, in this case the VRML forest populated by six flying fish. Telepresence provides access and a point of entry to a remote physical environment.
>
> (Kac 2006)

The construction of a virtual spectator is another of Kac's most interesting innovations. Traditionally, spectatorship in art and performance has been identified with presence. The present spectator brings with her a degree of choice, agency and self-determination and the art object is, therefore, constructed through the viewer's perception. Kac's transgenic art offers a model of spectatorship based on internet interactivity activated by streaming

media, virtual simulations of the actual art environment and telepresence through computer-mediation. The telepresent spectator inhabits a virtual environment where agency, choice and responsibility are available, but challenged. Clicking the javascript switch for an action that one cannot witness *in person* can invite an *impersonal* or alienated attitude to the activity. The privileging of presence in my binary of present versus virtual spectator may not be very useful, as so much of our daily lives are spent in virtual environments and communications. In fact, in contemporary commercial interactions, purchasers are encouraged and rewarded for doing business virtually, saving the seller or agent the time-consuming process and friction of face-to-face interaction. 'Talk to the machine', people are too expensive.

As discussed above, Kac's interactive and transgenic installation *Genesis* offers present and telepresent spectators alike the opportunity to effect a change in the biological entity (*E. coli* bacteria) through computer-mediated manipulation. The spectator of *Genesis* is capable, with the click of a mouse, to engage in a rudimentary biological alteration. Hardly earth-shattering, but it is evocative of the effortless activities of virtual action performed daily throughout the datasphere of digital culture. The San Francisco-based machine performance group *Survival Research Lab (SRL)* is using similar technologies that permit online users to tele-operate weapons during their performances. Since the mid-1970s, *SRL*, under the direction of Mark Pauline, has engaged in the development of radio-controlled and robotic machinery for destructive and combative performance. *Further Explorations in Lethal Experimentations*, presented at ZKM: Centre for Art and Technology in Karlsruhe, Germany on 18 October 1997, and *SRL Thoughtfully Regards the Arbitrary Calculation of Pathological Amusement*, presented at ICC in Tokyo, Japan, in December of 1999, were early experiments in tele-operative art. Web participants in the performances were allowed control of a combination of destructive machines, including the *Air Launcher*, which shoots explosive rounds at 500 miles per hour for a distance of one-fifth of a mile. Generally, the weapon/art object/performing machine is controlled via a head-mounted display or remotely operated via the Web. The *Pitching Machine*, which the SRL website claims is the most dangerous machine in the SRL arsenal, holds thirty 2 × 4 boards and shoots two boards per second at 135 miles per hour at a range of approximately 100 yards. The SRL website claims that the server facilitating the interactions is 'multi-threaded to enable chaotic, free for all control of the air-launcher. No login is required to provide for anonymous destruction' (SRL 2006). It is not difficult to compare these aesthetic practices with contemporary weapon systems, whose strategy consists of disengaging both the soldier and spectator from the *real* component of the action, namely the target. Anonymous destruction is the model of digital warfare, where enemy combatants are rarely to be encountered outside of a videated signal. The impersonal nature of the telepresent user alters both engagement with the activity and the ethics of behaviour in that action.

Perhaps it is only the artist in Kac's aesthetic field who evades the posthuman, postbiological condition. He remains in control, while offering irreversible body alterations for the animals and virtual multiple choice and javascript off/on switches for a telepresent and disembodied spectator. The ironic use of Biblical phrases that Kac has borrowed from the Judeo-Christian tradition point toward a construction of the artist as a God over his genetically engineered world. The language of the Biblical quotation, transposed and linked through the primitive technology of Morse Code to the new technology of genetic engineering points toward the ways in which the body and subjectivity are being reconceived and rewritten through biological interventions. Scientists in 2003 completed mapping the human genome and identified all the approximately 30,000 genes and determined the sequences of the 3 billion chemical base pairs that make up human DNA. Biomedical industrialists are using the map to patent and market the human code of life. The U.S. Human Research Institute states on its web site that:

> Another important feature of the project is the federal government's long-standing dedication to the transfer of technology to the private sector. By licensing technologies to private companies and awarding grants for innovative research, the project is catalyzing the multibillion-dollar U.S. biotechnology industry and fostering the development of new medical applications.
>
> (National Human Genome Research Institute 2006)

Like the California gold rush, the human genome project has led to claims being staked and territory marked out for ownership of our interiority. The human is being portioned and purchased. *Genesis* depicts the constructed character of the Judeo-Christian model of nature as natural and essential, while demonstrating the mutable structure of our biological coding. Kac's installation implies that life is a game of chance, but, in this artwork, who controls the aleatory experience? The telepresent spectator of *Genesis* is offered the opportunity to engage in the switching on of the alteration technology. They are not witness to, nor are they required to take responsibility for, their actions. Is there a cost to such telepresence wherein the participant creates an action to which they are neither witness nor caretaker?

The old question of whether the artist is offering a critique or promotion of a particular problem by re-enacting that dilemma arises in thinking through transgenic art. As I argued above, the work offers us the opportunity to think through some of the more pressing issues of the day. The artist's intentions are interesting, but not central.

Taking care

In *The Eighth Day*, Kac and his associates at Arizona State University have devised a biologically driven robot known as a biobot. The artist explains:

> A biobot is a robot with an active biological element within its body which is responsible for aspects of its behavior. The biobot created for 'The Eighth Day' has a colony of GFP amoeba called Dyctiostelium discoideum as its 'brain cells'. These 'brain cells' form a network within a bioreactor that constitutes the 'brain structure' of the biobot. When amoebas divide the biobot exhibits dynamic behavior inside the enclosed environment. Changes in the amoebal colony (the 'brain cells') of the biobot are monitored by it, and cause it to slowly go up and down, or to move about, throughout the exhibition. Ascending and descending motion becomes a visual sign of increase (ascent) and decrease (descent) of amoebal activity. The biobot also functions as the avatar of Web participants inside the environment. Independent of the ascent and descent of the biobot, Web participants are able to control its visual system with a pan-tilt actuator. The autonomous ascent and descent motion provide Web participants with a new perspective of the environment.
>
> (www.kac.org)

The amoeba works as a neural network affecting the actions of the machine. The amoeba's divisions cause the biobots to move about the installation. Further, the biobots are avatars for the Web participants who are able to control the visual system of the creature, thereby gaining different perspectives on the performance environment. Kac writes of an *ethics of robotics* that will need to be considered as the links between machine, animal and human are solidified. The biobot is a crude example of how the biological organisms and machine forms might create co-dependent entities. In a piece called *A-Positive*, Kac designed a system that would draw oxygen from the blood of an individual to power a flame. The traditional master/slave narrative of human and machine is troubled in Kac's work and suggests the time is ripe for a reconsideration of our ethics in regards to machines. As the machines are invited into our bodies and biological organisms introduced into machines, the neat boundaries of what marks a human are being complicated. Kac's use of animals and machines operates in a less dramatic system of difference, but suggests useful ways of thinking through how humans construct the world through the assistance of these animals and machines. As discussed above, The *GFP Bunny* 'Alba' is one of Kac's first transgenic creations. Alba is a rabbit fixed with the gene that codes for the green fluorescent protein. Alba glows green under a

UV lamp. Kac writes on his web site that the life of Alba is an artwork in three stages:

> The first phase of the 'GFP Bunny' project was completed in February 2000 with the birth of 'Alba' in Jouy-en-Josas, France [...] The second phase is the ongoing debate, which started with the first public announcement of Alba's birth, in the context of the Planet Work conference, in San Francisco, on May 14, 2000. The third phase will take place when the bunny comes home to Chicago, becoming part of my family and living with us from this point on.
>
> (www.kac.org)

The art is not placed in a physical or virtual installation, but framed through the existence of the rabbit, unless you consider all actions a performance; but that argument as an epistemology has limited usage. The art is not performed, presented or represented. It exists. The boundaries of art are extended to a presence that will only stop at death.

Martin Heidegger's notion of human existence as a phenomenon of *being-in-the-world* might be a useful model for understanding the problem that *transgenic art* offers us. Heidegger's being-in-the-world exists through an operation of *care*, which is articulated through time and surrounded by anxiety. *Caring* is structured as a three-part process of projection, wherein being-in-the-world 'projects upon or towards its possibilities to be', *throwness* 'into and among these possibilities', and *fallenness* among the possibilities 'to the neglect of [the being-in-the-world's] own deepest possibility to be itself' (Caputo 1998: 227). These movements are experienced in the being-in-the-world as anxiety. Within this structure, the human is responsible for her life and must take care of it. Similarly, the artist is responsible for her creation. She must take care of it. As the infinite quality of our possibilities accelerates in the advent of new science and technology, we must take care not to be overtaken by the anxiety of *projection*, *fallenness* and *throwness* and find that both ourselves and our creations are incapable of revealing our separate and unified destinies.

As Dr. Frankenstein learned, that which we create desires our care and responsibility. We are animals, and our machines are our extensions, supplementing and sometimes displacing ourselves. *Transgenic art* is a process for the manufacturing of monsters and machines, and thereby the artist must become the *care-taker* of these other beings. Without a concerned *care-taking*, these monsters and machines will return with desires and demands no posthuman can supply.

8 From simulation to embeddedness

Aestheticizing politics and the performance of 'bare life'

We must bring the masses illusions.

(Adolph Hitler quoted in Speer 1976: 103)

I became a politician against my will. For me politics are only a means to an end [...] If someone else had been found, I would never have gone into politics; I would have become an artist or a philosopher.

(Adolph Hitler quoted in Spotts 2002: 8)

'Now you all will have to reset your brain'.

(Karlheinz Stockhausen)

O those Greeks! They knew how to live. What is required for that is to stop courageously at the surface, the fold, the skin, to adore appearance, to believe in forms, tones, words, in the whole Olympus of appearance. Those Greeks were superficial – out of profundity.

(Nietzsche, *The Gay Science* quoted in Villa 1996: 80)

Throughout this book I have attempted to account for the history of the technological advances in the screened technologies of new media and computer environments, as well as the manners in which theatre and performance, culture and subjectivity, and material and metaphysical conditions have evolved within those systems. I have discussed the advances in media and computer technologies in the late twentieth century that brought forth unique exchanges and conversions between the recording technologies and live performance, which led to a reconsideration of how theatre happens (or does not) in mediated and virtual environments. I have tried to account for how the ideology of the will to virtuality manifested in performance and culture at large, and how subjectivity is contested in the space of technology.

Further still, I have questioned how the strategies of the virtual challenge the metaphysics of illusion.

Throughout this book I have followed the philosophical (Continental) and modern drama traditions of questioning and differentiating the illusions of the real and the realities of illusion. The trajectory of the arguments has followed much of postmodern theory that has worried over the performance of spectacle, the strategies of simulation, the fascinations with the surface, the problems of a culture of hyper-commodification and the manipulations of mediatized information. The arguments have noted the systemic problems of late capitalism, which create a circulation of simulations – mainly televisual, now cyber-spatial as well – which constantly evade any linkage to the real and which operate as coercive apparatuses for cultural domination. I am writing in a tradition drawn from the concerns found in Guy DeBord's notices on the spectacle's occurrence (1967), which in some respects was an addendum to Heidegger's supposition that the modern age is marked by the conquest of the world as picture. For Heidegger, picturing the world means that man is constructed as subject while everything else that exists is formulated as object. That assumption, I have argued, allows us to trace the manipulations of the world as image and aesthetic object from the Early Modern through to the contemporary period. Nietzsche outlined the problem earlier in *How the Real World at Last Became a Myth* (1889). Finally, to engage in the rhetorical strategy of infinite regression, it is hard not to see these late twentieth-century concerns as an echo of the founding statements of Plato's metaphysics regarding the shadows in the cave.

However, the full trajectory of this study follows Paul Virilio's model of an ever-accelerating world and considers that many of the critical questions posed by the collision of live performance and technology, although still important, have lost their urgency. I suggest that the era of virtuality (a problem of illusion and representation), the age of simulation (e.g. the televisual presentations of Gulf War I), has given way to a more troubling model of embeddedness, a problem of materiality and embodiment (e.g. American embedded reporting from Iraq). Led by new strategies of the performance of war and terror, mediatized and technologized cultural systems resist simulating signs of the real to mask the real and instead practice a technique of embeddedness (infecting the real from within information patterns and biological entities), which draws attention to a reconstructed material *truth* and ocular proof that seeks to coerce through a type of *shock and awe*. The strategy of simulation and spectacle has been extended and fundamentally altered. The linked performances of terror, war, propaganda and consumerism have not fully abandoned the strategies of illusory simulation, but have instead complicated their operation with an image regime and the bodily presence of a material embeddedness.

The core of the problem resides in the aestheticizing of politics, which was most usefully articulated by Walter Benjamin in his canonical essay *The Work of Art in the Age of Mechanical Reproduction* (1968). Aestheticizing politics and, by extension, aestheticizing life is problematic in that it constructs the world as stagecraft in a kind a 'cynical use of settings and props to elicit unthinking consent' (Greenblatt 113). In contemporary world politics there are two modalities of this aestheticizing. The first can be understood generally as a *repression of the real*. In this mode the real is either masked through simulation or infected through embeddedness. The second mode is that of *rebuilding a transcendental real* through a neo-iconoclasm bent on destroying heretical illusion. The issues of manipulating the real through simulation, embeddedness and neo-iconoclasm are grounded on the problem of aestheticizing politics and life.

In this chapter these suppositions are articulated through a performance analysis of various contemporary examples of war, terror, propaganda, science and theatre. The purveyors of war, terror, state propaganda and to a lesser extent the scientists and artists of bioengineering and nanotechnology are attempting to reengage the coercive and fascist tendencies of a metaphysics of absolute truth by challenging the regimes of illusory surface. The strategy is to lie and create through the manipulation of facts and representations of events a situation that appears as a *truth*. This is clearly nothing new. For as long as the human has had the power of speech, most of what has been said has been more or less a lie. What is new are the technologies of embedding that permit the liars broad control systems. The real-world evidence upon which I base this theory includes the expansion of biological and genetic manipulations of the Earth, animal and human, as well as an information system that has moved from ubiquitous surveillance and simulation to embedded infiltration, creating more complex infections of data flow and domination. The effect of simulation was that the real remained, hidden and coded but available. Embeddedness alters simulation's masking of the real with a dataflow that can inhabit the real itself and alter its essence. The problem is compounded by the aforementioned neo-iconoclasts who seek a reification of the real. The consequence of this cultural shift is that the borders and problems of theatre and performance have been challenged and altered. The problem at hand is that of the body's place of performativity in world culture and in contemporary theatre. What needs consideration is the functionality of theatre and theatricality (and more specifically, or synonymously, tragedy and the tragic) in the bio-politics of embeddedness, simulation and neo-iconoclasm. My conclusion is that only through an unveiling of the *bare life* of the subject on stage can a free relation exist between the performer and spectator. A study of *Società Raffaello Sanzio*'s *Tragedia Endogonidia* follows, to make the case for a theatre that responds uniquely to these issues and enacts these solutions.

The underlying political position of this essay, which is drawn from the ideas of Giorgio Agamben (1998) and Hannah Arendt (1958), is to question how individual autonomy, sovereignty and freedom, are challenged in an aestheticized culture of embeddedness. My argument seeks to promote a notion of art production, media and performance analysis and political action that is akin to Arendt's position of a non-sovereign, non-autonomous freedom that is worldly, plural, and whose position is marked by its distance from mastery, far removed from the tyranny of absolute truth. For it is the profanation of the notion and practice of freedom which has been cynically manipulated by current American ideology, foreign policy and homeland security, which argue for a freedom that is built on the notion of autonomy, isolation, mastery and ownership of *truth*. It is an unsustainable theory and a violent practice.

The chapter's questioning into the effects of the performative and mediated strategies of war and terror is concerned with the contemporary anxiety that much of liberal humanism holds for action (political? radical?) because of its perceived futility, and the fact that any action creates outcomes that are both boundless and uncertain. The ideal position or default setting for the liberal humanist is neutrality, which allows moral platitudes without any required action. The anxiety exists because, as we learn from the fifth century BCE Greek tragedies, it is the choices made and the actions followed that lead inevitably to our demise. From a tragic perspective, to live is to make choices, and through each choice our life is directed towards its ends. The terrorists of 9/11 had no such fear of the risk of a radical act and neither do the suicide bombers of Islam – nor has Bush's *war on terror* – but where does the cultural critic, the intellectual, the artist stand? What thing is there to do? What not to do? Is it still, *nothing to be done?* Hannah Arendt's affirmation of political action is encouraging. Dana R. Villa's enlightening book *Arendt and Heidegger* articulates Arendt's theory of action: 'Political action thus possesses a unique *revelatory* capacity, the ability to illuminate the realm of human affairs in its specific phenomenal reality, and to endow this reality with meaning' (1996: 85). This liberation model of action is tempered by Arendt's suggestion that the public realm, wherein action is performed in face-to-face communication, has been all but closed in contemporary culture, and thus political action is increasingly harder to perform. Written in 1958, Arendt's thesis is exacerbated in the current televisual and technocultures.

It is a common perception in twentieth-century critical theory that the mixing of art and politics is dangerous, and that art is not the problem, but the solution to the problem of aesthetics. However, Jacques Ranciére offers a recouping of aesthetics. He writes in *Politics of Aesthetics*:

> There is thus an 'aesthetics' at the core of politics that has nothing to do with Benjamin's discussion of the 'aestheticization of politics' specific to the 'age of the masses'. This aesthetics should not be understood as the perverse commandeering of politics by a will to art.
>
> (2005: 13)

Žižek, in commenting on Ranciére's thesis, warns to be 'careful not to succumb to the liberal temptation of condemning all collective artistic performances as inherently *totalitarian*' (77). Thus tempered, my analysis is not a condemnation of the whole of aesthetics as a constant corruption of politics or vice versa, but rather a questioning of specific instances of bio-politics, which are increasing prevalent when life and politics are captured in an aesthetic framing that limits and controls.

What is meant by bio-politics? Giorgio Agamben's philosophy and political theory of post-Holocaust Western subjectivity suggests that the personal sovereignty of the subject is challenged within contemporary bio-politics, in which embedded technologies challenge the body forth toward a troubling dis-empowerment. According to Giorgio Agamben through Foucault, bio-politics is 'situated at the point at which the species and the individual as a simple living body become what is at stake in a society's political strate-gies' (1998: 3). Quoting Foucault, Agamben suggests that the new bio-power exerts a 'bestialization of man achieved through the most sophisticated polit-ical techniques. For the first time in history, the possibilities of the social sciences are made known, and at once it becomes possible both to protect life and to authorize a holocaust' (3). He states further:

> In particular, the development and triumph of capitalism would not have been possible, from this perspective, without the disciplinary control achieved by the new bio-power, which, through a series of appropriate technologies, so to speak created the 'docile bodies that it needed'.
>
> (3)

How can the theatre respond to the production of *docile bodies* whose bare life is the new site of political power and control? To redraw my conceptual map there is a new bio-politics in which the life of the individ-ual is at stake. Layered on to this culture is the ongoing problem of the aestheticization of politics, which operates through simulation, embedded-ness and neo-iconoclasm. It is a struggle for control of the real.

Embeddedness (exterior): televisual terrorism

The work of simulation, modelled as a masking of the real, has been well-documented and appears daily in the relatively benign works of TV in real-ity programming and confessional talk shows, abusive game shows and manipulative comedy setups, real-time broadcasting and 24-hour news cycles. More troubling actions of simulation took place in the mediated representations of the 1991 Gulf War, on which Baudrillard (1995) and Virilio (2002) had much to say. More troubling still are the recent examples of the exterior process of embedding and infecting the real with misinfor-mation, including the works of the American military's techniques of embed-ded reporters during the Iraq war (2003–?), which I will discuss below. Simultaneously, a counter-movement to the repression of the real is present in a neo-iconoclasm promoted primarily by radical elements of Islam. One particular event can be read as a fictive beginning of a reinstalling of the real through the obliteration of graven images of illusion. In 2001 the Islamist Taliban government of Afghanistan was concerned over UNESCO's renovation work on the 1,500-year-old monumental Buddhas of Bamiyan located in the Bamiyan valley of central Afghanistan, approximately 230 km northwest of Kabul. The Taliban began a month-long bombing of the Buddhas in March of that year. Like medieval iconoclasts, they performed a reiteration of the profanation not to speak the name of God. The Taliban later claimed to be concerned primarily with the material needs of the Afghani citizen and, therefore, elected to destroy the Buddhas to bring world attention back to *real* issues. Standing like twin towers, the Buddhas, one 55 metres and the other 37 metres, were eradicated in order to insist that no mere appearance could represent the real of the transcendental signifier of God. The obliteration of the statues was an unsettling prefiguring of the World Trade Center's collapse, a spectacle which itself served to interrupt, if only briefly, the circulations of simulations in mediatized culture.

If the demolition of the Bamiyan Buddhas was the opening gesture of radical Islam to restore the real, the parading of the corpses of Uday and Qusay Hussein by the American military on 24 July 2004 during the Iraq war was the flipside of the problem. At the same time as the Taliban and Al-Qeada were rending the power of illusion from the surface of appearance and reestablishing a metaphysical truth of God, the American military authorities in Iraq were undertaking their own exhumation of the real through a mediated ritual and a fictive laying to rest of the strategy of simulation. When the sons of Saddam Hussein, Uday and Qusay, were killed in a firefight with the American 101st Airborne unit and U.S. Special Forces near Mosul it was not enough to simply report the death. *Live video* evidence was required. The autopsied bodies were displayed for journalists to witness the scene, while satellite video feeds streamed the images.

To read the event as a ritual reengagement with the real after the meticulous simulations of Gulf War I is interesting. The silver autopsy tables draped with medical blue sheets rise up as sacrificial altars. The bodies of the brothers, bloodied, bruised, autopsied and embalmed, are draped so as not to offend the viewer with exposed genitalia. They lay immobilized in a death staged for the cameras to assure the spectator of the veracity of the claim. Three cameramen lean over the bodies to get a close-up and send their visual feed to the satellites for worldwide broadcast, working like Caravaggio's *Doubting Thomas* (1602–3) whose finger is placed in the wounds of Christ for confirmation. Like priests or shamans, the cameramen and their cameras peer directly into the face of the Husseins' death and channel its occurrence to the congregation. All this takes place within a white but shabby field morgue, like a temple or ritual circle that enacts a phony death of simulation and a fictionalized reengagement of direct reality through the faces of death. It is as if the white room were the *skene* building of the ancient

Greek theatre wherein the hidden primal scene or crime was committed. But rather than repress that scene the audience is invited inside, and the hidden is made visible so that no illusion can be imagined, no truth concealed. The images of the event can be read, as all documents can be, from multiple perspectives. There is the obvious goal of the grotesque parading of the war dead, which is an age-old performance strategy such as was enacted in the displaying of the decapitated heads at Traitor's Gate at the Tower of London. However, I would argue that this action is the signature moment when the strategy of simulation was itself laid to rest and the process of exhuming the real through a mediated ritual took place. Over the past twenty years, mediated manipulations of the real have been *too* successful. Many of the world spectators simply no longer believe what they see. Thus it has been necessary to re-engage a circulation of the real, or an embedded real that can persuade. But, of course, this event is no real presentation of any actuality or any unconcealing of truth, but a more subtle and contrived manipulation of facts (a theatre) to create a pliable and plastic truth for coercive purposes. The next event in my narrative was more conclusive and traumatic to some; equally as conclusive, but victorious to others.

The impossible ruins of a virtual environment: the aesthetics of 9/11

The aestheticizing of politics lies at the root of these movements of simulation, embeddedness and new iconoclasm. The sovereignty of the subject, the bare life of the individual, lies at the core of that aestheticizing process. The events of September 11, 2001, as event, even as performance, illuminate this problem graphically. 9/11 is not so much an example of simulation, embeddedness or a recalling of the real, but reveals the aestheticizing of politics and life.

In what can only be explained as either the worst public relations misstep in the history of Western civilization or confirmation that some elements of modernist aesthetics and fascism are indeed complimentary phenomena, it was reported in a German newspaper that Karlheinz Stockhausen, renowned electronic music composer and theorist, suggested in a press conference in Hamburg on September 16, 2001 that the terrorist attacks on September 11, 2001 were 'one of the world's greatest works of art'. His statement as reported:

> What happened there is – now all of you must adjust your brains – the biggest work of art imaginable [...] but what happened spiritually, this jump out of security, out of the self-evident, out of the everyday life, this sometimes also happens in art [...] or it is worthless [...] so that we see the world in a way that we have not seen it. But, please, do not publish this. People might not understand this.
>
> (Stockhausen quoted in *The New York Times* 2001)

Stockhausen is certainly correct on his last point. He is also right that the most useful function of art is to move outside the everyday so as to see from a new perspective. In this way, Stockhausen is linking the process of art with that of the economy of sacrifice. Dennis King Keenan glossing the theory of sacrifice in the work of Julia Kristeva, writes: 'Art mimics sacrifice in order to preserve one "suspended" on the edge of nothingness' (2005: 44). Stockhausen's linkage to actual human sacrifice took readers off-guard. Sacrifice in Western culture has been primarily relegated to the mimetic acts of art and religion. Actual sacrifice is sublimated in mimesis. In fact, much writing on sacrifice – from Nietzsche to Bataille to Kristeva – suggests that what is needed is not a return to sacrifice, but rather a sacrifice of sacrifice. Žižek notes that the goal of Lacanian psychoanalysis is to rid the subject of the false response of sacrifice. However, Stockhausen was arguing that the events of 9/11 were returning the world to a pre-societal model of sacrifice through its usage of the actual and of the real, without recourse to mimesis, revealing a truth of the aporia of death.

Stockhausen prepared a follow-up statement on September 19, 2001.

> In my work, I have defined Lucifer as the cosmic spirit of rebellion, of anarchy. He uses his high degree of intelligence to destroy creation. He does not know love. After further questions about the events in America, I said that such a plan appeared to be Lucifer's greatest work of art. Of course I used the designation 'work of art' to mean the work of destruction personified in Lucifer.
>
> (Stockhausen 2001)

Stockhausen was digging a deeper hole from himself by drawing on Christian metaphysics to promote a notion of works of art as agents of Lucifer's destructive potential. But, again, he was making intriguing associations between sacrifice and art firstly, and between destruction and art secondly. According to Stockhausen, he was misquoted and taken out of context. As quoted above, he claims to have qualified his original statement by saying that the atrocities were '*Lucifer's* greatest work of Art'. Either/or, the shock of the statement resulted in a scapegoating of Stockhausen that led to concert cancellations, hate mail and much condemnation and revulsion. Since 9/11, in an America less and less tolerant, other decidedly less controversial artists such as the Dixie Chicks and Steve Earl have dealt with similar backlashes as a result of making what was perceived as anti-American comments. Nonetheless, whether or not Professor Stockhausen drew upon Christian metaphysics to mitigate his comments, he was, according to the rhetoric of some elements of the historical avant-garde and aesthetic theory, correct. Which is, of course, a condemnation of these modernist aesthetics.

A glance back at the manifestos of the historical avant-garde reveals incessant calls for burnings, destruction and dismantlings of all past aesthetic precepts, art objects and cultural forms. Only through the destruction of the past could a future be given birth. Perhaps it is unfair to link the historical avant-garde and its response to its own historical moment to the impulses of contemporary *unlawful* terrorism and *sanctioned* wars. However, Stockhausen's modelling of the events of 9/11 as destructive art works does foreground some of the militaristic and destructive tendencies in the history of the avant-garde of the nineteenth and twentieth centuries. Stockhausen's art of destruction suggests that the sadist, or agonistic, or nihilistic desire constructs a deadening and *truthful* aesthetic that sees war, terror and murder as beautiful. Nietzsche's aesthetic may give us an opportunity to reclaim illusion and art from the truth of sadism.

The aesthetics of destruction has a rich history in twentieth-century art. The cleansing and cathartic role of war was celebrated by Italian Futurist Filippo Tommaso Marinetti (1876–1944), who declared in *The Founding and Manifesto of Futurism* (1909) that 'We will glorify war – the world's only hygiene – militarism, patriotism, the destructive gesture of freedom-bringers, beautiful ideas worth dying for' (1991: 50). Contemporary artists, such as San Francisco's Survival Research Labs, utilize the images and technologies of machine violence to stage scenarios of technological destruction. The genre of *war film* is likewise demonstrative of the aesthetic pleasures afforded war. Perhaps Marinetti is right. We should not brand war as anti-aesthetic, because it isn't. War is horrifying, but *aesthetically pleasing* to many eyes (but who is willing to admit that, even to themselves?). Destruction is appealing (some danced in the streets of Palestine as the towers collapsed). Murder is a masterpiece (*natural born killers* reach celebrity status in the US). The sadist desire runs amok in our world. If we aren't ready to face this horrible truth, we won't be able to combat it. Perhaps Mark Pauline and his Survival Research Lab have a point. Machines are being set in struggle against one another, and it is the human body that pays the cost of the struggle. The spectacle is the theatre of war, which is viewed as a simulation, but experienced in reality. The terrorists inscribed the image of 9/11 for the infidels of the world. How does an infidel read the writing of the holy ones? No reading required. Slaughter and the genocidal impulse speak unequivocally. The image is voiced, whether it be a tower collapsing or a cluster bomb exploding, as an anti-Aristotelian, anti-cathartic, neo-theatre of cruelty that accelerates pity and fear, with no resolution or dénouement, and rather than challenge the field of representation, concretizes the signs.

Many of the arguments I construct in this study are in some manner or another built on or near traumatic incidents of violence and loss. This troubles me, and it is not my intention to build a facile theory on the bodies of the dead or to engage in a callous or facile theory in the face of real suffering. I am struggling with the issues surrounding the politics and performance of war, terror, science and technology, which all involve the life and death of the individual. In the case of 9/11, I am attempting to understand the image and reality of absolute collapse, the shock of accelerated history within the crushing of bodies and buildings in the instant creation of a ruin; and I try, as Stockhausen suggested, to 'reset my brain' in order to question how one might understand the moment through the damaged and weakened systems of art and aesthetics. Perhaps since all communication is structured through sound, image, motion, and read through the senses and processed through the perceptual mechanism of the brain, all is subject to an aesthetic, to a judgement regarding its value within the realm of the beautiful. Unfortunately, no image, no thing, escapes our judgement, unfortunately.

As suggested above, my critique draws from Benjamin's important equation that fascism is the aestheticizing of politics, while communism is the politicizing of aesthetics. I am not suggesting a return to the master narrative of Marx, although a little more historical materialism would greatly help this current study, but I am working toward understanding the corruption involved in a politics based in the aestheticizing of the world and of the life of the subject. Perhaps I am trying to admit that some aesthetic strategies are trivial and trivializing at best and, at worst, coercive and limiting, while not falling into the liberal trap of conceiving an inevitable linkage between aesthetics and fascism.

The history of modelling the work of the State as a work of art is as old as that of Western philosophy. Plato inaugurated the notion of the State as a work of art. Dana Villa writes, 'Plato's Republic stands as the initiator of the state as "collective masterpiece", as artwork, trope' (1996: 108). Villa links the establishment of the notion of the state as artwork with the extensions and critiques by Schiller, Hegel and Nietzsche, who, Villa claims, do not fundamentally challenge Plato's formulation. Villa holds Hannah Arendt's theory as an exception to the rule, asserting that Arendt 'studiously avoids the figure of the state as a work of art' (108). Again, the argument is not with art but with aesthetics. Like Brecht or Boal's theatre, it is a theatre for sure, and thus a mode of aesthetic praxis, but it is also a non-aestheticized theatre that promotes a model of action, agency and dialogue.

Why were Stockhausen's comments cause for such consternation and concern? Why was it wrong to frame 9/11 as an art object? Is it because such a judgement trivializes the suffering of the victims? Art trivializes the event? An art object would not degrade memory, but considering the event as art does. The real bodies of the dead equated to an art object or event is deeply unsettling to the memories of the survivors. But was this not a partial goal or result of the terrorist act: to create an image of such shocking proportions which would be reflected infinitely through televisual reproduction? Writing about 9/11 Baudrillard states:

> The role of images is highly ambiguous. For, at the same time as they exalt the event, they also take it hostage. They serve to multiply it to infinity and, at the same time, they are a diversion and a neutralization (this was already the case with the events of 1968). The image consumes the event, in the sense that it absorbs it and offers it

for consumption. Admittedly, it gives it unprecedented impact, but impact as image-event.

(2002: 27)

9/11 as image-event creates an object that omits any autonomy to the subject implicated; it folds the lives of the dead into an aesthetics that challenges and limits. Does it count if we encounter death televisually? Does survivor status entail physical proximity? The process of televisualizing and virtualizing the world picture is a manner of arresting, avoiding, or undoing the human as a *being-toward-death*, and a way of missing materiality's ruinous nature. The virtual construction of reality has allowed for simulations such as the Gulf War to be enacted, far removed from the actualities of human destruction. Yet the image-event of 9/11 short-circuited the televisual simulation. It presented the unpresentable in presentation itself. Simulation theory momentarily collapsed along with the buildings and the lives they contained. However, this contradicts my thesis as I am arguing that it is not as simple as one regime (i.e. simulation or embeddedness) closing and another opening. Regarding 9/11 Baudrillard suggests, 'In the present case, we thought we had seen (perhaps with a certain relief) a resurgence of the real, and of the violence of the real, in an allegedly virtual universe' (2002: 28). It would work too neatly into the manipulations of current US policy to imagine that simulation's work was over and that now the US is facing real enemies that require the real solution of war: 'The terrorist violence here is not, then a blowback of reality, any more than it is a blowback of history. It is not 'real'. In a sense, it is worse: it is symbolic' (2002: 29). The symbolic structure of 9/11 allowed for the turning of the event from a distressing and irredeemable loss to a call to arms and a moment of being 'proud to be an American, where at least I know I'm free'. As Žižek argues, the problem with cyberspace is its being a symbolic order. Baudrillard is making a similar claim regarding terrorism.

The designers of the *mise-en-scène* of the Third Reich were fully aware of the power of art in politics. Benno von Arent was appointed *Reich Stage Designer* by Hitler and Albert Speer; Hitler's architect was named *Chief of Artistic Production of Mass Demonstrations*. Why were Hitler's *night rallies* so successful? Because Albert Speer, scenographer of the fascist *mise-en-scène*, knew that the events could be enhanced with art and that the appropriate image would lead to a compliant people. Speer, in his Spandau diaries, commented on Hitler's 'passion for the theatre'. He wrote how fellow prisoner Schirach

[...] recalled Hitler's amazing knowledge of stagecraft, his interest in the diameter of revolving stage, lift mechanisms, and especially different lighting techniques. He was familiar with all sorts of lighting systems and could discourse in detail on the proper illumination for certain scenes.

(1976: 102)

Hitler himself sketched set designs for Wagner's *Tristan und Isolde* and *Der Ring des Nibelungen*. His passion for theatre need not lead to a condemnation of theatrical practice, but rather to a reminder of how theatre, when applied to politics, can be so persuasive and dangerous. The terrorists who staged 9/11 did so in a spectacular fashion, in what Baudrillard saw as the 'spectacle of terrorism [that] forces the terrorism of spectacle upon us' (2002: 30). The image was central. The spectacle was designed to sear the image in the memory of the spectator.

The theory of ruin value and the cult of the picturesque

As I argued earlier in the book, the impulse to *picture* the world and all of its objects is the essence of the modern age, or so Heidegger claims. Walter Benjamin, in *The Origin of German Tragic Drama*, wrote: 'in the ruin history has physically merged into the setting. And in this guise history does not assume the form of the process of an eternal life so much as that of irresistible decay' (1977: 177–8). Isn't history always a part of the setting? Or is history a human inscription on the face of materiality? And by *history* do we mean, simply *time*? What of an instant ruin, where within several hours time shifts so irrevocably like at ground zero of 9/11, or more decisively at ground zero of Hiroshima, or at the site of any of the other world calamities and atrocities? The crushing of time in the destruction of a nuclear warhead or the planes within the World Trade Center, in a sudden catastrophe, creates an instantaneous ruin.

The accumulation of time viewed on the face of a ruin can stimulate an uncanny experience of mortality of presence and absence. The Romantic poets and painters were keenly aware of the power and seductive force in the timeless stillness of the ruin. Disturbingly, Albert Speer, chief Nazi architect, developed what he called *a theory of ruin value*, which he presented to the Fuhrer. In *Inside the Third Reich*, he wrote:

> The idea was that buildings of modern construction were poorly suited to form that 'bridge of tradition' to future generations, which Hitler was calling for. It was hard to imagine that rusting heaps of rubble could communicate these heroic inspirations, which Hitler admired in the monuments of the past. My theory was intended to deal with this dilemma. By using special materials and by applying certain principles of statics, we should be able to build structures, which even in a state of decay, after hundreds or (such were our reckonings) thousands of years would more or less resemble Roman models.
>
> (1970: 56)

Speer illustrated his idea with a drawing of his design for the Zeppelin Field in a state of ruin. Impressed, Hitler gave orders that future Nazi buildings should follow this *law of ruins*. The cityscape and signs of the state of the Third Reich were to become permanent and persuasive art objects.

The ruin was a central element in the primarily British cult of the picturesque, which peaked during the late eighteenth and early nineteenth centuries, roughly running along the Romantic period. Rejecting neo-Classicism and working in landscape painting, landscape architecture, garden and park design, purveyors of the picturesque privileged irregularity, roughness and variety. Ruinous structures were often a feature of landscape and garden architecture, illusionist painting for interior design, stage design and landscape painting. Tourists of the picturesque in the British Isles searched out suitable scenery in such areas as Wales, the Lake District and Scotland. Using a *Claude Glass*, a tinted mirror that controlled and framed a suitable portion of scenery, the tourist of the picturesque enjoyed a formula for studying and recording nature and thus adjudicating the landscape. William Gilpin, nineteenth-century English painter, attempted to codify what made a work picturesque. He considered the objects of the world as appendages to the overall aesthetic of the picturesque. He wrote in 'The Principles of Painting Considered, So Far as They Relate to Prints', that:

> The last thing included in design is the use of proper appendages. By appendages are meant animals, landscape, buildings, and in general, whatever is introduced into the piece by way or ornament. Every thing of this kind should correspond with subject, and rank in a proper subordination to it.
>
> (823)

The composition is the chief concern of Gilpin, as well as how the picture is taken or how the picture takes place. All else – the landscape, animals, buildings – are mere appendage to the pictorial impulse, to the eye of the beholder. Is Gilpin ordering the world as representation, neutralizing the natural through art, or simply celebrating and seeking to imitate the beauty of the world? In 'Observations on the River Wye' (1782) he wrote:

> Every view on a river, thus circumstanced, is composed of four grand parts; the area, which is the river itself; the two side-screens, which are the opposite banks, and mark the perspective; and the front-screen, which points out the winding of the river.
>
> (837)

The thing being pictured is not the primary concern; it is the picture itself that demands attention. The picturesque is defined 'as in or like a picture', and the philosophers of the form such as Gilpin, who also wrote 'On Picturesque Beauty' (1792), suggested that the picturesque might be considered the third term to Kant and Burke's model of the beautiful and the sublime. The purveyors of the picturesque identified what could and could not be considered picturesque. Human figures and cultivated land were not picturesque; wilderness and ruins were.

I want to make two opposing points here in thinking around the picturesque. A stated goal of the Romantics was to bring individuals away from their alienation from nature to enjoy a new and more open relation with the Earth. And yet the tendency was to picture the world and limit it as a representation. What is seen is possessed, framed and naturalized. Secondly, the contemplation of ruins, as Benjamin argues, reveals the markings of history and time upon the material of the world. The ruin demonstrates the transitory position of the subject in the world and signals the process toward death and decay. The unnatural acceleration of the force of 'irresistible decay', as witnessed on 9/11, afforded no moment of reflection and cheated time of its course. Such is the art of destruction, the art of war. The radical, violent act leaves the survivor like Agave, searching for the dismembered body parts of her son, Pentheus, whom she earlier rent asunder, and that which was held dear is destroyed.

The picturesque and the age of the world picture represent a desire to regulate the world through image and to defer the human authenticity of *being-toward-death*. The unremitting picturing of digital culture is an obvious extension of the cult of the picturesque, and yet can we image a *virtual ruin* or a *picturesque cyberspace?*

More than once in this volume, I have pointed to Nietzsche's theory as read by Heidegger that 'art is worth more than the "truth"'. The argument goes that there is a liberation through illusion and the *will to art* of the *Übermensch* entails an ability to love everything that happens in one's life and in the world. The *truth* brings misery and a suicidal perspective. Understanding *illusion* is to embrace the material, the sensual, which is the way toward an accurate metaphysics. Nietzsche writes, 'The will to semblance, to illusion, to deception, to Becoming and change is deeper, more "metaphysical", than the will to truth, to reality, to Being' (Nietzsche quoted in Heidegger 1979: 74). In the courage to remain at the surface lies the power of art. The collapse of the two towers is the terrorists' will to truth, which seeks to destroy the will to semblance and install a super-sensuous, which 'lures life away from invigorating sensuality, drains life's forces, weakens it' (Heidegger 1979: 75). It is anti-art truth-telling. Fascistic. Corrupted religion equals nihilism, and nihilism rejects the surface and sensuousness of life in favour of a promised metaphysical realm. The will to the sensuous is metaphysical.

As I put forth in the previous chapter in discussing the work of Eduardo Kac, much of modernist aesthetics has attempted to converge art and life, on the one hand and to circumvent representation on the other, but perhaps what matters most in art is its world of illusion, the sheer utopian joy of playfulness, thought and emotion that exists only in dreams. Perhaps what matters most in life is its limits of time and space, its presence now, its spirit tarrying with the negative. Perhaps art and life find their destiny in discrete existences, in separate spheres.

The work of terrorism and war is aimed at undermining the economics and security of power in order to break the will of the authority or people under attack. The terrorists of radical Islam embrace an iconoclastic drive to destroy appearance and the technologies of illusion in order to serve a transcendental real. The same can be said of the fundamentalism that underpins the militaristic ambitions of the administration of George W. Bush's White House. The strategies of the current American administration are different and perhaps a bit more cynical, as there is not an attempt to install the real, but instead to promote fabricated ideologies of fictional freedoms for dominance and control.

Another example of the reinstalling of the real took place in Moscow on 23 October 2002, when Chechen rebels undertook a horrific restaging of the real during a popular musical theatre production. Forty terrorists seized 700 audience members during the production of a Russian musical, *Nord-Ost*, at the House of Culture theatre near Dubrovka. The in-house cameras trained on the stage showed a performance underway, with actors dressed as Russian soldiers dancing. Suddenly, terrorists entered the stage from the wings, firing their weapons in a seamless blurring of the illusions of the stage and the reality of the rebels. Two and a half days later, all of the terrorists and 170 of the hostages were killed, primarily as a result of the gas used by Russians to subdue the rebels. The clearly stated goal of the Chechen rebels is to remove the Russian troops from Chechnyan land. But the effect of the staging of terrorism in the popular theatre was to blur the border between the fantasy stage and the real world, to break down the illusory and to promote a harsh reality, or to establish the terrorists' symbolic nature on the stages of illusion.

It is not just the ubiquitous presence of recording media that makes so much information available to us; it is also the drive to document, save and make it real by capturing it on tape. Like Citizen Kane's basement, we collect things to be stored on hard drives and rarely, if ever, to be recalled or put into use. But since our irredeemable loss, our *Rosebud*, will never be redeemed, the collection, the object and commodity fetishism continues. There are two issues at hand here: the ongoing drive to document and capture the world as picture and the drive to defeat that picture, that appearance, with a transcendental real. On the one hand there are the repulsive photo-documentation of prisoner abuse at Abu Ghraib; on the other hand there are the barbaric decapitations of hostage by various terrorist organizations.

The photo evidence of a virulent violence crowds the televisual flow: the disintegrated bodies of the many suicide bombers and their victims, the Grand Guignol street theatre of Falluja in March 2004, the shackled and blindfolded prisoners of Guantanamo Bay, and the reality programming of snuff video in the multiple video documents of hostage takings and decapitations. These 'performances of terror and war' unsettle the mind profoundly. I read them not only as atrocities, but also as depictions of an iconoclastic impulse to destroy the illusions of material surface and simulation and to install a metaphysics of the truth through a presentation of the real. It is, as others have stated, a clash of fundamentalism, of true believers who are brokering for control of a preconceived truth. These changes represent a radical shift in mediated propaganda strategy that as recently as Gulf War I sought to use simulation as a primary model of information control and circulation. Recall the green screen technology of representation of the Gulf War in 1991. Recall what might be read as another assault on simulation when on 7 April 2003, as the coalition forces were entering Baghdad, the Iraqi minister of information, Muhammad Saeed al-Sahhaf, or *Comical-Ali* as he became known in the Western press, stood on a rooftop announcing 'victory is at hand' and the 'American forces were committing suicide at the gates of Baghdad'. As he spoke, artillery rounds of the American troops were heard *off-screen* and smoke was seen rising behind him. The real was seeping in from the edges of the screen. However, a more insidious technique is of the embedded reporters joining the 'fighting men and women of the coalition' and reporting the news from within, with a slant toward the position the reporter holds. One is a model of illusion and simulation: 'what you see is not real'. The other is the new work of embedded information infection: 'what you see is the real, we made it that way'.

Throughout history, mediated representations of war, terrorism and atrocities have often been circulated with the associated militaristic campaigns and propaganda systems. Napoleon's conquests and triumphs on the battlefields were routinely captured in heroic and romantic paintings of the period, the goal being to glorify the man and to establish his visibility as hero and leader. Journalists were embedded with the troops in all of the major conflicts of the United States since the Civil War. Reporters aggressively documented the actions of the troops in World War II and the Vietnam conflict. Each of these events carries their own level of propagandistic support and manipulative persuasions. By focusing on the current situation, I understand the precedents set by the previous actions, but wish to foreground the shift from the simulated presentation of war (exemplified by the first Gulf War), an unprecedented series of simulations, to the ongoing Iraq conflict of representations of reality. This marks a shift in strategies of simulation toward a metaphysics of truth.

Let me reiterate: the age of simulation in which media replaced the real with the signs of the real (e.g. the televisual presentations of Gulf War I) has given way to the advance of embeddedness. The effect of simulation was that the real remained, hidden and coded, but available. Embeddedness, making its appearance in the recent American invasion of Iraq (Gulf War II), altered simulation's masking of the real with a dataflow that could inhabit the real itself and alter its essence. I want to suggest the end of the reign of virtual data by the usurpation of embedded technology, and consider how the material bodies of the earth (through GM crops) and the human (through similar genetic modifications) are the new site of conflict. Mediatized culture has moved from the simulated screens of the virtual to the modified bodies of embeddedness.

Embeddedness (interior)

The problem of embeddedness is not simply an informational disruption, but a harvesting or colonization of the human, other animals and the Earth. The technical achievements of genetic engineering, splicing and modification are allowing researchers and science to redirect life. The promises of nanotechnology and molecular manufacturing and design might one day make computers as para-biological entities, with human–computer interfaces of intimate and invisible structures. Both of these advances – the redirection of life and the further blending of the human and machine interface – are creating profound challenges to subjectivity. The boundaries of the body are now so porous that the usages of the term *posthuman*, over which I worried in Part I of this book, seem now positively positivist within the models of subjectivity promoted in Part II. Google the term 'genetic modification', and a bewildering avalanche of information is detailed. Websites that consider the 'technical challenges of cloning pigs for biomedical research', 'homologous recombination and genetic engineering of transgenic recombinant animals', 'enhancing transgenics through cloning' and 'human germline engineering – the prospects for commercial development' give a glimpse of the work being done. The possibility for gene-pool enhancement or eugenics is now an option. I do not attempt a thorough investigation of these scientific and technological innovations, but instead point to three recent experiments that make clear the revolutions and what is at stake in the embedding of technologies within the human body.

First, researchers at America's National Institute of Mental Health developing genetic alterations in rhesus monkeys have succeeded in blocking a gene called D2 to interrupt the link between monkeys' motivation and a perceived reward. The result is an inability in the animals to become bored with simple repetitive tasks. Humans have the same gene. Disturbing, but when presented with a pile of undergraduate essays on theatre history, such a triggered response might be welcomed. Second, as reported 13 October 2004 on the *News at Nature* website, researchers at the Sargent Rehabilitation Center in Rhode Island, USA, reported that a pill-sized brain chip has allowed a quadriplegic man to check e-mail and play computer games using his thoughts. The device can tap into a hundred neurons at a time, and is the most sophisticated such implant tested in humans so far (*News at Nature*, 2004). Finally, Žižek cites in *Organs without Bodies* an experiment undertaken at New York University in 2002 in which scientists 'attached a computer chip able to receive signals directly to a rat's brain so that one can control the rat (determine the direction in which it will run) by means of a steering mechanism' (2002: 16). All three of these experiments indicate the wide capacity for genetic manipulations and direct machine integration within the neuronal network of the brain. Under such interface control, where does identity, freedom, free will and autonomy stand?

Tragedia Endogonidia

In a previous chapter I made the case that the virtual represented a model in late twentieth-century performance practice defined by Lyotard as 'a kind of para-experience in which the dialectic meets a "non-negatable negative" and abides in the impossibility of redoubling it into a "result"' (Lyotard 1989: 363). I maintain that until recently, the dialectic confronted by the model of the virtual was the reality/illusion pairing, and the impossible redoubled result is the representational act of theatre. The model of embeddedness challenges the dominance of the virtual, and what stands as impossible is not a problem of representation, but the sovereignty of the subject. What concern me are not the aesthetic challenges to theatre, but rather the obstacles constructed to block the sovereignty of the autonomous, *free* subject within the bio-politics of digital culture. I am not claiming that the politics and metaphysics of identity constructed through immersion in the domain of the virtual are fully understood or do not continue to offer unique problems of oppressive control, opportunities for philosophies and practices of discontinuity. And there are artists and theorists who continue to confront the field of the virtual usefully not through essentialized constructions of failed subjectivities, antiquated technologies, or a romantic claim to the 'live and present body', but rather through a strategic manipulation of the performing body converging and colliding with the virtual. However, the questions I now pursue are, on the one hand, methodological, concerning how our field of performance analysis can help understand the theatres of war, terror and science. And how, on the other, theatre and performance, or theory and philosophy, might consider the effects of embedded information and materiality and re-establish a link with the philosophical path of freedom through a re-consideration of a substractive logic of theatre, of a theatre minus theatre. The final chapter of this study will take on that notion.

The end of the reign of virtual data is signalled by the usurpation of embedded technology, and the material bodies of the earth (through GM crops) and the human (through similar genetic modifications) are the new sites of conflict for free and autonomous subjectivity. If mediatized culture has moved from the simulated screens of the virtual to the modified bodies of embeddedness, I suggest that the notion of a virtual theatre was dead even as it first appeared, and that the more interesting works of contemporary performance that are concerned with the problems of digital culture are in fact not disturbed by the illusions and aesthetics of the virtual, but are dealing with the material and bio-politics of embeddedness. Important work in the problem of embeddedness includes Orlan's surgical interventions, Stelarc's prostheses, and Eduardo Kac's transgenic art not as conditions of virtuality, but as bodily explorations of embeddedness. Theatre and artists such as *La Fura del Baus*, *dumb type* and *SRS* are creating work not as reflections on the conditions of computer virtuality, but as bodily explorations of embeddedness. Other artists will hopefully attempt to understand what *embedded* information infection will mean to human communication and to propaganda. Art and theatre will remain the most useful of epistemological modalities for this process.

Società Raffaello Sanzio's Tragedia Endogonidia is a research project and performance cycle on the future of tragedy carried out over several years under the direction Romeo Castellucci. The project has consisted of eleven *Episodes* devised in different cities throughout Europe. Each of the performances carries with it the traces and suggestions of the city in which it was created. The final installment was performed December 2004 in the company's hometown of Cesena, Italy. During 2006, various episodes were presented throughout Europe. I will discuss the fourth episode of the cycle, a work created in Brussels and later performed at the Samuel Beckett Centre in Dublin, October 2004.

The performance is minimal in action, consisting of five scenes that roughly depict one lifetime from infancy to death. Language is used sparingly, with only a few letters uttered by a mechanical head and a muted and mumbled recitation of the *Hail Mary*. Castellucci's stage in *BR.04* is a closed space of white marble, illuminated by fluorescent lights hung from the ceiling (Figure 8.1). The playing area is a room with no doors or windows,

Figure 8.1 BR.#04 Bruxelles/Brussel. IV Episodio della Tragedia Endogonidia, dir. Romeo Castellucci.
Pictured: Sonia Beltran Napoles.
Photo: Luca del Pia, Courtesy *Società Raffaello Sanzio*.

entrances or exits, a space within the space of the theatre. The traditional theatrical technology of a white, centre-drawn curtain separates the stage and the audience. The curtain is used to open and close each scene.

The first scene opens with a black woman alone on the stage. She wears the uniform of cleaning staff with a grey dress and white apron, gloves and socks. She mops the floor quietly and picks up pieces of crumpled paper. No other sound is heard but the faint echoes of her movement. Perhaps she is cleaning the residue of the later scenes of violence. After nearly four minutes of silent cleaning, she drags the mop in a large circle around the edges of the stage. She returns upstage centre next to her blue cleaning cart and very slowly inscribes figure eights along the floor with the mop. She stops and looks out toward the audience as the lights brighten and the curtain closes.

The cleaning and the circle and figure inscriptions in an empty room emote a timelessness, a mood of re-occurrence, a ritual preparation and a waiting. On the material level, they speak of servitude, of race and class, asking who it is that cleans up the mess of culture? Like the plumber in Genet's *The Balcony*, someone has to clean out the pipes. The scene sets the stage in a rhythm that invites the audience to a quiet contemplation.

The curtains are drawn back to reveal the second scene of an infant, perhaps one year old and wearing a white full-body sleeper suit (Figure 8.2). He crawls about the stage. Upstage right is a flat, wooden, white, free-standing head and shoulders, approximately two feet high. The eyes and nose of the figure are black squares and the mouth a black rectangle. The eyes open and shut while it slowly speaks the alphabet, a few letters at a time. The opening of the eyes and the voice are radio-controlled from the sound booth by the director. During the performances at the Beckett Centre, Castellucci was also running the lights and sound, conducting the work in a similar fashion to the stage incursions of Kantor and Foreman.

The child crawls to the figure, lifts himself up and even reaches into the eyes. Given the age of the child, his actions could not be choreographed and were open to a wide degree of chance. During the first night performance of the run, the child fell and began to cry, creating a palpable anxiety in the audience, whose natural response was to assist the seemingly helpless and solitary child. However, the child remained on stage, and no one moved in the audience, although Castellucci quickly had the curtain pulled and the next scene omitted to accommodate the distressed child.

The situation that occurred with the child highlights the concerns of the stage of *Societas Raffaello Sanzio*. The spectator watches a child whose knowledge of its performance is rudimentary, or at best playful. The child apparently has no awareness of its place in an aesthetic work. Does this lack of consciousness of performance, what Blau calls a *universal*, on the part of the performer, void its process as theatre? Or does the spectator's reading of the activity as performance suffice? If so, is that not a troubling aestheticizing of the unwitting performer? A similar problem occurs when

Figure 8.2 BR.#04 Bruxelles/Brussel. IV Episodio della Tragedia Endogonidia, dir.
Romeo Castellucci.
Pictured: The *bebé*.
Photo: Luca del Pia, Courtesy *Societas Raffaello Sanzio*.

animals enter the stage and their performance is likewise misunderstood.
If we are not seeing a performance or a moment of theatre, what are we watching? I suggest that if the spectator maintains a *free* relation to the subject,
and if the spectator can resist an aesthetic frame, one can witness a *bare-life*,
an immanence, and a becoming. As stated on the Romaeuropa 2005 website,
'the figures that live on stage [of Raffaello Sanzio] don't rely on any recognizable myth; you don't see any biographies emerge, but instead you see
biological matters, bio-political themes' (Fondazione Romaeuropa 2005).

All this talk of *life*, of *bare life*, of *immanence*, of *becoming*, is treacherous
and lies in a danger zone: 'Like Foucault, Deleuze is perfectly conscious of
the fact that any thought that considers life shares its object with power and
must incessantly confront power's strategies' (Agamben 1999: 162). Life is
a political object, and the political is invested with its own aesthetic that
turns on and reconfigures that life.

When a scene is revealed, the audience is often as watched as watching
by the actors. There is a mood of suspension, of narrative time avoided
and a real time evoked. The performers' bodies are *actual* moments in time
(the very old and the very young, the very black and the very white). The
toddler is as amused by the audience, as he is enchanting to watch, while
the old man is distraught, seemingly lost and dazed, but evocative of his

own chronology. On the traditional stage of wings and drops, entrances and exits, there remains much that is hidden and subsequently revealed. In the claustrophobic space of this white room all that is revealed is the *bare life* of the performer.

What does this child do? Is it performing? Will it repeat the letters from a machine? What is this machine?

> Technology is present on the stage as metaphor and spirit. Technology and machines are bearers of phantoms who inhabit the set, the stage – the concept is animistic. So a machine has an entrance and an exit, it lights up, it takes up a chunk of the world; in short, it creates its own world. So it's quite clear that it's not merely a gadget, a decoration, because it is energized and it is triggered by argument with the actor, and thus it has in some way a dehumanizing function. It dehumanizes the actor, puts him in danger, places him in the paradoxical position of deuteragonist, so that finally it creates an inhuman tension.
>
> (Castellucci 2004: 17)

Yet the unknowing machine, manipulated by the director by means of a radio-controlled device from within the lighting booth, meets its performative double in the naïve toddler, creating a very human moment which had a restraining influence on the audience reception of the performance. The figure is a language machine, a teacher who has become a machine, a product of language and the law communicating the brokerage of the past with the agent of the future. *BR.04* was devised in and for Brussels, the seat of government control for the European Union, and the interchange of language, the law and the *bare life* of the individual is played out through the performance in response to that locale.

> The machine, unlike the animal, is inhuman because it's pure function without experience. The actor falls exactly between these two camps, between animal and machine, he's both things at the same time, pure function and pure exposed body, pure being. Technology becomes a central metaphor and, as such, it's often more useful to hide it in order to make it effective: it's the operation or action of the machine that's important, not the machine itself.
>
> (Castellucci 2004: 17)

When the lights come up on the third scene, the curtain remains closed. Standing in front, her back to the audience, is a woman in a long black Victorian-styled dress with bustle and black gloves. Her brunette hair is long, but noticeably thinning on top. She holds her left arm behind her, her hand holding the right arm. The curtain quietly opens, and the child is again on-stage. Upstage left is a freestanding large white screen, and downstage right is a high stand with a film projector. The projector turns on and spools a film-loop of a bonfire, which runs throughout the scene. The woman enters the stage and points to the film with a rod she carries. Along a diagonal, parallel to the line of the film projection, she repeats four steps forward and four steps back. She picks up the child, and standing downstage-centre she holds him to her torso, facing him and herself to the audience. The curtain closes.

What is on or in the film of the fire? Is it a traumatic memory, a scene of primal violence that reappears on celluloid as a new eccyclema, rolling out a *tableau vivant* of the long or newly repressed? Is the image an inheritance, a gift to the child who will forever have to face its occurrence? The effect of the stage image is to present a loss of the primal scene, to rid the *tragedy* of the choral response, or narrative order and to leave within that absence the sacrificial event of life.

The life established through the law is performed in the fourth scene, which opens on an empty stage save a chair placed downstage-left (Figure 8.3). Garments are draped over the chair. An old man enters through the proscenium at downstage right. His white beard is long and his head is bald on top but long on the sides. He wears an orange- and red-flowered bikini with sandals, upon each of which is one pink flower. He wanders about the stage watching the audience and wringing his hands. He shakes his head and taps his forehead, appearing confused, anxious and distraught. He goes to the stage-right and upstage walls and quietly and slowly pounds the wall. On his hands and knees at centre-stage, he crawls toward the audience. The humiliating attire of the garish costume and the dignity of the performer's presence collide in this solitary white room; like a Beckettian figure absurdly experiencing some profane truth or divine illusion, the old man draws us uncomfortably close. He rises from his crawl and walks to the chair, beginning to dress himself in white garments of a rabbi or priest. He puts on an armband with the number two on it. The robe he dons is inscribed with Hebrew text. Over the top of these white sacred garments, he begins to dress himself in the uniform of policeman, soldier or security guard. Oddly, the blue uniform he puts on is strikingly similar to those worn by the police in Stanley Kubrick's film *A Clockwork Orange*. The allusion is backed up or hinted at by the fact that an image of the film advertising, the well-known picture of Malcolm McDowell, appears on the performance's programme. The stage set itself resembles the white room of the climactic scene of Kubrick's *2001*, and even the narrative itself seems like an extension of the infinite or eternal moments in *2001*'s white room.

The process of the old man dressing is very slow, taking nearly ten minutes from his first entrance. This is not a theatrical time, like what might happen on the stage of Robert Wilson, tortuously drawing time out to a virtual stand still, but rather a real time. The old man dresses himself, neither hurriedly nor retarded. The movement from child-like naiveté to uniformed authority, from playful clothing to spiritual garb, and ultimately to uniform of the law, communicates clearly. Upon the body we place the signs of the self,

God, and the law, and with each layer the subject's life is further removed, further subject to control and party to the repression. After he is dressed in the uniform with shoulder holster and cap, he sits and waits. Two metal rings are lowered on wires from the fly space. He gets up, grabs the rings and fails to lift himself up. Another man in the same uniform enters downstage right. He carries a plastic bottle filled with red liquid, which he pours out on the floor upstage right. Around the perimeter of the *blood* he places four folded cards with a single letter printed on them: 'B', 'D', 'J', and 'C'. He takes out a tape measure, measures the distance between the lettered cards and jots down the information in a small notebook. He moves to the old man and whispers in his ear. He loosens the old man's hands from the rings and walks him off-stage at the downstage left proscenium.

Two more men in similar uniforms enter from downstage right. One of them carries a white object shaped like a traditional image of the tablets of Moses. He places the object next to the side of the blood pool. The other man with his back to the audience and facing the blood, removes his gun and undresses himself to his underwear. He sits in the blood. The other man begins to beat him with a baton, and each blow is accompanied by a thunderously loud crash that shakes the theatre. The beating continues for nearly five minutes as the victim wallows in the blood. The aggressor

Figure 8.3 BR.#04 Bruxelles/Brussel. IV Episodio della Tragedia Endogonidia, dir. Romeo Castellucci.
Pictured: Luca Nava (in uniform) and Sergio Scarlatella.
Photo: Luca del Pia, Courtesy *Societas Raffaello Sanzio.*

pours more blood on the victim, whose face is swollen and bruised in highly realistic stage makeup. The other policeman, who escorted the old man off-stage, reenters and joins in the beating. The first policeman dons white gloves and unzips the canvas covering over the white tablets, which are blank. The sounds of the beating morph and dissolve into an intense crackling sound as the violence heightens. The police drag the victim to the tablets and use one of his bloodied feet to mark the tablets red and turn them over. As the tablets fall, the room returns to silence. They carry the man to the chair and sit him down facing the audience.

The victim peers through his swollen eyes at the always-already implicated audience as more blood is poured over his face (Figure 8.4). The police place a microphone on a stand in front of him. He trembles and rocks in the chair. He is pushed lightly to the floor, and one of the police drags his body into a black trash bag, sealing the top. The bag is tied off, and his heavy breathing makes the black plastic rise up and down. The policeman places

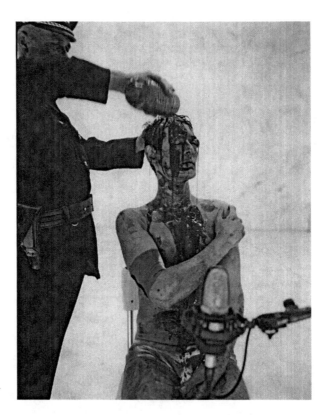

Figure 8.4 BR.#04 Bruxelles/Brussel. IV Episodio della Tragedia Endogonidia, dir. Romeo Castellucci.
Pictured: Sergio Scarlatella and Claudio Borghi (in uniform).
Photo: Luca del Pia, Courtesy *Sòcietas Raffaello Sanzio.*

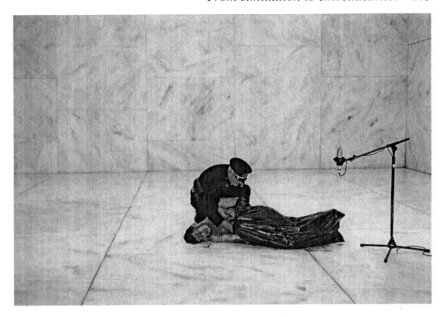

Figure 8.5 BR.#04 Bruxelles/Brussel. IV Episodio della Tragedia Endogonidia, dir. Romeo Castellucci.
Pictured: Claudio Borghi (in uniform) and Sergio Scarlatella.
Photo: Luca del Pia, Courtesy *Societas Raffaello Sanzio.*

the microphone on the floor in front of the bagged body. The figure inside quietly chants the *Hail Mary* between choking and gasps of breath, for nearly three minutes (Figure 8.5). At this point in the Dublin performance, a number of audience members left the theatre, perhaps twelve to fifteen people out of the two hundred present. The rest remained in what seemed a rather stunned silence.

The policemen pours out the blood, sets up a perimeter marking the spots of trauma, and measures the distance between two of the letters. What is the distance between two letters? What lies in the gap? It is the blood trace of the body. The blood is spilt first, then the letters are placed around the borders of the blood. Measurements are taken as to the distance between the letters and the blood. A message, conveyed; a secret is whispered from one authority to the other. The policeman who undresses is not forced. He prepares himself as a willing sacrifice. He abandons himself recalling Jean-Luc Nancy's model of a 'compulsion to appear absolutely under the law' (Nancy quoted in Agamben 1998: 58). The tablets that are revealed are blank. The words will come later. First the blood, then the letters, next the body, then the *tabla rasa,* finally the words scrolled on the darkened screen separating the stage from the disappearing old man. What we see presented on this stage is the intimate relation of violence and the law. Violence is used to establish and maintain the law. Culture, as articulated by

Benjamin in *Critique of Violence*, 'establishes as law not an end immune and independent from violence, but one necessarily and intimately bound up with it' (Benjamin quoted in Agamben 1998: 65) in order to control life.

BR.04 enacts the sacrifice of the body to the demands of the law. On this stage language forms the boundary upon which the body is brutalized. Without the body, the language has no mark. The performance dispenses with narrative and character for a corporeal embodiment of time and space. Drawing on classic forms of tragedy the work sheds the critique of the chorus and the death of the hero in favour of fact-based episodes. What type of tragedy sees its hero never die, loses the wisdom of its chorus and remains rooted in the state of things as they are? It is, in my estimation, a tragedy of bio-politics about the positionality, function and freedom of life as a pure immanence.

The fourth scene continues with the bagged body of the victim still trembling on the stage. The fluorescent lights begin to flicker and flash. The effect is created in part by a slowly rotating fan placed in front of a projection lamp positioned at Castellucci's lighting and sound table. An adolescent boy wearing a black top hat, Edwardian style overcoat, and high-heeled boots enters from the downstage left proscenium. He carries a cane and a black, long, cloth sack, which he places against the stage-right wall. A black, foot-long, horn-like protrusion is strapped to his chin, and he wears a small black mask. The woman in black from the third scene enters the stage and hands the boy an envelope on a white dish, which he opens and reads. A string hangs from the woman's mouth. The boy tugs on the string, and the woman's head bobs with each pull. She takes hold of the string and pulls out a bloody object, spitting blood onto the white dish. The black woman from the first scene enters. She is dressed in a similar fashion to that of the other woman, with a long black bustled dress and gloves. She has her cleaning cart with her, and she carries a black trash bag over to the bagged victim. She reaches into her bag and removes what appear to be animal organs, laying them in front of the victim. The white woman presents the white dish stained with blood to the black woman who places it on the stage next to the victim. The white woman kneels, and the black woman whispers in her ear and then combs her hair.

The boy opens the cloth sack to reveal an illuminated fluorescent light, which he shines on the women. The black woman pulls hair from the brush, which has fallen from the other woman's head (Figure 8.6). She places the hair in the open hand of the white woman, who stands, drops the hair to the ground, runs her hand over her balding head and screams. The boy breaks the light in the sack with his foot. Metallic sounds scrape the air. The black woman, in stylized movement, mimes hitting the boy with the hair-brush. The white woman turns to the audience smiling a hideously pained and demented grin. The boy places the top hat on the black woman as she ties a leather choker around the neck of the other woman. A black double of the white tablets descends from the fly space upside down, and upon

Figure 8.6 BR.#04 Bruxelles/Brussel. IV Episodio della Tragedia Endogonidia, dir. Romeo Castellucci.
Pictured: Sonia Beltran Napoles and Claudia Castellucci.
Photo: Luca del Pia, Courtesy *Societas Raffaello Sanzio.*

them are hung locks of black hair. The boy runs his hands through the hair from the black tablets. The black cords that hang from the choker on the white woman are tied by the boy to the animal organs on the victim. The three figures walk upstage, dragging the organs behind them. A small white house that resembles the alphabet figure in the second scene rolls across the length of the downstage proscenium.

The torture of the victim has brought a cruel complexity to the stage. Up to this point in the performance, a simplicity, a quiet, held sway. At this point in the performance, amidst the trauma, it is as if all connections of the body in pain were severed. The scene is a piling up of unprocessed traumas, and an abyss of psychic terrors is unearthed. A precipitation of a tragic moment rains in the theatre. No reflective or tragic consciousness appears, but rather the violent moment where seeds are planted in the wounds of all witnesses to the event. The spectre of the law first revealed as the white tablets that seek the sacrifice of blood to write the text now return blackened, reversed and upside-down, carrying the traces of disease and death. Life escapes the law in the reversal of death.

Our intention with this production is to rethink tragedy, bring it into the here and now. In ancient Greece, the Episodes were sections of a tragedy that presented only the facts, without commentary; commentary was left to the Chorus. In Tragedia Endogonidia there is no Chorus. Out of the Episodes emerge basic recurring figures and forms, themes and ideas, which make the spectators aware of their existence, their state of being.

(Castellucci 2004: 17)

Life, now un-sacrificeable, is crushed and exterminated in the work of bio-politics. *BR.04* confronts the will to truth of the neo-iconoclast with a sacrificial semblance. The work takes on the challenge to individual sovereignty in a presentation of bare life, appearing as it must through a here and now in time and space. The performance shows the life that is no longer sacrificeable, but simply placed out with the garbage; the production of a corpse: the terminal point of modern technology.

The performance concludes with the old man sitting on hospital bed eating bread from a paper sack. His uniform is draped on a chair next to the bed, and he wears white underwear. He covers his head with a white balaclava and gets under the sheets of the bed. Slowly, imperceptibly at first, in a brilliant bit of stage illusionism, he sinks and disappears into the bed. A black scrim closes across the stage. The boy in the top hat enters and stands by the bed. A video projection of illegible, Hebrew-like text scrolls across the scrim as a meditative and plaintive piano plays.

A very real and tender moment, a bit of grace is afforded the figure that vanishes in the bed. Like Oedipus at Colonus, whose apotheosis through suffering concludes his life, this figure descends past the world to disappear in the impossible moment of his own death. However, the stage continues the fiction of the narrative, even though the event is over and the hero now absent. The curtains pull shut to play at the simulation of a closure in the end credits scrolling. But behind the scrim lurks the little man with the big hat inspecting the remains of the corruptible flesh.

Lukacs, quoting Paul Ernst, wrote in *Soul and Form* that 'only when we have become completely godless shall we have tragedy again' (1974: 154). So perhaps when considering the worlds that lay ahead, we can say we have become just that and, therefore, we might just regain that which has been lost. Romeo Castellucci, in an interview published in the *Performing Arts Journal*, states:

My tragedy project is called *Tragedia Endogonidia* or *Endogonidial Tragedy*. 'Endogonidial' is a word taken from microbiology; 'gonidial' refers to simple living forms that have inside them two gonads, thus both sexes, and they consequently reproduce through an endocrine system. The price they have to pay for being able to reproduce themselves is not conjunction, union, but division, a perpetual division of themselves. These living things are immortal. The interesting thing was to contrast these two words. Tragedia or tragedy is something that is part

of our history (or at least the history of this side of the planet); its structure has a place at the origin of our consciousness and our culture.
"Endogonidial" on the other hand, is a word that falls completely outside
culture, in the sense that there is no culture in this process of reproduction and survival. So while tragedy is a mechanism to expose the
dead body, a mechanism whose fundamental aim is to display death,
these micro-organisms are in fact immortal and reproduce themselves
ad infinitum. "Tragedia" or "tragedy" on the other hand, presupposes an
end (of the hero).

(Castellucci 2004: 17)

Castellucci, in an almost surrealist fashion, links the opposing terms of
tragedy – which is culturally, geographically, and historically specific, grounded
on death – and endogonidial, which is outside culture, biological, but figured
as immortal. Thus we have the cultural specificity of a historical biology, an
immortal death, which seems profoundly similar to Nietzsche's eternal return
or Hegel's good infinity. Our biology is tragic, or as Artaud wrote, 'I tell you
microbes have been invented. . .' (1995: 305–6). The event that takes place
in *BR.04* is a godless sacrifice of sacrifice that reveals the possibility of a
free relation to life. The primal scene is not repressed historically or
compressed in time, but obsessively gazed upon here and now. An empha-
sis on the event and not on the re-presentation of that event through a choral
re-appraisement is the manner in which the spectators are made 'aware of,
their existence, their state of being' (Castellucci 2004: 17).

When we combine the art works, propagandistic manipulations and
atrocities above with the embedding technologies of genetically modified
and technologically supplemented plants and animal, Western culture finds
itself at a new stage of 'the era of the spectacle' where the site of power
has shifted from the exterior screens of simulation to the interior body of
the material subject.

After decades of televisual simulations and mediatized misinformation,
the will to truth has become an equally dangerous impulse. Perhaps it is
time to re-learn the *jouissance* of the sensual surface of illusion and have
done once and for all with the fascistic tendencies of the true believers who
seek the metaphysical domains of truth.

Embeddedness threatens, beckons and promises; beckoning extensions
and improvements to the body that might aide the disabled, assist in
curing disease, ease some suffering while promising to develop the
human/machine interface to an enlightened level. It threatens to allow
undesirable manipulations of information and biological borders. Standing
at the centre is the immanent life, whose freedom we can either value and
let live or repress and control.

9 The theatre and its negative
Event, truth and the void

> There is perhaps no discourse more entangled with what it would address than discourse on the essence of truth. There is perhaps no questioning less capable of detachment from what it would interrogate.
>
> (Sallis 1993: 28)

> [...] we can reach what truth is, and how it presences, only by *interrogating* it in respect of its own *occurrence*; above all by asking after *what* remained *un-happened* in this history and which was closed off, so much closed off that ever since it has seemed as if in its primordiality it *never was*.
>
> (Heidegger 2002: 228)

> For the process of truth to begin, something must happen. What there already is – the situation of knowledge as such – generates nothing other than repetition. For a truth to affirm its newness, there must be a *supplement*. This supplement is committed to chance. It is unpredictable, incalculable. It is beyond what is. I call it an event. A truth thus appears, in its newness, because an evental supplement interrupts repetition.
>
> (Badiou 2003: 62)

A question in response to this book

Throughout this study I have tried to position theatre and performance in technoculture and to articulate the processes of their aesthetics, metaphysics and politics while considering various subject positions within the phenomena. Employing the writings (primarily) of Agamben, Badiou and Heidegger, alongside the dramas of Beckett, Genet and Shakespeare, and the theatre of Kantor, Foreman, *Socìetas Raffaello Sanzio* and *The Wooster Group*, I have driven the argument to the following question: if contemporary technoculture operates under the regime of embeddedness that seeks to infect information from within while colonizing the body through science and technology, and if the new site of the struggle for sovereignty within bio-political systems is the *bare life* of the individual, how can the theatre produce an effective response?

In answer to the query above, I offer a prolegomenon to a new line of inquiry regarding the theatre and its negative, or a theatre of negation. I pursue a questioning around the artistic configurations of the theatre as a *singular* event of thought, a *truth-procedure* and possible site of an *event*, which, through a process of subjectification of the individuals who nominate the event, contributes to the appearance of the radically new, a truth, an exceptional break with the state of things as they are. I am using Alain Badiou's and Martin Heidegger's divergent philosophical models to understand what is meant by an *event*, a *situation* or *structured presentation* of be-ing as in the case of Badiou and *Ereignis* (event) in terms of Heidegger, both of whom see it as a moment of radical potentiality. Against this event theory, I fashion and, finally, reject, a theatre regarded as a sacrifice, considering instead what a sacrificing of theatre within itself might mean by supplementing sacrifice with a subtractive logic of a negative theatre (theatre minus theatre). I do this to bring the questioning toward how the theatre event might re-establish a link with the philosophical questions regarding *truth* and *freedom*.

My theory, or my best guess (if the truth of my thesis be fully disclosed), is that the sacrificing of theatre within itself and the thinking of the theatre thought *can* take place and clear a sacred space (the void), in which a freedom, in Heideggerian terms as *a comportment to allowing things to be in and of themselves*, and a truth, in Badiou's terms as a radical potentiality for transformation and innovation, can *happen*. If it can happen, then it will happen rarely, admittedly, no doubt, rarely, if ever.

Structurally, I begin the argument with a parsing of Badiou's notion of the truth event and how that system can modulate our understanding of theatre practice.[13] I bring in, but only briefly, Heidegger's assessment of *truth* and *freedom* to develop this model further. In considering the event of theatre as a thinking of the sacrificing of theatre that creates a space for the *bare life* of the subject to be illuminated, I construct my own cult of ruins by building a bricolage of fragments on the idea of sacrifice. I arrange these portions and segments, or glimpses and glances, of various theories of sacrifice from Hegel to Agamben in order to position how social practice and psychic process is understood. The discourse surrounding sacrifice is understandably far-reaching and crosses multiple fields of research; it is, therefore, a highly contested concept. The various theories of sacrifice can be ordered under the categories of metaphysical, cultural, psychological, mimetic and bio-political. I do not attempt a thorough commentary of each class, but instead draw the sources together to form a picture of sacrifice that I think is useful in thinking through the theatre, or, more precisely, thinking the theatre. The sacrifice that concerns me here is one that can be built on transgression, but circumvents the barbarism, violence and repression, or the fascism that Benjamin accused Bataille's theory of sacrifice of practicing. I thereby respond to the appeal of Jean-Luc Nancy regarding the need to engage 'both the end of real sacrifice and the closure of its phantasm' (38). Noting the problems inherent in the logic of sacrifice, I substitute and supplement (yet another sacrifice?) the model of sacrifice for a strategy of subtractive logic.

I hope to demonstrate the possibility of a theatre that, in words borrowed from Artaud, will *have done with the judgement of god* and an onto-theological theatre of sacrifice, toward a sacrificing of theatre itself, a theatre and its negative, so that the theatre may yet again *take place.* Beckett is already there, of course, as a paradigm of subtractive staging practices: less, always less, towards worsening. Castellucci is thinking the theatre as an event that can absorb tragedy, so that the possibilities, situations, and conscious-ness, are moments of potentialities, not exhausted aporias. Specifically, I draw on Beckett's late television play *Ghost Trio* (1976) and its inculca-tion of the presence of the void to disclose my point.

It seems that there is too much for this chapter to contain, and should likely be considered a prolegomenon to indicate the starting point of this ending. The chapter, in posing a question in response to the rest of the book, asks: if all of what has been argued, or even a portion of what has been argued, is true, then what comes next?

Badiou and Heidegger/truth and freedom

The terms, *truth* and *freedom* are impossibly loaded, nearly comical and nearly finished; nearly comical, aping the intro to a *Superman* comic, and nearly finished in the postmodern and poststructuralist critique of any posi-tion not radically relative. The terms are ideas whose power has been co-opted and profaned in contemporary political rhetoric and should not be left to falter on the terms of a questionable ideology. In Heidegger's philos-ophy, truth and freedom are interwoven phenomena and activities. Truth is not a simple correspondence of thing and concept, but rather is the occurrence of the *unhiddenness of beings.* Freedom is not unfettered liberty past all social barriers, but a *comportment to letting things be.* In other less, only slightly less, tortuous Heideggerian phrasing, *truth* is when something is fully disclosed, fully illuminated in and of itself; and freedom is the ethi-cal will and the capacity to let that happen, which requires sacrifice. Simply put, in Heidegger's thought the metaphysics of truth and freedom are grounded as ethical considerations. I am aware of the difficult associations attached to the terms, not just to truth and freedom, but to concepts like sacrifice, and *unhiddenness* and *comportment to letting things be.* Perhaps I should place all these terms *sous rature* or under erasure. But that runs against my project to regain their power within theatre. I know I threaten to alienate the theatre specialist who may find this theory all too theoretical, and displease the philosopher who may find the borrowing of Heidegger and Badiou too reductive. I can only point toward the conclusions and func-tions of the concepts, not the complexities of their processes, and it is my hope that the theory will illuminate the conditions and utility of a theatre responsive to the bio-political systems of technoculture.

As I noted in Chapter 6, in challenging traditional metaphysics, various philosophers such as Heidegger, Badiou and Žižek argue for a conception of being not as transcendental structure or objectivity, but as *event, act, happening, occurrence, structured presentation* or *situation*. These notions of the *event* model a historicity of being, which suggests an engagement with truth as a decisive moment, a turning, a fundamental change or interruption to the *state of things as they are*. These occurrences of being are based on performative choices and chance and are similar to what, traditionally, one might think of as the essence of drama (e.g. *Antigone*). The event and performativity of being that these philosophical models propound can help expand our knowledge of how the theatre and drama function.

Badiou is working within the twilight of poststructuralism and postmodernism, and thus insists on a resistance to the sophistry of deconstruction's fatal strategies – of the linguistic limitations of the 'language games' of nothing but opinions – and a saturation of the polyvalence of meanings. Badiou's notion of truth is highly nuanced and challenging to a poststructural or postmodern theoretical framing. It taunts what Žižek states is a 'psuedo-Nietzschean "deconstructionist's" notion that "truth" is a fixed, constraining order imposed by some Power on to the free thriving of our life-sustaining imagination' (2000: 79). Badiou poses a challenge to rethink what we have thought for a long time. The *event* articulates a *truth*, which is contingent, historical and subjective, and which represents a radical break within a given situation, a 'boring of a hole in knowledge' (repetition) to allow a truth (newness) to be nominated by the subjects to that truth. The truth-event *happens*, according to Badiou, at the edge of the void, the unknown of any situation, and that void is constitutive of the event itself. Later I will discuss Beckett's *Ghost Trio*, which can help us see how the presence of the void, or the presence of its edge, is presented as unpresentable in the presentation itself. *Ghost Trio*, like Badiou's model of a truth-event, presents the figuration of an un-decidable event summoning an indiscernible subject who nominates the procedure as a generic truth, which is forced through fidelity and ethical consistency, toward an unnameable good or evil, 'a pure choice between two indiscernibles' (Badiou 2003: 63).

Badiou considers truth to be a revolutionary progression of newness, a radical potentiality for transformation and innovation, beginning through an evental site, occasioning through artistic configuration, romantic love, scientific discovery or political action (and *only* through art, love, science and politics), and operating as a supplement not a component. The undecidedable event recognized and nominated is a process of subjectification as it calls forth individuals who, through fidelity to the idea, constitute themselves as subjects to its truth.

For example, in Badiou's model of romantic love, you ask yourself, 'is this real, am I in love'? There is an undecidable event: you meet someone and something happens, something incalculable, unpredictable. 'What there already is – the situation of knowledge as such – generates nothing other than repetition' (2003: 62) In that something that is happening are now two indiscernible subjects operating within a finite structure of the event, which may or may not be nominated or recognized. 'A truth must be submitted to thought, not as a judgement but as a process in the real.' (2003: 61). Nominating the truth is a groundless decision as it begins with an undecidable event, because the 'rules of established knowledge' are not in play. If the answer is 'yes' it will require a fidelity to that unexpected something that happened, that truth of love. Through commitment, fidelity, naming and performing: 'I love you and I promise myself to you' (and here one can see the performative nature of this whole process), the event of something happening becomes a truth to which the individuals, through fidelity, establish themselves as subject. 'This event has taken place, it is something which I can neither evaluate, nor demonstrate, but to which I shall be faithful' (2003: 62). It cannot be proved. A decision has to be made and a choice hazarded (a universal of drama?). You take a chance. Badiou suggests another example of a truth procedure:

> For example, the work of Sophocles is a subject for the artistic truth – or procedure – of Greek tragedy, a truth begun by the event of Aeschylus. This work is a creation; that is, a pure choice in what, before it, was indiscernible. And it is a finite work. However, Tragedy itself, as an artistic truth, continues toward infinity. The work of Sophocles is a finite subject of this infinite truth. In the same way, the scientific truth decided by Galileo is pursued to infinity.
>
> (2003: 63)

The trajectory of many of the *heroes* in the canon of Western drama are built on this model, or, more correctly argued, Badiou's model is built on the drama. Narratives such as Antigone's commitment to the burial of Polyneices, or the devotion to love of Romeo and Juliet, Hamlet's resistance to the call for revenge, or even Gogo and Didi's cyclical waiting game are illustrations or preceding models for Badiou's thought. Each of these characters fashion their subjectivity around an indiscernible event or thing (a belief, a love, a ghost, a Godot). The drama unfolds as the deviances and detours to their commitment are tested and challenged.

Badiou is aware of the dangers of this model. He argues that forcing from generic truth to an unnameable limit is the danger zone of any truth event (e.g. the romantic problem of absolute love, the scientific problem of science as integral truth and the political problem of totalitarianism). The unnameable is the Real of any truth, and the evil of any truth is 'always a desire for omnipotence of the true. 'Evil is the desire for "Everything-to-be-said"' (2003: 67). It is the negative of this becoming that needs to be held to: 'The event is undecidable, the subject linked to the indiscernible, truth itself is generic, untotalizable; and the halting point of its potency is the unnameable' (2003: 67). All these negatives of the undecidable, indiscernible, untotalizable and unnameable are the subtractive logic whose remains represent the ground, the void upon which a subject is constructed. It is the theatre of the negative being, the human, who is, according to Hegel in the *Phenomenology of Spirit*, 'that which he is not and not that which he is' (quoted in Agamben 1991: xii).

Badiou, a playwright himself, writes of the theatre:

> I do not believe the main question of our time to be that of horror, suffering, destiny, or dereliction. We are saturated by these notions, and besides, their fragmentation into theater ideas is truly incessant. On all sides, we are surrounded by a choral and compassionate theater. Our question instead is that of affirmative courage, of local energy. To seize a point and hold it.
>
> (2005: 75)

I would argue that theatre and performance theory need a similar shot in the arm or poke in the face to work against the constant recourse to paradigms of exhaustion, endings and failures, and seize the point, in this case, to think the theatre.

I want to draw one more idea from Badiou, to which I have been alluding, regarding the nature of the theatre. Alain Badiou's model of the *thinking of theatre* states that the theatre, as an artistic procedure, embodies a unique *theatrical-idea* and *theatre-thought*, which can appear only through performance and acts as 'an illumination of history and life', an *eventful site of truth*. The ideas created in the theatre are singular theatre-ideas, and 'they cannot be produced in any other place or by any other means' (2005: 72). Badiou states, 'the idea arises in and by performance, through the act of theatrical representation. The idea is irreducibly theatrical and does not preexist before its arrival "on stage"' (72). The event of thought that takes place as a theatre idea and which may become the eventful site can be thought of as housing a truth that is both immanent and singular: immanent, in that truth is internal to the effects of theatre and that theatre is not an instrument of an external truth; and singular, in that the truth that happens in theatre is given nowhere else but on the stage.

The theory of sacrifice

Economic model

The primary model of Western sacrifice is an economic one. I sacrifice something of value so that I will receive something in return. According to Marcel Mauss on the *gift* or Georges Bataille on the *potlatch* ceremony of North American first peoples, a sacrificial expenditure is a manner of gaining power, control or wealth. St. Thomas Aquinas outlines the Christian notion of sacrifice, which is itself based on expenditure and return. According to Aquinas, the three paths of sacrifice include martyrdom, austerity and works of justice and worship. The exchange value for these activities includes remission of sins, preservation of grace and acquisition of glory. It is the law of return that has held sway for so long. I will sacrifice so long as I win out in the end. René Girard, in *Violence and the Sacred*, works from a similar Christian perspective and sees sacrifice as means of production, a method of purification. He distinguishes *good* violence from *bad* violence and argues both for and against the formalist perspectives of sacrifice as a deliberate act of collective substitution performed at the expense of the victim, and absorbing all the internal tensions, feuds and rivalries pent up within the community.

Theorists such as Freud and Girard model the theatre as a cultural strategy for the representation of, and substitution for, the sacred horror of ritual sacrifice and violence. For Freud the founding of Western culture is based on the sublimation of sacrifice, and this is the ground upon which the subject and culture are constructed. According to Freud in *Totem and Taboo*, the sacrifice or substitution killing of the father is the repressive basis of culture. Sacrifice and, later, the theatre, are constructed as collective substitutions performed at the expense of the victim, while resolving the tensions and dramas of the wider community. The theatre carries the trace, or ghost, of the sacrifice, but also the same model of expenditure and return.

Western theatre and drama are built primarily on these notions of the exchange value (and sacrificial logic) of entertainment and knowledge. There have been challenges to the commodification of theatre in performance art (Vito Acconci) and sometimes, the theatre itself (*The Living Theatre* or even perhaps Grotowski's practice of para-theatrics, or Beckett's philosophical interruptions), nonetheless, the exchange mode of production remains dominant. Is our only viable paradigm of theatre basically a business model, a manager's view of art production (i.e. 'how many bums are there in the seats, tonight'?)? Are there alternatives to a capitalist model of consumption theatre, to what Brecht called a *culinary theatre*? Or are we back to the logic of late capital?

The model of sacrifice as the basis of theatre and drama is a rather unproblematic equation, folding as it does on much of the birth of democracy, legal systems and literary theory of Aristotle. Each and every social system requires the letter and the law, which in turn grants a limited agency. But the Greeks held no illusion of an absolute free will but understood choice as an over-determined process contextualized by community, the polis, the divine and the interiority of the subject. For any freedom enacted that might exhibit the hubris of mastery or autonomy, like Agamemnon's stroll on the purple carpet, or Oedipus's torturing of Teiresias for the answers he already knows, or Creon making the demands of the law of the state upon the individual, there is a precipitous fall. The outcome is a process in which a new freedom is brought to a polis, not an individual right that aspires to unfettered free choice, but an agency embedded in a polis wherein actions are enlightened by others.

> The tragic turning point thus occurs when a gap develops at the heart of the social experience. It is wide enough for the oppositions between legal and political thought on the one hand and the mythical and heroic traditions on the other to stand out quite clearly. Yet it is narrow enough for the conflict in values still to be a painful one and for the clash to continue to take place. A similar situation obtains with regard to the problems of human responsibility that arise as a hesitant progress is made toward the establishment of law. The tragic consciousness of responsibility appears when the human and divine levels are sufficiently distinct for them to be opposed while still appearing to be inseparable.
>
> (Vernant 1990: 27)

The birth of the theatre arrives through a tragic consciousness and a litigious chain of events that pits individual agency against the concerns of society. The pattern set out by Vernant above is a series of choices leading to a moment of sacrifice that has the potential for tragic consequences, and hopefully for tragic consciousness. Just as every thought is a negation of the former idea, so every action or event requires a choice, which necessitates a sacrifice. Agamemnon chooses to sacrifice his daughter, Iphigenia, so as to advance to Troy. Agamemnon chooses to step upon the carpet, sacrificing his humility and character. The sacrifice sets the stage for the tragic action constructed on choice, with combat between the individual and the polis, necessity and fate, the material and metaphysical, between two equally balanced rights. If we consider what Blau outlines as universals of performance (e.g. consciousness of performance, etc.), have we not uncovered an even more fundamental order, or at least contributor? And if not in the world of performance, then certainly of the theatre and its drama, which as Blau notes haunts all performance? The order of choice, sacrifice and tragedy are the equation or nuclear structure of theatre. Sacrifice and tragedy – but also excess and comedy – orchestrate the theatre. In the end, every action is a sacrifice, as something is given up, given away, but for what or to whom, with what returns or demands?

Sacrifice, mimesis, transgression

> And what is meant by this proximity between unspeakable sacrificial wisdom, as the initiation into destruction and violence, and the negative foundation of philosophy? Here the problem of the absolute foundation (of ungroundedness) reveals its full weight. The fact that man, the animal possessing language, is, as such, ungrounded, the fact that

he has no foundation except in his own action (in his own 'violence'), is such an ancient truth that it constitutes the basis for the oldest religious practice of humanity: sacrifice.

(Agamben 1991: 105-6)

Cultural theorists and many aestheticians claim that there is an obvious link between sacrifice and mimesis. Sacrifice is the violent ground upon which culture and subjectivity is constructed, but is sublimated as mimesis in the form of ritual, which is in turn sublimated into the theatre, and further to art, television, virtuality, etc. Each step is a move away from the sacred horror of sacrifice and the authentic experience of the body in time toward a comfortable and evasive abstraction. Agamben's thesis above is clear, drawn from Heidegger and Hegel: that the human is foundationless, an ungrounded being, a negative. The human is ungrounded in the sense of possessing no foundational truth or transcendental signifier as support. We make it up from scratch, from our actions, our violence performed through sacrifice, our thoughts through negation. That supposition coupled with Heidegger's implication that the human is always in error and Hegel's notion (again) that the human always appears as one 'who is that which he is not and not that which he is' (quoted in Agamben 1991: xii), sets up a subtractive logic whose remains seem very close to the landscape of Beckett. This model of identity suggests the need for a performative gesture or act, a theatre or an art, a happening, which can redouble the negative of the human, to turn the *that is* toward a that which *is not*, an epistemological modality of momentary freedom that allows the *other* and the self to be. Nancy writes, '"sacrifice" means appropriation of the Self in its own negativity' (25). Is that not one way to see Beckett's theatre, as an *appropriation of the Self in its own negativity*, and thus a sacrifice, in Nancian terms?

Theatre is one modality of the negative foundation of philosophy of which Agamben is speaking. Its function can be to construct the fictive ground upon which a sacrifice, or a sacrifice *sous rature* – or better yet, a subtraction, a negative, a negation – can be performed that might present a glimpse of a process capable of staging the unspeakability of sacrificial mystery, a *structured presentation* of the *situation* of be-ing, a corporeal metaphysics. If there is this proximity between 'unspeakable sacrificial wisdom' and 'initiations through destruction and violence', and the 'negative foundation of philosophy', thought and subjectivity, the theatre should be an occasion and situation for that matrix to be mimetically activated, understood and lived through. The language of the theatre is a platform or stage for the negative beings, what Heidegger calls 'the placeholder for nothingness' (quoted in Agamben 1991: xii) to be present to an event: an *Ereignis*, a clearing, a freedom, a grounding truth of letting things be.

The negative logic of the stage is the redoubled reflection of the subject, which firstly presupposes the world of appearance as mere appearance, what Hegel calls (and Žižek glosses) the *positing reflection*. The second stage of Hegel's perceptual system of reflection is the presupposition of the thing itself as aware of itself, as otherness or *external reflection*. Finally the thing presupposes itself as positing, or the subject for whom consciousness considers itself considering, the *determinate reflection* of the subject. The process is one of a *no there there*. The redoubling begins as 'I' sees 'it' as mere appearance, then 'I' sees 'I' as part of the mere appearance, and then 'I' sees 'I' seeing 'I' as mere appearance, thus staging a negation of 'I'. Basically, it is the dramaturgy of Beckett's *Film*. Everything on the stage is sacrificed and appears as that which *is not*, and the redoubling reflection of the theatrical reappears as that which primordially, or materialistically-metaphysically, *is*. The theatre is a redoubled, negative reflection in which the groundlessness, the situation of be-ing of the human, finds a here and now, a home and dwelling place in the world. Theatre is the sacrifice and appropriation of the self in its own negativity, as Nancy intimates, and it is a sacrifice of the self that negates and makes the nothingness apparent.

As I mentioned in an earlier passage, Georges Bataille and Julia Kristeva understand art as a mimicry of sacrifice that remains a transgression, which has the potential (danger?) to appropriate death and violence, to return to what Genet models as art's trajectory from cruelty to absence to death. The pattern repeats and is seen in multiple models of art, including Kant's sacrifice of the imagination in his idea of the sublime, or as Nancy writes: 'isn't one dominant representation of art that of the transgressive exposition of a subject, who thereby appropriates himself and lets himself be appropriated? (28). Much of my own discussion in this book has exercised a sacrificial logic of a self sacrificing the self, for an otherness as salvation. The quote below was briefly referenced in the preceding chapter:

> For Kristeva, as for (Nancy's reading of) Bataille, art lets one commune, by means of a transgression that is still effective, with the enjoyment of instantaneous appropriation of death. Art mimics sacrifice in order to preserve one 'suspended' on the edge of nothingness. But art maintains the sacrificial moment, and sacrificial logic does not leave off re-appropriating (trans-appropriating) death.
>
> (Keenan 2005: 44)

Sacrifice is that suspension between the simulacrum and nothingness, a liminal moment of doubling vision that challenges the subject. Bataille sought the liberative potential in the conjunction of violence and an atheistic 'religious spirit' that necessarily remains lodged in a mimetic field. He argues against the construction of sacrifice as a mode of production. Bataille's theory of sacrifice is essentially an Artaudian model (actor's signalling through the flames) and an operation of loss, of failure, which entails the *throwing of the self* toward an *otherness*, with little chance of a return.

Sacrifice functions as a technology for placing things outside the world of things and is constituted by an operation of loss.

Bataille's theory of sacrificial violence is seductive, but its intimacy with fascism, barbarism and terror is unacceptable and has been critiqued by Benjamin and Nancy. However, neither is the Christian idea of sacrifice of much use, enacting as it does the sacrifice of God, which serves all mankind, severing individuals from their own ritual sacrifice of sovereignty, stealing the essential moment of crisis, choice, agency and freedom. The role of sacrifice in the radical political actions of suicide bombers, working to right the wrongs of the physical world while gaining paradise and 72 virgins in the bargain, seems likewise suspect. The sacrificial demands of America's military industrial complex demonstrates yet another crisis for the concept. These problems are why recuperating a practice of sacrifice is of concern. Nancy, in his article 'Unsacrificeable', challenges Bataille's attraction to the horror in the transgression of taking a life in sacrifice. Nancy is concerned with the horror of sacrifice and even the ghosting of that horror in the sublated sacrifice of art. I agree with Nancy's model, coupled with Agamben's extension of the 'demystifications of sacrifical ideology' (1998: 113). But I realize, to paraphrase a line from Paul Taylor Anderson's great film *Magnolia*, 'we might be through with the sacrifice, but sacrifice isn't through with us'.

Out of those critiques, what could be useful in the notion of sacrifice? Hegel's model of reflection? Or, what if we were to follow the admonitions of sacrificing sacrifice? What would we witness? To burn down all the elements of the machinery of the stage, the technologies of representation of the theatre, to see a theatre that posits itself, that is doubled over, which vanishes, reappears, transformed. What remains is a sacrifice that is not repressive, but transgressive, that is useful through its uselessness. By creating a negation of theatre as Beckett and Castellucci do, an entirely new model of art and performance takes place, a negative space upon which a comportment to letting things be can occur.

The sacrifice of theatre

I am trying to imagine a theatre event constructed on a subtractive logic (theatre minus theatre) whose remainder is the void, 'the unpresentable link that connects, or "suture", any situation to its pure be-ing' (Hallward 2003: 65) and from which radical change might appear, in order to make visible, as Badiou writes, that which cannot be seen by Empire. Recall Badiou's theses quoted in an earlier chapter that the goal of art is to 'render visible to everyone that which, for EMPIRE (and so by extension for everyone, though from a different point of view), doesn't exist' (2004: 86). My questioning draws from Badiou's philosophical logic, mathematical theory, and Beckett's theatre that seizes, in the case of philosophy, articulates in the case of set theory, and presences, in the case of Beckett, the void. The void is the nothing that *is*, that which remains undecidable, indiscernible, untotalizable, and unnameable, but whose being makes a sacred space for the thingness, materiality, and historicity of the event. In turn, it is the evental site that pursues (welcomes, witnesses) a subject to truth through convocation, fidelity and commitment. Beckett's *Ghost Trio* is a demonstration of a subtractive theatre (television) whose remainder is a void that engages not a fatalistic nihilism, but a last stage, a final worsening that propels, such as the comma of 'I can't go on, I'll go on'. *Ghost Trio* can be read as a metaphor of the loss of the other, the horror and suspense of the void, but that reduces its importance. It is not representation of the approach of the void, but is an evental site for the presentation of the void. It is the remainder, the void that remains, which leads us to the place where Beckett's stage is inaugurated and it determines the eliding of the stage to the screen of the cinema and television, making distinctions between live performance and mediated representations all the more difficult. The logic of subtraction and the appearance of the void is a concept echoed through much of the history of Western philosophy, including Žižek's Hegelian discussion of the negation of negation, or Jean-Luc Nancy's sacrifice of sacrifice. It is, as Rex Butler argues glossing Žižek glossing Badiou, 'the truth is what reveals the void from which the existing situation stands in' (Butler 2005: 88).

Beckett is not the only one to follow this model. Consider the mid-career theory of Jerzy Grotowski and his notions of *encounters* in his own subtractive theatre (theatre minus illusion) of what he called *Holiday* or the day that is holy. By removing notions of spectacle, stage, audience, etc., he worked toward an actual meeting or occurrence. The interesting point is that it began through a negation of theatre. I am interested in understanding the negative equation of removing something from itself (a present absence) resulting in a remainder of a void, which leads to an art-procedure of the making or placing of an evental site for the appearance of a truth as a radical break with the state of things as they are: to make invisible things and situations appear. *Societas Raffaello Sanzio*'s performance cycle *Tragedia Endogonidia* would likewise operate under this regime. Remember from the last chapter Castellucci's thoughts on a tragedy without a chorus, with only episodes in uncontextualized situations.

The ontology of the theatre

To begin thinking a theatre idea or thinking the thought of theatre we need to begin by discussing the ontological nature of the phenomenon then expand to its appearances and material operations: 'Ontology always gathers up what remains to thought once we abandon the predicative, particular determinations of "that which is presented"' (Badiou quoted in Hallward, 51).

> What can be said of a being as a be-ing says nothing about its material
> qualities (its shape, purpose, history, and so on). The discourse that
> claims to present presentation in general must withdraw from any
> constituent relation with what is presented.
>
> (Hallward 2003: 57)

Subtract all that is presented to attain the remainder of what essentially *is*.
In theatre and performance studies there has been much discussion of the
ontology of performance in recent years, most famously put forward by
Peggy Phelan in *Unmarked*. However, what is theorized is non-ontological,
speaking not of its essence, but rather identifying its operational processes
such as disappearance.

Badiou speaks of what occurs as a *situation* in which all that exists
happens in a structuring and counting operation. To exist is to belong to a
situation. And all that is within the situation can be counted as *one*.
However, each *one* is only structured in that manner; each one is actually
multiple. A prop is placed in an empty set. It is counted as one: one hat.
One glove. One staircase. But each is ghosted by its multiplicity. And
because this multiplicity is unpresentable, it figures as nothing; but it does
figure as nothing. In Badiou's mathematical modelling, drawn from the set
theory of Georg Cantor and others, suggests that it is 'perfectly coherent to
affirm the being of the nothing. The nothing is, it is not nonbeing'
(Hallward, 65). In an immanent potentiality the ghost figures as nothing,
not absence of being. The void is pure immanence, the gate at which
everything stands waiting.

Mathematical set theory can help us to understand how this void exists
and operates as generative of all that is. A set is a collection whose
members could be any things: words, numbers, names. We can imagine a
set of Aeschylus, Sophocles, Euripides. Subsets of this set would be any
combination of the three, such as a set with only Aeschylus, or a set of
Aeschylus and Euripides, etc. A bigger set is created of all the subsets of
one set. But it is the concept of the empty set that is illustrative of what we
are approaching.

The remarkable result of the invention or discovery of the empty set is
the ability to generate all natural numbers from nothing.

> Define the number zero, 0, to be the empty set, $\emptyset$, because it has no
> members. Now define the number 1 to be the set containing 0; that is
> simply the set {0} which contains only one member. And since 0 is
> defined to be the empty set, this means that the number 1 is the set that
> contains the empty set as a member {$\emptyset$}. It is important to see that this
> is by no means the same thing as the empty set. The empty set is a set
> with no member whereas {$\emptyset$} is a set containing one member.
>
> (Barrow 2000: 166)

An easier way to go at this, as described by John Barrow in his popular science title *The Book of Nothing*, is to think of an empty cartoon thought bubble as the empty set. Now think of that thought, which is like creating the set that contains the empty set, which is what we call the number 1. Now think the thought of the thought of the empty set. This is the mathematical model for creating structure out of nothing.

To reiterate there is a situation (a stage set, if you will) within which all is counted as one, but which is ghosted by its infinite, unknowable multiplicity (and multiplicity is a banal fact of any situation, not a referral to a transcendental signifier). The multiplicity, which cannot be represented, figures as the being of nothing. Badiou calls it the unstructurable something that haunts the situation and threatens to erupt, such as a rising of the masses in revolution. In the theatre it is perhaps all that we leave offstage hidden in the *skene*, that might erupt as the tragic or the comic. This spectre of the void is ominous and threatening, and the State (politically speaking) and the state of things (situationally speaking) employ mechanisms of foreclosure to challenge any event taking place that exceeds the boundaries of the power of what is known. The void requires control from the state of things. This unhinging or interruption of the state of things as they are, which reveals an invisible impossible thing, is the event of a truth. 'The central idea of my ontology is the idea that what the state seeks to foreclose through the power of its count is the void of the situation, and the event that in each case reveals it' (Badiou quoted in Hallward, 100).

Ghost Trio

Written in 1975 and first presented on the BBC in 1977, I am working from a video of the German television production for SDR, *Geistertrio*, which Beckett directed himself. The play, or the tape, begins as Beckett's text demands, on a general view of a grey room 6 metres by 5 metres. A female voice, a faint voice, states, 'Look [*Long pause.*] The familiar chamber. [*Pause.*] At the far end a window. [*Pause.*] On the right the indispensable door. [*Pause.*] On the left, against the wall, some kind of pallet. [*Pause.*]' (Beckett 1986: 408). The picture shows, barely, the 'sole sign of life a seated figure'. A series of inserts shows formal perspectives of the floor, window, door and wall. All are shades of grey rectangles of varying dimensions (*nice dimensions, nice proportions*). The voice asks, or requires, the viewer to look again. Look again, as more than likely, you have not seen it all, or perhaps, look again, *as you have not seen what is not there.* The window, the door, the pallet, all of whose edges seem nearly invisible, a grey on grey, undecipherable, indiscernible, mark the edge of the void, which is locatable 'even if the void itself is not' (Hallward, 117). On the stage that is screened on the television, recognizable differences are nearly imperceptible, until the objects are used when the door or window are opened.

The camera pushes in toward the figure who holds a cassette player on his lap, and the sound of Beethoven's Fifth Piano Trio, *Ghost Trio*, is heard. A cassette tape is played by the figure on the videotape, an electronic recording of an electronic recording, always receding from presence, as the female voice states, 'He will now think he hears her' (410). The disembodied voice (over) of the other states what she thinks he thinks he hears. And what he hears is that nobody is there: 'No one'. In the first section of the tape, the camera eye presents the pallet, floor, window, and door. In the second section, the figure visits what had been displayed, and finds no one, no thing there. In the third section, which repeats parts of the preceding action, the male figure listens at the door, makes his way to the window and pushes it open to the 'rain falling in dim light', observes the palette (with a camera zoom), and looks into the mirror on the wall and sees not much there. He opens the door, and in the corridor a small boy in 'black oilskin with hood glistening with rain' shakes his head faintly to the 'invisible f' or figure (413). What is outside the window, the door, and in the corridor? Nothing? Everything? Both? Loss? Gain? Pure immanence? Is it the be-ing of the nothing that is?

Deleuze writes of *Ghost Trio* that, 'Even the pallet is so flat that it bears witness to its void' (1997: 172). But Deleuze sees the work as a process of depotentialization, the undoing of potential, as an artifact of metaphysical exhaustion.

> And when the little silent messenger suddenly appears, it is not to announce that the woman will not be coming, as if it were a piece of bad news, but to bring the long awaited order to stop everything, since everything is truly finished.
>
> (1997: 171)

Deleuze loses the thread of potentiality and immanence of the void. The voice from the first part states, 'the light; faint, omnipresent. No visible source. As if all luminous.' All luminous, but the light issues from where? Is it from an unnameable limit? 'Now look closer. [*Pause.*] Floor'. (408). The smooth, vague rectangles are presented on the screen like the abstract paintings of Mark Rothko or Kasimir Malevich. What is on the screen is the infinite struggle or seduction of the thing and the void of the situation. There is a boundary, but only barely. But then the crux (the dénouement?) is played out, the decisive moment at the beginning of the play, which signals the ending. 'Now look closer. [*Pause.*] Floor. 3. Cut to close up of floor. Smooth grey. Rectangle. 0.70 m × 1.50 m. 5 seconds. 4. Dust. [*Pause.*] Having seen that specimen of floor you have seen it all' (408). Has the viewer seen all of the floor or seen *it* all? What can be seen is a generic floor like a generic truth, for which all the rest of the floor is but infinite repetition, duplication. 'Wall', she says. Cut to wall. 'Dust'. From dust to dust, from floor to wall, the edges seem less defined.

Every truth thus proceeds from that point in a situation where all recognizable differences are at their most imperceptible, at that place where, according to the criteria of distinction operative in the situation, there is 'almost nothing'. Every truth begins in the place that the situation represents as desert or wasteland, a place devoid of what the situation recognizes of value and promise.

(Hallward 2003: 120)

Beckett's insistent subtraction takes us to a point where all recognizable differences are at their most imperceptible, at a point where this almost nothing appears and little happens. In the clearing is a wasteland, corpsed, and then redoubled, negated toward the field of opportunities and the occasion of the end as the eventual site for the beginning of a radical newness through the theatre and its negative.

Notes

1 I am making reference to Merleau-Ponty's distinction between 'physiological facts which are in space and psychic facts which are nowhere' in Maurice Merleau-Ponty, *Phenomenology of Perception* (1962: 77).

2 See Michael Walsh, 'Jameson and "Global Aesthetics"' in *Post-Theory: Reconstructing Film Studies*, ed. David Bordwell and Noel Carroll (Madison: University of Wisconsin Press, 1996), 481-500, for further reading on the topic of post-Lacanian, post-theoretical film studies.

3 See Herbert Blau, *The Audience* (1990) and Peggy Phelan, *Unmarked* (1993), as useful examples of Lacanian theory applied to the field of theatre and performance studies.

4 See 'The Most Concealed Object' in Blau, *The Audience* (1990: 50–94), for an analysis of the scopic drive in theatre practice and spectatorship.

5 The gaze, or more specifically the male gaze, may be one of the most misused terms in the critical theory of performance. Lacan writes this of the gaze, 'In our relation to things, in so far as this relation is constituted by the way of vision, and ordered in the figures of representation, something slips, passes, is transmitted, from stage to stage, and is always to some degree eluded in it, that is what we call the gaze' (Lacan, 1981: 73).

6 Lacan has this to say regarding the nature of the split subject: 'In my opinion, it is not in this dialectic between the surface and that which is beyond that things are suspended. For my part, I set out from the fact that there is something that establishes a fracture, a bi-partition, a splitting of being to which the being accommodates itself, even in the natural world' (Lacan, 1981: 106).

7 See Robert Ayers (1999).

8 The history of automata construction and fascination is well rehearsed in *Living Dolls* (2002) and *The Mechanical Turk* (2002).

9 Video of the automata is available through T.I.L. Production in Paris at www.automates-anciens.com.

10 A theme that runs through this essay can be paraphrased as the 'liquidation of subjectivity in the space of technology'. Troublingly, this notion seems to follow the nightmare scenario of the evolution of technology toward the Final Solution. The danger of technology lies in its consumption of the destinies of the human and it is not difficult to see the destiny of the machine at the collapse of the human and the destruction of the earth. I can sense this pressure on my thesis. I, and others who follow the call of technology, should be cautious.

11 *Principium individuationis*, the principle of individuation, is drawn from the writing of Schopenhauer and Nietzsche and refers to the illusion of identity as a separate and autonomous entity.

12 See Virilio (1986).

13 Badiou's philosophy has profound implications for how we think the theatre and several theatre scholars have recently addressed his ethics and ontological models. These include a cluster of articles in *Performance Research* (9: 4) December 2004, by Janielle Reinelt, Adrian Kear and Alan Filewod. Reinelt questions how political theatre practice can usefully encounter Badiou's thought, but remains sceptical, especially to any discussion of a *universal* operating in theatre. Her critique of Badiou's theory argues for why Badiou does not serve the

concerns of political theatre. But it is my impression he is speaking to a different process at the inauguration of a truth, as opposed to the negotiations of earlier established states of things. Reinelt chastises Badiou for drawing on 'great' moments in history and Western art to draw his conclusion, while missing the smaller moments of political resistance and commitment, such as the Dixie Chicks's episode of criticizing the US president. Reinelt is further concerned with any recourse to a notion of universality, and she is, perhaps, right to be so. Adrian Kear gives a more supportive reading and astute gloss of Badiou's thinking, drawing on his ontological and ethical models to understand how performance operates as an event of timed interruptions inherent in theatre practice. Amanda Stuart Fisher in an article titled, 'Developing an Ethics of Practice in Applied Theatre; Badiou and Fidelity to the Truth of the Event' in *Research in Drama Education* Vol. 10, No. 2, considers, in an affirmative manner, if Applied Drama practices of community drama would benefit from understanding its processes through Badiouian ethics of fidelity to the truth.

Works cited

Adorno, T. W. (2000) *Metaphysics: Concept and problems*, ed. R. Tiedemann, trans. E. Jephcott, Cambridge: Polity.

Aeschylus (1953) *Aeschylus I: Oresteia*, trans. R. Lattimore, Chicago: University of Chicago Press.

Agamben, G. (1991) *Language and Death: The Place of Negativity*, trans. K. E. Pinkus with H. Hardt, Minneapolis: University of Minnesota Press.

—— (1998) *Homo Sacer: Sovereign Power and Bare Life*, Stanford: Stanford University Press.

—— (1999) 'Absolute Immanence' in *An Introduction to the Philosophy of Gilles Deleuze*, ed. J. Khalfa, London: Continuum, 151–69.

Arendt, H. (1958) *The Human Condition*, Chicago: University of Chicago Press.

Artaud, A. (1958) *The Theatre and Its Double*, New York: Grove Press.

—— (1995) *Watchfiends & Rack Screams: Works from the Final Period*, trans. C. Eshleman, ed. B. Bador, Somerville: Exact Change.

Auslander, P. (1992) *Presence and Resistance: Postmodernism and Cultural Politics in contemporary American performance*, Ann Arbor: University of Michigan Press.

—— (1997) *From Acting to Performance: Essays in Modernism and Postmodernism*, London: Routledge.

—— (1999) *Liveness: Performance in a Mediatized Culture*, London and New York: Routledge.

Ayers, R. (1997) 'Orlan: A Woman who Refuses to Suffer', in *Live Art Letters* (18: 1), 4–6.

Bablet, D. (1962) *Edward Gordon Craig*, New York: Theatre Arts Books.

Badiou, A. (2002) *Dissymetries: On Beckett*, eds. N. Power and A. Toscano, Manchester: Clinamen Press Limited.

—— (2003) *Infinite Thought: Truth and the Return to Philosophy*, trans. O. Feltham and J. Clemens, London: Continuum.

—— (2004) 'Fifteen Theses on Contemporary Art', in *Performance Research* (9: 4), 86.

—— (2005) *Handbook of Inaesthetics*, trans. A. Toscano, Stanford: Stanford University Press.

Barrow, J. (2000) *The Book of Nothing*, London: Vintage.

Barthes, R. (1977) *Image Music Text*, trans. S. Heath, New York: Hill and Wang.

Bataille, G. (1991) *The Accursed Share, Vols. II and III*, trans. R. Hurley, New York: Zone Books.

—— (1991a) *The Impossible*, trans. R. Hurley, San Francisco: City Lights Books.

Baudrillard, J. (1988) *Selected Writings*, Stanford: Stanford University Press.

—— (1995) *The Gulf War Did Not Take Place*, trans. P. Patton, Bloomington: Indiana University Press.

—— (1996) *The Perfect Crime*, trans. C. Tucker, London: Verso.

—— (2002) *The Spirit of Terrorism*, New York: Verso.

Beckett, S. (1964) *Endgame*, London: Faber and Faber.

—— (1986) *Samuel Beckett: The Complete Dramatic Works*, London: Faber and Faber.

Benjamin, W. (1968) *Illuminations*, ed. H. Arendt, trans. H. Zohn, New York: Schocken Books.

—— (1977) *The Origin of German Tragic Drama*, New York: Verso.

Berghaus, G. (1998) *Italian Futurist Theatre 1909–1944*, Oxford: Clarendon Press.

Bhabha, H. K. (1994) *The Location of Culture*, London: Routledge.

Blau, H. (1987) *The Eye of Prey: Subversions of the Postmodern*, Bloomington: Indiana University Press.

—— (1990) *The Audience*, Baltimore: Johns Hopkins University Press.

Blau, H. (1992) *To All Appearances: Ideology and Performance*, New York: Routledge.

Boal, A. (1985) *Theatre of the Oppressed*, New York: Theatre Communications Group.

Bourdieu, P. (1990) *The Logic of Practice*, trans. R. Nice, Cambridge: Polity Press.

Brecht, B. (1964) *Brecht on Theatre*, ed. J. Willet, New York: Hill and Wang.

Butler, J. (1993) *Bodies That Matter: On the Discursive Limits of Sex*, New York: Routledge.

Butler, R. (2005) *Slavoj Žižek: Live Theory*, London: Continuum.

Callens, J. (ed.) (2004) *The Wooster Group and Its Traditions*, Bruxelles: Peter Lang Publishers.

Case, S. (1996) *Domain-Matrix: Performing Lesbian at the End of Print Culture*, Bloomington: Indiana University Press.

Castellucci, R. (1999) Programme Notes to *Genesi: from the Museum of Sleep*.

—— (2004) 'The Universal: The Simplest Place Possible,' interviewed by V. Valentini and B. Marranca in *Performing Arts Journal*, PAJ 77, 16–25.

Causey, M. (2001) 'We Shall Be Monsters: The Performance Technology Research Laboratory (PTRL),' in *Theatre Forum*, 18, 42–51.

—— (2003) 'Cyber-theatre' in *Oxford Encyclopedia of Theatre and Performance, Vol. 1*, ed. D. Kennedy, Oxford: Oxford University Press, 341.

Craig. E. G. (1983) *Craig on Theatre*, ed. J. M. Walton, London: Methuen.

Cooper, S. (2002) *Technoculture and Critical Theory: In the Service of the Machine?*, London: Routledge.

Cronenberg, D. (1983) *Videodrome*, Universal Pictures.

D'Amelio, J. (1984) *Perspective Drawing Handbook*, New York: Van Nostrand Reinhold.

D'Arcy, E. (1993) 'The eye and the projectile,' in ed. T. Fry, *RUA/TV?: Heidegger and the Televisual*, Sydney: Power Publications, 104–16.

Damisch, H. (1995) *The Origin of Perspective*, trans. J. Goodman, Cambridge, MA: MIT Press.

DeBord, G. (1983) *Society of the Spectacle*, Detroit: Black and Red.

Deleuze, G. (1986) *Cinema 1: The Movement-Image*, trans. H. Tomlinson and B. Habberjam, Minneapolis: University of Minnesota Press.

—— (1989) *Cinema 2: The Time-Image*, trans. H. Tomlinson and R. Galeta, Minneapolis: University of Minnesota Press.

—— (1997) 'The exhausted', in *Essays: Critical and Clinical*, trans. D. W. Smith and M. A. Grotto, Minneapolis; University of Minnesota Press, 152–74.

Derrida, J. (1978) 'The Theatre of Cruelty and the Closure of Representation' in *Writing and Difference*, trans. A. Bass, Chicago: University of Chicago.

Derrida, J. (1991) *Of Spirit: Heidegger and the Question*, trans. G. Bennington and R. Bowlby, Chicago: University of Chicago Press.

Diderot, D. (1974) 'Encyclopedia', in *Dramatic Theory and Criticism: Greeks to Grotowski*, ed. B. Dukore, New York: Holt, Rinehart and Winston, 287–91.

Dienst, R. (1994) *Still Life in Real Time: Theory after Television*, Durham: Duke University Press.

Dyens, O. (2001) *Metal and Flesh: The Evolution of Man: Technology Takes Over*, Cambridge, MA: MIT Press.

Eagleton, T. (2003) *Sweet Violence: The Idea of the Tragic*, Oxford: Blackwell.

Filewod, A. (2004) 'Impurity and the Postcolonial Subject' in *Performance Research* (9: 4) 95–8.

Fisher, A. S. (2004) 'Developing an Ethics of Practice in Applied Theatre; Badiou and Fidelity to the Truth of the Event', in *Research in Drama Education* (10: 2) 247–52.

Flaubert, G. (1980) *The Temptation of St. Antony*, trans. Kitty Mrosovsky, London: Secker and Warburg.

Fondazione Romaeuropa (2005) *Romaeuropa Festival 2005*, http://www.romaeuropa.net (accessed on 10 August 2005).

Foreman, R. (1976) *Plays and Manifestos*, ed. K. Davey, New York: New York University Press.

—— (1985) *Reverberation Machines: The Later Plays and Essays*, New York: Stanton Hill Press.

—— (1992) *Unbalancing Acts: Foundations for a Theatre*, ed. K. Jordan, New York: Pantheon.

Foucault, M. (1983) *This Is Not A Pipe*, trans. J. Harkness, Berkeley: University of California Press.

—— (1970) *The Order of Things: An Archaeology of the Human Sciences*, New York: Pantheon Books.

Freud, S. (1950) *Totem and Taboo: Some Points of Agreement Between the Mental Lives of Savages and Neurotics*, trans. J. Strachey, New York: W. W. Norton and Co.

—— (1955) 'The Uncanny', in *The Standard Edition of the Complete Psychological Works of Sigmund Freud, Vol. 17*, trans. and ed. J. Strachey and A. Freud, London: Hogarth Press and the Institute of Psycho-analysis, 217–52.

Fried, M. (1968) 'Art and objecthood', in *Minimal Art: A Critical Anthology*, ed. G. Battcock, New York: E. P. Dutton and Co.

Fry, T. (1993) *RUA/TV: Heidegger and the Televisual*, Sydney: Power Publications.

Genet, J. (1962) *The Screens*, trans. B. Frechtman, New York: Grove Press.

—— (1991) *The Balcony*, trans. B. Wright and T. Hands, London: Faber and Faber.

Giannchi, G. (2004) *Virtual Theatres: An Introduction*, London: Routledge.

Gilpin, W. (2000) 'The Principles of Painting Considered, so Far as they Relate to Prints', 'Observations of the River Wye', 'On Picturesque Beauty', 'On Picturesque Travel', in *Art in Theory 1648–1815: An Anthology of Changing Ideas*, ed. C. Harrison, P. Wood, and J. Gaiger, Oxford: Blackwell, 820–3, 836–8, 857–861.

Greenblatt, S. (1988) *Shakespearean Negotiations: The Circulation of Social Energy in Renaissance England*, Berkeley: University of California Press.

Gropius, W. (ed.) (1961) *The Theater of the Bauhaus*, trans. A. Wensinger, Mittletown, CN: Wesleyan University Press.

Grosz, E. (2001) *Architecture from the Outside: Essays on Virtual and Real Space*, Cambridge, MA: MIT Press.

Hallward, P. (2003) *Badiou: A Subject to Truth*, Minneapolis: University of Minnesota Press.

Hansen, M. (2004) *New Philosophy for New Media*, Cambridge, MA: MIT Press.

Haraway, D. (1990) 'A Manifesto for Cyborgs: Science, Technology and Socialist Feminism in the 1980s', in ed. L. J. Nicholson, *Feminism/Postmodernism*, New York: Routledge, 190–233.

Hayles, K. (1993) 'The Seductions of Cyberspace', in ed. V. A. Conley, *Rethinking Technologies*, Minneapolis: University of Minnesota Press, 173–190.

———————— (1999) *How We Became Posthuman: Virtual Bodies in Cybernetics, Literature, and Informatics*. Chicago: University of Chicago Press.

Hegel, G. W. F. (1977) *Phenomenology of Spirit*, trans. A. Miller, Oxford: Oxford University Press.

Heidegger, M. (1977) 'The question concerning technology', trans. W. Lovitt, in *Basic Writings*, ed. David Farrell Krell, San Francisco: HarperSanFrancisco, 287–317.

———————— (1979) *Nietzsche, Vol. I: The Will to Power as Art*, trans. D. F. Krell, San Francisco: Harper Collins.

———————— (1996) 'The Age of the World Picture' in ed. T. Druckrey *Electronic Culture: Technology and Visual Representation*, New York: Aperture, 47–61.

——— (2002a) *The Essence of Human Freedom: An Introduction to Philosophy*, trans. T. Sadler, London: Continuum.

———————— (2002b) *The Essence of Truth: On Plato's Parable of the Cave Allegory and Theatetetus*, trans. T. Sadler, London: Continuum.

Heim, M. (1993) *The Metaphysics of Virtual Reality*, Oxford: Oxford University Press.

Hoberman, P. (1995) *Exhibition Notes to Barcode Hotel*, unpublished.

Hoberman, P. (1996) 'Barcode Hotel', in *Immersed in Technology*, ed. M. Moser and D. MacLeod, Cambridge, MA: MIT Press, 287–90.

Howard, R. (1999) *Edtv*, Universal Pictures.

Ihde, D. (2001) *Bodies in Technology*, Minneapolis: University of Minnesota Press.

Jameson, F. (1991) *Postmodernism: The Cultural Logic of Late Capitalism*. Durham: Duke University Press.

Kac, E. (1998) 'Transgenic art' in *Leonardo Electronic Almanac* (6: 11), http://mitpress.mit.edu/e-journals/LEA/ (accessed 20 March 2002) and http://www.ekac.org/transgenic.html (accessed 20 March 2002).

Kac, E. (2006) *Kac Web*, http://www.ekac.org (accessed 10 January 2006).

Kantor, T. (1993) *A Journey Through Other Spaces: Essays and Manifestos, 1944–1990*, ed. and trans. M. Kobialka, Berkeley: University of California Press.

Katz, D. (1999) *Saying I No More: Subjectivity and Consciousness in the Prose of Samuel Beckett*, Evanston: Northwestern University Press.

Kaye, N. (1994) *Postmodernism and Performance*, London: Palgrave.

Kear, A. (2004) 'Thinking Out of Time: Theatre and the Ethic of Interruption' in *Performance Research* (9: 4) 99–110.

Keenan, D. K. (2005) *The Question of Sacrifice*, Bloomington: Indiana University Press.

Kernodle, G. R. (1944) *From Art to Theatre: Form and Convention in the Renaissance*, Chicago: University of Chicago Press.

Kershaw, B. (1999) *The Radical in Performance: Between Brecht and Baudrillard*, London: Routledge.

Kirby, M. (1971) *Futurist Performance*, New York: E. P. Dutton.

——— (1987) *A Formalist Theatre*, Philadelphia: University of Pennsylvania.

Kleist, H. v. (1994) 'On the Marionette Theatre', in *Sources of Dramatic Theory*, ed. M. Sindell, Cambridge: Cambridge University Press, 235–40.

Lacan, J. (1977) *Ecrits: A Selection*, trans. A. Sheridan, New York: W. W. Norton and Company.

—— (1981) *The Four Fundamental Concepts of Psycho-analysis*, trans. A. Sheridan, New York: W. W. Norton and Company.

Lacoue-Labarthe, P. (1990) *Heidegger, Art and Politics: The Fiction of the Political*, Oxford: Blackwell.

Land, N. (1992) *The Thirst for Annihilation*, London: Routledge.

Larijani, L. (1993) *The Virtual Reality Primer*, New York: McGraw-Hill.

Laurel, B. (1993) *Computers as Theatre*, Reading: Addison-Wesley Publishing.

Levinas, E. (1969) *Totality and Infinity: An Essay on Exteriority*, Pittsburgh: Duquesne University Press.

Levinson, B. (1997) *Wag the Dog*, Tribeca Productions.

Lippard, L. R. (1973) *Six Years: The Dematerialization of the Art Object from 1966 to 1972*, London: Studio Vista.

Lukacs, G. (1974) *Soul and Form*, trans. A. Bostock, London: Merlin Press.

Lyotard, J. (1976) 'The Tooth, the Palm', trans. A. Knap and M. Benamou in *Sub-Stance* (15) 105–110.

——————— (1984) *The Postmodern Condition: A Report on Knowledge*, trans. G. Bennington and B. Massumi, Minneapolis: University of Minnesota Press.

——————— (1988) *The Inhuman*, trans. G. Bennington and R. Bowlby, Stanford: Stanford University Press.

—— (1989) 'Discussions, or Phrasing, "After Auschwitz"' in ed. A. Benjamin, *The Lyotard Reader*, Oxford: Blackwell, 360–92.

MacDonald, E. (1993) *Theatre at the Margins: Text and the Post-structured stage*, Ann Arbor: University of Michigan Press.

McKenzie, J. (1997) '*Laurie Anderson for Dummies* + *The "Puppet Motel"*, an Interactive CD-ROM', in TDR (41: 2) 30–50.

McMahon, M. (2005) 'Difference, Repetition', *in Gilles Deleuze: Key Concepts*, ed. C. J. Stivale, Bucks: Acumen.

Mann, P. (1991) *The Theory-Death of the Avant-Garde*, Bloomington: Indiana University Press.

Marcuse, H. (2001) *Technology, War and Fascism: Collected Papers of Herbert Marcuse, Vol. II*, ed. D. Kellner, London: Routledge.

Marinetti, F. T. (1991) *Let's Murder the Moonshine: Selected Writings*, ed. R. W. Flint, Los Angeles: Sun and Moon Classics.

Mascia-Lees, F., Sharpe, P. and Cohen, C. (1989) 'The Postmodernist Turn in Anthropology: cautions from a feminist perspective', *Signs: Journal of Women in Culture and Society*, (15: 1) 7–33.

Mazlish, B. (1993) *The Fourth Discontinuity: The Co-evolution of Humans and Machines*, New Haven: Yale University Press.

Merleau-Ponty, M. (1962) *Phenomenology of Perception*, trans. Colin Smith, London: Routledge and Kegan Paul.

Nancy, J.-L. (1991) 'The Unsacrificeable', in *Yale French Studies* (79) 20–38.

National Human Genome Research Institute (2006) *Genome.gov*, http://www.genome.gov (accessed 10 January 2006).

New York Times (19 September 2001) 'Attacks Called Great Art' in Arts/Culture Desk.

News at Nature (2004) http://www.nature.com/news/2004/041011/full/041011–9.html. Published online and accessed: 13 October 2004.

Nietzsche, F. (1967) *The Birth of Tragedy and the Case of Wagner*, trans. W. Kaufman, New York: Vintage Books.

Penny, S. (1994) 'Virtual Reality as the Completion of the Enlightenment Project' in *Culture on the Brink: Ideologies of Technology*, eds. G. Bender and T. Druckrey, Seattle: Bay Press, 231–48.

Phelan, P. (1993) *Unmarked: The Politics of Performance*, London: Routledge.

Pimentel, K. and Teixeira, K. (1994) *Virtual Reality: Through the New Looking Glass*, New York: Windrest, McGraw-Hill.

Pirandello, L. (1952) *Naked Masks: Five Plays*, ed. E. Bentley. New York: E. P. Dutton.

Rancière, J. (2004) *The Politics of Aesthetics: The Distribution of the Sensible*, trans. G. Rockhill, London: Continuum.

Reinelt, J. (2004) 'Theatre and Politics: Encountering Badiou' in *Performance Research* (9: 4) 87–94.

Rheingold, H. (1991) *Virtual Reality*, New York: Touchstone.

Ronell, A. (1989) *The Telephone Book: Technology, Schizophrenia, Electric Speech*, Lincoln: University of Nebraska Press.

Ross, G. (1998) *Pleasantville*, New Line Cinema.

Rutsky, R. L. (1999) *High Techne: Art and Technology from the Machine Aesthetic to the Posthuman*, Minneapolis: University of Minnesota Press.

Sallis, J. (1993) 'Deformations: Essentially Other than Truth', in *Reading Heidegger: Commemorations*, ed. J. Sallis, Bloomington: Indiana University Press, 29–46.

Savran, D. (1988) *Breaking the Rules*, New York: Theatre Communications Group.

Sayre, H. (1989) *The Object of Performance: The American Avant-Garde since 1970*, Chicago: University of Chicago Press.

Schechner, R. (1973) *Environmental Theatre*, New York: Hawthorn Books.

—— (1988) *Performance Theory*, New York: Routledge.

Scheibler, I. (1993) 'Heidegger and the Rhetoric of Submission: Technology and Passivity', in *Rethinking Technologies*, ed. V. C. Conley, Minneapolis: University of Minnesota Press, 115–42.

Schlemmer, O. (1961) 'Man and Art Figure', in *The Theater of the Bauhaus*, ed. W. Gropius, Mittletown, CN: Wesleyan University Press.

—— (1990) *The Letters and Diaries of Oskar Schlemmer*, ed. T. Schlemmer, trans. K. Winston, Evanston: Northwestern University Press.

Speer, A. (1970) *Inside the Third Reich*, trans. R. Winston and C. Winston, New York: Macmillan Publishing Co.

—— (1976) *Spandau: The Secret Diaries*, trans. R. Winston and C. Winston, New York: Macmillan Publishing Co.

Stelarc (1984) *Obsolete Body/Suspensions/Stelarc*, ed. J. Paffrath, Davis: JP Publications.

Stockhausen, K. (2001) 'Message from Professor Karlheinz Stockhausen', in *Karlheinz Stockhausen Homepage*, http://www.stockhausen.org/message_from_karlheinz.html (accessed on 10 January 2006).

Stone, A. R. (1995) *The War of Desire and Technology*, Cambridge, MA: MIT Press.

Survival Research Lab (2006) *SRL: Survival Research Lab*, http://www.srl.org (accessed on 10 January 2006).

Tomas, D. (1991) 'Old Rituals for New Space: Rites de Passage and William Gibson's Cultural Model of Cyberspace', in *Cyberspace: First Steps*, ed. M. Benedikt, Cambridge: MIT Press, 31–48.

Turkle, S. (1995) *Life on the Screen: Identity in the Age of the Internet*, New York: Simon and Schuster.

Vanden Heuvel, M. (1993) *Performing Drama/Dramatizing Performance: Alternative Theatre and the Dramatic Text*, Ann Arbor: University of Michigan Press.

Vanderbilt, T. (2004) 'The Real da Vinci Code', in *Wired Magazine* (12: 11).

Vernant, J.-P. and Vidal-Naquet, P. (1990) *Myth and Tragedy in Ancient Greece*, New York: Zone Books.

Villa, D. R. (1996) *Arendt and Heidegger: The Fate of the Political*, Princeton: Princeton University Press.

Virilio, P. (1986) *Speed and Politics*, trans. M. Polizzotti, New York: Semiotext(e).

—— (2002) *Desert Screen: War at the Speed of Light*, trans. by M. Degener, New York: Continuum Publishing.

Walsh, M. (1996) 'Jameson and "Global Aesthetics"', in *Post-Theory: Reconstructing Film Studies*, eds. D. Bordwell and N. Carroll, Madison: University of Wisconsin Press, 481–500.

Weir, P. (1998) *The Truman Show*, Paramount Pictures.

Williams, R. (1973) *Television: Technology and Cultural Form*, Glasgow: Fontana.

—— (1975) *Drama in a Dramatised Society*, Cambridge: Cambridge University Press.

Wittgenstein, L. (1981) *Tractatus Logico-Philosophicus*, trans. C. K. Ogden, London: Routledge and Kegan Paul.

Wolford, L. and Schechner, R. (eds) (1997) *The Grotowski Sourcebook*, London: Routledge.

Wolska, A. (2005) 'Rabbits, Machines, and the Ontology of Performance', in *Theatre Journal* (57: 1) 83–95.

Wood, G. (2002) *Living Dolls: A Magical History of the Quest for Mechanical Life*, London: Faber and Faber.

Woolley, B. (1992) *Virtual Worlds*, London: Penguin.

Wooster Group, The (1989) Programme Notes for *Frank Dell's The Temptation of St. Antony*, unpublished.

—— (2002) Programme Notes for *To You, The Birdie!*, unpublished.

Žižek, S. (1994) *Mapping Ideology*, London: Verso.

—— (1997) *The Plague of Fantasies*, London: Verso.

—— (1999) *The Ticklish Subject: The Absent Centre of Political Ontology*, London: Verso.

—— (2000) *The Fragile Absolute: Or, Why is the Christian Legacy Worth Fighting For?*, London: Verso.

—— (2003a) *Organs Without Bodies: Deleuze and Consequences*, London: Routledge.

—— (2003b) *Welcome to the Desert of the Real: Five Essays of September 11 and Related Dates*, London: Verso.

Index

eBooks – at www.eBookstore.tandf.co.uk

A library at your fingertips!

eBooks are electronic versions of printed books. You can store them on your PC/laptop or browse them online.

They have advantages for anyone needing rapid access to a wide variety of published, copyright information.

eBooks can help your research by enabling you to bookmark chapters, annotate text and use instant searches to find specific words or phrases. Several eBook files would fit on even a small laptop or PDA.

NEW: Save money by eSubscribing: cheap, online access to any eBook for as long as you need it.

Annual subscription packages

We now offer special low-cost bulk subscriptions to packages of eBooks in certain subject areas. These are available to libraries or to individuals.

For more information please contact
webmaster.ebooks@tandf.co.uk

We're continually developing the eBook concept, so keep up to date by visiting the website.

www.eBookstore.tandf.co.uk